The Origins of Modern Spin

Democratic Government and the Media in Britain, 1945–51

Martin Moore

macmillan

First published 2006 by
PALGRAVE MACMILLAN
Houndmills, Basingstoke, Hampshire RG21 6XS and
175 Fifth Avenue, New York, N.Y. 10010
Companies and representatives throughout the world

PALGRAVE MACMILLAN is the global academic imprint of the Palgrave Macmillan division of St. Martin's Press, LLC and of Palgrave Macmillan Ltd. Macmillan® is a registered trademark in the United States, United Kingdom and other countries. Palgrave is a registered trademark in the European Union and other countries.

ISBN 13: 978–1–4039–8956–7   hardback
ISBN 10: 1–4039–8956–7   hardback

This book is printed on paper suitable for recycling and made from fully managed and sustained forest sources.

A catalogue record for this book is available from the British Library.

Library of Congress Cataloging-in-Publication Data
Moore, Martin, 1970-
    The origins of modern spin : democratic government and the media in
Britain, 1945–51 / Martin Moore
        p. cm.
    Includes bibliographical references and index.
    ISBN 1–4039–8956–7 (cloth)
        1. Mass media–Political aspects–Great Britain. 2. Great Britain–Politics
and government–1945–1964. I Title.

P119.32.G7M66 2006
302.2'340941–dc22   2006046588

10   9   8   7   6   5   4   3   2   1
15   14 13 12 11 10 09 08 07 06

Printed and bound in Great Britain by
Antony Rowe Ltd, Chippenham and Eastbourne

To Mum, Dad and Jo

Contents

Acknowledgements

In the years that it has taken me to research and write this book I have been to countless libraries and scores of archives. Short of thanking each archivist and librarian in person I would like to thank all of you together for your help and support – in particular those at the BBC archives in Caversham, those at the Churchill archives in Cambridge, and all those at the Public Record Office in Kew.

At the LSE both Arne Westad and David Stevenson gave me invaluable advice. Particularly important were David Stevenson's searching questions and his remarkable knowledge of sources. I have received lots of additional guidance from Linda Kaye and Luke McKernan at the BUFVC, Alban Webb, Jean Seaton, John Ramsden, Peter Hennessy, and Dominic Wring – for all of which I am very grateful. Mr Donald Haley has kindly given me permission to quote from his father's diaries in my chapters on broadcasting. At Human Capital, where I worked while doing much of my research, everyone was very patient and supportive. In their astonishing willingness to discuss, debate, advise, read and edit my work I cannot thank my parents enough. Finally, I'd like to thank my wife Jo, who has seen this book through from its origins to its completion and provided me with so much encouragement and reassurance throughout.

List of Abbreviations

BBC – British Broadcasting Corporation
CAB – Cabinet Records, Public Record Office
CEA – Cinema Exhibitors Association
COI – Central Office of Information
DG – Director General
EAU – Empire Advisory Unit
EIC – Economic Information Committee
EIU – Economic Information Unit
EPC – Empire Publicity Committee
FO – Foreign Office, Public Record Office
HO – Home Office, Public Record Office
IH – Home Information Services (Ministerial) Committee
IH(O) – Home Information Services (Official) Committee
IH(O)(E) – Economic Information (Official) Committee
INF – Central Office of Information, Public Record Office
IRD – Information Research Department
IS – Information Services Committee (Ministerial)
ME-RCP – Minutes of Evidence to Royal Commission on the Press
MH – Ministry of Health, Public Record Office
MOI – Ministry of Information
NRA – Newsreel Association
NUJ – National Union of Journalists
PEP – Political and Economic Planning
PC(O)C – Prosperity Campaign (Official) Committee
PRO – Public Relations Officer
RCP – Royal Commission on the Press
RG – Social Survey, Public Record Office

List of Abbreviations

Introduction: What is Modern Spin?

1945–51 was a seminal period in the development of communication between the government, the media and the people in Britain. The Attlee government was the first British government to engage fully with the dilemma of how a government communicates with its citizens to sustain a credible democracy. The concepts and methods it pioneered then became the organisational framework for all subsequent British governments. This book tells the story of this government's journey from idealism to pragmatism, from a vision of an informed electorate to a worldly acceptance of the manipulation of communication to engineer consent – what has now come to be known as modern 'spin'.

The term 'spin' has now become ubiquitous and is normally used pejoratively. But spin, in the political sense, is simply the way in which a government, any government, seeks to present its actions in the most favourable light. Every government spins. It is the means by which they maintain and enhance their power. Henry VIII led a large scale propaganda programme to convince his subjects that Catholicism was no longer the true religion. The Victorians very successfully diverted industrial unrest at home by extolling the successes of imperialism abroad.

Information management, and its iniquitous offspring – modern spin, are more recent phenomena. They are phenomena that have neither been properly examined nor sufficiently understood, by their practitioners or by their targets. And yet they are integral to the practice of modern government. Information management involves the constant, systematic control of the flow of information from government. It would not be necessary without substantial national governments with large scale administrative bureaucracies and easily accessible mass

1

media. It requires state machinery and personnel whose primary function is not execution or administration but simply communication. It requires the ability not just to provide information but to measure the effectiveness of that information. It requires an institutionalised series of methods for delivering that information to the mass media, and an awareness of those methods across government. Most importantly, it requires a new conceptual understanding of communication as a distinct function of governance.

Modern government communication is not simply about the provision of information but also its deliberate management. Such management can be for entirely benign and constructive reasons. Democratic governments have information that they believe is important for people to know, but they are conscious that in its raw form this information may be indigestible by the majority of the people to whom it is aimed. They know that most people will receive this information from the independent mass media. They therefore have to consider how best to select, shape and distribute the information to increase its chances of being properly received, and to take account of the way in which it will be presented by the mass media. In practical terms this might mean targeting sections of the population with specific information through particular media outlets, commissioning an advertising campaign to raise awareness about a health issue, or releasing information in such a way and at such a time that it will be integrated into the independent news media. Many of these, and other techniques, are now very familiar. But this conscious separation of policy from presentation, and the constant management of information in order to engineer consent, emerged as a feature of government in the aftermath of the Second World War.

But not all information management is benign and constructive. Modern spin evolved from information management but is distinct from it. It involves the deliberate distortion of information and manipulation of the independent media in order to achieve government objectives. In modern spin the information itself is no longer considered to have inherent value but is regarded as malleable raw material in the service of an eventual goal. How it is perceived and its predicted response are considered more important than any ideals of objective truth. Modern spin developed in response to the government's acceptance that it had to rely almost entirely on the independent mass media as the primary means of political communication. Yet, at the same time, the government recognised that it was severely constrained in the overt control it could exert over that media. It therefore felt justified in maximising what control it had and exerting whatever covert influence it could – concealment being critical since once this influence becomes public the information loses its credibility.

The methods of information management and modern spin are similar, but their motivation is different. The purpose of information management is to clarify government information, to target it at specific audiences who need or could use it, and to make it more comprehensible. The purpose of modern spin, on the other hand, is to sustain government popularity and to secure popular consent no matter what the content of the information. For this reason modern spin is inordinately focused on the government's relationship with the media, and the presentation of its policy within the media.

Over the past decade there has been a significant increase in writing devoted to the subject of political communication and spin. Margaret Scammell, Pippa Norris, Bob Franklin, Dominic Wring, Martin Rosenbaum, Dennis Kavanagh, Nicholas Jones, Michael Cockerell, Bernard Ingham and others have all written about the phenomenon.[1] Much of this work, however, concentrates on party political communication. Though fascinating, this has to be distinguished from government communication. Party political communication is about partisan propaganda, and normally focuses on elections. It is characterised by books such as Norris et al.'s *On Message: Communicating the Campaign* (1999).[2] But, as Edward Bernays, 'the father of public relations', wrote back in 1928, 'campaigning is only an incident in public life. The process of government is continuous'.[3] This book is about the continuous process of government and its ongoing attempts to manage the information its citizens receive.

There is also a propensity in the literature on spin, especially in journalism about it, to focus on the recent past. But modern spin did not suddenly appear in 1997, as some people have suggested. To understand its origins one must go back to the period immediately following the Second World War. It was in this period that the institutional, methodological and conceptual frameworks for both information management and modern spin were first developed. Since then they have been immeasurably enlarged and enhanced, and yet their outline remains much the same and many of the problems associated with the framework remain unresolved.

In 1945 the Labour government did not think too much about the dilemma of how to communicate within a democracy. It had much else on its mind. The war was ending and there was the huge task of making the transition to peace. Moreover, the government had plans to overhaul the entire economic infrastructure of the country.

Yet it is important to recognise that Labour was in a distinctly different position from its predecessors as regards communication. Pre-1914 governments had not engaged with the dilemma because they had not needed to. They did not feel it necessary to communicate with the whole population because, prior to 1918 less than a third of the adult population, under eight million people, could vote.[4] So although political rhetoric referred to democracy and the 'will of the people', the government only needed the support of a significant minority of the nation. Yet by the 1930s the franchise had been extended to 30 million people, just under the whole of the adult population.[5] Moreover, prior to the Second World War the size of the state and the number of places where it touched people's lives was still limited. Equally, before the 1920s, it was not possible to deliver a similar message to virtually the whole population simultaneously.[6]

By 1945 this had all changed. Not only did almost the whole adult population have the vote but their political consciousness had been raised by the war. Everyone had a more immediate relationship with the state at the war's end than at its beginning. This was not surprising since the 'bureaucratic empire' had, in Richard Crossman's words, 'been both enormously enlarged and dangerously centralised during the war'.[7] Between 1939 and 1947 the total number of civil servants rose from 397,570 to 722,294.[8] In addition, the penetration of the contemporary news media was approaching saturation point. The national daily press, whose circulation had jumped from 3.1 million in 1918 to 10.6 million on the eve of World War Two, was now read by 87 per cent of the adult population (its circulation would continue to rise to its all time peak in 1950).[9] Over 30 million people went to the cinema, and saw the newsreels, each week.[10] Almost ten million homes had a radio.[11]

The significance of these structural developments should not be underestimated. For the first time it seemed as if the democratic ideal, of 'common information' for the whole community, could, theoretically, be fulfilled. Walter Lippman wrote in 1922, that whereas 'the pioneer democrats did not possess the material for resolving the conflict between the known range of man's attention and their illimitable faith in his dignity', the material, in the form of the mass media, was now available.[12] By 1945 it was therefore possible for a Political and Economic Planning broadsheet to state that 'it is high time, in consonance with democratic principle, that fuller and simpler explanations be given to the great majority of people, who have a right to know why and what their government has done, is doing, and wishes to do'.[13]

In addition to these structural changes, Labour's attitude in 1945 was fundamentally different from its pre-war predecessors. Communication, if not at the forefront of its mind, was implicit in much of the new government's thinking. The war had generated a huge confidence in the potential positive influence of the state. Peter Hennessy has said of the new Ministers in the administration that, 'They really did think that Jerusalem could be builded here'.[14] But it could only be built if the government organised it, planned it, and led it. This was what Ministers believed the war had shown and what they believed the electorate had voted for in July 1945. As Hilary Marquand, the Secretary for Overseas Trade, said in a speech in autumn 1945, 'The verdict of the election was unmistakably in favour of planning'.[15] Though they were not conscious of it yet, they would soon come to believe that communication would be vital in translating planning into action.

Labour was also committed to a much closer partnership with the people. The Party's legitimacy was based very consciously on its belief in its role as the representative of the people's interest, as compared with the Conservative representation of 'Big Business' (according to the Labour manifesto). Nationalisation meant an unprecedented alliance of the people with the state. The war and the election landslide gave Labour the confidence that such an alliance was both necessary and attainable. Just as the war 'persuaded Government that victory hinged upon a frank and acknowledged partnership between the Government and the people' so too, they believed, would success in the peace.[16]

Therefore at the end of the war, motivated by idealistic intentions and democratic principles, the government decided to establish the machinery of communication; the Central Office of Information, the departmental press offices, and the Prime Minister's public relations adviser (examined in detail in Chapter 1). At this point Ministers assumed that packaging the information would be simple, that channelling it to the public via the mass media would be straightforward, and that ensuring it was seen, understood and accepted by the public would not be a problem. All these unexamined assumptions would be challenged over the following six years.

1945 was, therefore, a critical turning point in the history of government communications. It was the moment at which the government recognised the need for communication within a democracy, though not yet the obstacles to it or the difficulties of achieving it.

The subsequent experience of that administration proved immensely instructive for subsequent governments. It learned, over the course of its first term in office, how disruptive the mass media could be to what it thought should be communicated, how difficult it was to produce effective government information without resorting to persuasion, and how hard it was to make people 'informed' (an experience described in Chapters 2 and 3). In the process of trying to resolve some of these difficulties it began to think of presentation as distinct from policy making. It began to consider how it could and should relate to the independent mass media within a democracy and then how to use these media to its advantage. And, for the first time, it began systematically to measure the public's attitudes to its policies; not just to inform policy making, but also to make its presentation more effective. Information management became a new tool of governance, as outlined in Chapter 4.

Ministers within the administration had become convinced that they were justified in taking such action. They were simply trying to gain the consent of the people to plans which they were persuaded would be to everyone's benefit. Indeed the period, for the most part, is characterised by sincere politicians and earnest officials struggling to deal with overwhelming economic and social adversities as best they could.

Therefore it was only when Ministers like Herbert Morrison felt that the nature of the press had begun to inhibit political communication and was leading to the misrepresentation of the government's policies, in mid-1946, that they considered restructuring the newspaper industry (see chapters 5 and 6). It was only when the Cabinet saw the failures of government communication in the wake of the 1947 fuel crisis that it sanctioned its centralisation and the employment of communications specialists. And it was only when Ministers began to realise the constraints on their original ambitions regarding information that they sought to infiltrate their messages through the existing media disguised as independent news. But the effect was that in trying to find solutions to these difficult situations, Ministers and officials began to devise and institutionalise the techniques of information management and modern spin (as illustrated in chapters 7 and 9).

The way in which these emerged in the aftermath of the Second World War was not inevitable. Had a government informed by a less radical ideological agenda been elected in 1945 its development would have been different. As it would had Labour not produced such enormous amounts of information in an effort to inform and persuade the electorate. Over six years, this administration made over 500 films, ran upwards of 30 advertising campaigns each year, organised over 100,000 lectures nationwide, set up over 170 exhibitions and published numerous pamphlets and books (particularly on economic information). 'No former Government of the United Kingdom had allocated so great a proportion of its resources to the tasks of informing and cajoling its citizens'.[17] Examining how it came to do this is crucial to understanding why it eventually abandoned this approach, and why the experience had such a profound impact.

Prior to the First World War the British government expended little effort in trying to communicate with the population at large (though considerable effort trying to influence small sections of it). The Stationery Office, though established in the late eighteenth century, printed a limited number of government papers, and these were aimed specifically at MPs and officials. Those wanting political information were most likely to look to the press. This, though diverse, could not be considered independent. Most publications relied, for part of their funding and much of their readership, on political patronage. Moreover, throughout the 18th and first half of the 19th centuries the press was so heavily taxed and regulated that its circulation remained small. It was not until after 1855, with the repeal of stamp duty, that newspapers began to appeal to a much wider readership.

The First World War represented a watershed in the government's approach to communication. The war was of such length and intensity that the government devoted much more attention to propaganda, at home and abroad, than it ever had previously. Intellectuals and writers were employed at Wellington House, writing articles to appear in foreign journals, particularly in the US. Departments brought in journalists to act as press advisers. In 1917 the Lloyd George administration went as far as to create a Department of Information. This was transformed, in 1918, into Britain's first Ministry of Information, headed by the Canadian newspaper baron, Lord Beaverbrook.

The Ministry was, however, shortlived. It was disbanded after the end of the war and the nascent departmental press offices were also closed down due to spending cuts in the early 1920s. The government was as yet not convinced of the necessity of communication in peacetime although there were certain people who were starting to recognise its value and to promote it. Foremost amongst the early evangelists of publicity was Sir Stephen Tallents, who in 1926 was asked to run the newly created Empire Marketing Board. As well as conducting research, the Board promoted the idea of Empire abroad through films and publicity (spawning the renowned documentary film movement). From 1933, when the EMB was closed down, Tallents led discussions within Whitehall about the legitimate use of propaganda by the State.

Other progressive groups, such as the think tank Political and Economic Planning (PEP), did the same. PEP had been formed in 1931 to emphasise the importance of planning. It published regular 'broadsheets' on issues ranging from the control of national utilities to the state of the press, written by committees of between three and ten people and published anonymously. During the Thirties its 'inquiries played a vital part in the emergence of what has been called a "consensus on social responsibility"'.[18]

In November 1933 PEP published a broadsheet on 'Government Public Relations'. This rationalised the new role of the State, arguing that due to the growth of the population and enlargement of the electorate there was an 'acutely felt need... for more and more knowledge and informed criticism in regard to government and its function'. At this stage, however, it recognised that such a role remained conceptual. 'Very little indeed has been done', the article said 'or even seriously contemplated in the direction of creating a full scale and alert public relations service as an essential and specialised part of the machinery of government'.[19]

This was no exaggeration. In 1931 there were only 44 people employed on publicity work within government.[20] Even these, Mariel Grant has shown, are difficult to identify. One was George Steward, previously of the Foreign Office news department, who was seconded to Downing Street and the Treasury to liaise with the press. His role had similarities to the future Number 10 press secretary but he remained a 'peripheral figure'.[21] Others began to be employed across a number of government departments, in a sporadic and haphazard way. By 1937 'seventeen departments maintained permanent public relations and/or press divisions'.[22] But there remained no central direction, and many people were highly suspicious of the whole idea of government communication.

One of the reasons for this was the use of propaganda by the British state in the First World War. A myth had grown up, most famously promoted by Hitler in *Mein Kampf*, that the war had been won as much by propaganda as by arms. In this view the British government had undermined the spirit of the German army, lied to its own people about German atrocities, and convinced Americans to join the war under false pretences. As has been shown since, though propaganda was a much greater factor in this war than in previous ones, its effectiveness was hugely exaggerated by contemporaries.[23] Their perceptions, however, led directly to the use of propaganda by fascist states in the 1930s and added further to Britons' concerns.

Such was the level of suspicion of government propaganda that even when another world war seemed imminent the government was very reluctant to set up any central machinery of communication. Discussions began as early as 1935, but little was done over the following five years.[24] When the Ministry of Information was eventually established, in 1939, it was made clear that it was a temporary measure, and done with such haste and ill-preparedness that it became the object of general ridicule.[25]

When the war broke out there was, therefore, still only a small number of people who saw communication as a responsibility of democratic government. Many still thought such an idea was dangerous and unnecessary. Certainly few of the politicians who would later lead the 1945 government were yet convinced of its necessity. Clement Attlee, leader of Labour from 1935 and Prime Minister from 1945, was famously uncommunicative and dismissive of the media. His Downing Street press secretary, Francis Williams, tells the story of how he only managed to convince Attlee to install a teleprinter in Number 10 by saying it would enable them to find out the cricket scores. It is particularly ironic that someone as unaffected and as unforthcoming as Attlee should have overseen the development of modern government communication.

But some of Attlee's colleagues were already much more conscious of the value of communication. One of these was Herbert Morrison, Lord President in the 1945 Labour government, head of its information policy (and grandfather of Peter Mandelson). Anthony Eden later said Morrison was the 'the lynch-pin of the post-war Labour government'.[26] Some have also said he was its engine. Short, stocky, with only one working eye and a trademark quiff (beloved by cartoonists), Morrison powered the Labour administration through its first two most radical years in office. He organised and led Labour's legislative programme, he co-ordinated economic planning (until 1947), and he directed Labour's nationalisation measures.[27]

Three factors connect the lead actors in this story and provide an important insight into what informed the change in the approach to communication. The first was that almost all the key figures were linked in some way to Herbert Morrison. Some were officials in the Lord President's office, such as Max Nicholson, the head of the office,

John Pimlott, Morrison's Private Secretary, and 'Puck' Boon, his public relations advisor. Others had worked closely with Morrison in the past. Clem Leslie, head of the influential Economic Information Unit from 1947, had been Morrison's Principal Assistant Secretary at the Home Office during the Second World War. Robert Fraser, the first Director General of the Central Office of Information, had helped on Morrison's London election campaigns while at the London Press Exchange in the Thirties (where he also worked with Leslie). Others were Members of Parliament who shared Morrison's attitude to communication and who he appointed as his Parliamentary Private Secretaries. His first PPS, Christopher Mayhew, became chairman of the Overseas Information Services Committee and formed the secret Information Research Department of the Foreign Office. His second, Patrick Gordon Walker, became deputy in charge of Information Services in October 1947 and took over as head of information policy in 1951. His third, Stephen Taylor, was instrumental in convincing the government to continue using public opinion surveys after the war. Finally, there were the Prime Minister's two PR advisors during this period, Francis Williams and Philip Jordan. These were the only two without close ties to Morrison.

The second factor connecting these figures was their extensive media experience. Almost all of them had worked in the press, broadcasting or advertising. Nicholson, Jordan, Williams and Gordon Walker had all been journalists. Nicholson had written briefly for the *Week-End Review* and *New Statesman* before helping to found PEP. Jordan made his name writing for the *News Chronicle* from Spain during the civil war, while Gordon Walker made his writing for the *Daily Telegraph* from Germany (after which he joined the European Service at the BBC). Williams wrote for and then edited the *Daily Herald* in the 1930s before going onto the Ministry of Information, at which he worked with Robert Fraser and Stephen Taylor. Both Fraser and Clem Leslie also worked in advertising.

The third and final connection was ideology. Even though more than two thirds of these figures were government officials more than half of them were also committed socialists. Robert Fraser stood as a Labour candidate in the 1935 election at York.[28] Francis Williams' left-wing credentials were so strong that he was offered the Labour candidacy of no fewer than 26 Parliamentary seats prior to the election in 1945, but decided not to stand.[29] Clem Leslie had a 'lifelong devotion to progressive democratic socialism'.[30] Max Nicholson was a committed planner, as demonstrated by his intimate connections with PEP.

Even if they tried to keep their ideology out of their work, there is no question that it helped to inform their subsequent actions.

This book argues that 1945–51 was a decisive period in the development of communication in Britain and that the organisation and practice of modern government communication date from this period. In order to substantiate this, the book first needs to show how and why the government set up the machinery of government communication immediately after the war and how its initial attempts to use this machinery to create direct communication were fraught with difficulties. The book then needs to show how the government tried, and essentially failed, to re-cast the existing media of democratic communication (newspapers and broadcasting) to make it easier to channel government information to the people. In the process it developed the frameworks and techniques of modern government communication that exist to this day – one of the most important among them being modern spin. The first part of the book, therefore, is about the organisation of communication, and the latter two about the practice. The reason the book concentrates on newspapers, journals and broadcasting is because they were by far the most dominant media of political communication at the time. The reason it focuses almost exclusively on the BBC in the third part is because the BBC held the broadcasting monopoly in the UK until 1954.

This argument has not been made before. Although there have been many books written about the 1945–51 Labour government, very few of them deal with government communication. Even those that do, tend to refer to it only in the context of other policies. William Crofts' dense and valuable book on the Attlee government's economic campaigns is an exception and provides an essential background to this study. But it is a subject that remains, as yet, chronically under-researched, despite its increasing centrality to democratic governance. Hopefully this book will generate further interest and encourage more research to help explain and illuminate the current situation.

Part I

Organising Government Communication

Part 1

Organising Government
Communication

1
Idealistic Intentions: Striving to Speak to the People

There is a famous David Low cartoon from June 1945 in which Rodin's Thinker holds out the options open to the British people after the war. On the left is 'Haphazard enterprise for private profit'. On the right is 'Planned development for the higher good'. The cartoon wonderfully captures the attitude of many of those on the left of the Coalition government in the latter stages of the war. They believed there was a straightforward choice between a return to the chaos and confusion of the 1930s or the creation of a new, planned and ordered society. The choice was as clear and the answer as obvious to them as Low's cartoon implied.[1]

The election result seemed like a triumphant endorsement of this choice. More important still, it was a choice made rationally, they thought, by an informed electorate. 'The significance of the election,' Aneurin Bevan wrote in *Tribune*, 'is that the British people have voted deliberately and consciously for a new world, both at home and abroad... For the first time we have an electorate, adult and responsible, knowing what it wants, with some notion of the difficulties involved in attempting it, and ready to pay the price for the effort'.[2]

That people had voted 'deliberately and consciously' was critical to the incoming government. It corroborated Labour's belief in the importance of information and education, and the centrality of the rational citizen to a genuine democracy. Attlee, Greenwood, Dalton, Morrison, and others were convinced of and committed to this ideal; and theirs was not just a theoretical commitment. Attlee and Dalton had taught at the London School of Economies (LSE) and Greenwood at Leeds University. Fourteen members of the 1945 Labour government had been Workers' Educational Association tutors or executives.[3] Ernest Bevin transformed the dying *Daily Herald* into a two million selling campaigning mass market tabloid to ensure workers at least had a choice between a right-wing and a left-wing popular newspaper.

For years the Fabians, the Independent Labour Party (ILP) and socialist politicians had been arguing that government planning, a welfare state, and comprehensive national insurance were rational solutions to the problems of modern society. Once these were properly explained to people they would see this and support them. They were only held back by a lack of information and by right-wing propaganda. Tell them the facts and they would listen.

The war seemed to bear this out. After a slow start (mainly due to MOI blunders) the public seemed both able and willing to understand and digest official information. From 1942, after the release of the Beveridge report, they even began to demand it. From 1943 political engagement and civic participation increased and accelerated. Public meetings on esoteric subjects like the meaning of democracy and the process of reconstruction were packed out.[4] Soldiers clamoured to find out more about the welfare state through the Army Bureau of Current Affairs.

This was an enormous, radical change and had a profound effect on the establishment. Harold Nicholson, writing in his diary in 1942, confessed that he was 'amazed at the intelligence of the public'.[5] Stephen Taylor, head of home intelligence at the Ministry of Information, wrote that 'The British public shows a very high degree of common sense. Given the relevant facts, they will listen to and accept explanations when they will not accept exhortations'.[6] As long as policies were explained to people they seemed perfectly capable of understanding and acting upon them.

They saw the ultimate affirmation of the people's rationalism as the rejection of the emotional vote in the election. By voting for a Labour government they proved that they had listened to the reasoned arguments of the Workers Education Association (W.E.A.), the Left Book Club, the socialist summer schools and the Army Bureau of Current Affairs and rejected the appeal of the war hero Winston Churchill. This gave those on the left even greater confidence in the people. It buoyed their conviction that a full and participatory democracy was realisable. It convinced them that the people were ready to help build a New Jerusalem. Labour politicians were elated. 'Socialists saw it as the dawn of a new world'. The Parliamentary Labour Party 'was really full of hope and glory', Douglas Jay wrote, 'we were on a mission, a crusade'.[7]

The decision to keep the government machinery of information

It was in this context, with overflowing optimism in the aptitude of the electorate, and a firm belief in the benefits of government information, that Ted Williams, the post-war Labour Minister of Information, asked the Cabinet whether it wanted to keep the machinery of wartime communications. 'A decision is urgently required' Williams told them in September 1945, 'on the post-war organisation of Government publicity at home and abroad'.[8]

The responses to Ted Williams' question, particularly that of the Lord President, Herbert Morrison, reflected this belief in the people and idealistic intentions of the government. 'It is the right and indeed the duty of the Government' Morrison wrote, 'to inform the public of the facts necessary for the full understanding of its actions and decisions'. Only if the public were given the facts could they be expected to accept and act upon government policy. 'It is in the national interest' Morrison continued, 'that the citizen and taxpayer should be adequately informed by the Government on its administration and policy. The people "have a right to know"'.[9]

The Prime Minister formed a small committee to discuss the issue and invited Herbert Morrison, 'to review, in consultation with the Minister of Information, the technical publicity services which ought to be continued in peace; and to submit a report... clarifying the issues involved and recommending how Government publicity services as a whole should be organised if the Ministry of Information were abolished'.[10] Morrison's task was, as Mariel Grant has written, 'quite monumental'.[11]

More than that, it was revolutionary. Morrison was being asked to decide whether the British government should adopt an entirely new role. A role which the government had consciously turned away from after the First World War. A role that it had shunned in the run up to the Second World War. Never before had Britain had permanent domestic government communications machinery in peacetime and many felt strongly it still should not. Yet Morrison decided to keep virtually all of the huge wartime structures – home and overseas information services, the departmental press offices and a central office of communication. Such a decision would have been unthinkable in 1939.

In Morrison's plan, which he wrote up and sent to Ministers on 14 November 1945, the Ministry of Information (MOI) would be dissolved but a Central Office of Information (COI) set up in its place. This would closely resemble the Ministry, retaining many of its personnel and its production divisions, but it would no longer be a separate department or have a dedicated Minister.[12] Responsibility for departmental information policy should revert to departments themselves who would then be expected to use the new Central Office to produce their information. The Central Office would be funded on a Treasury vote.[13]

Though Information would no longer be a department in its own right, there would be a Minister of Cabinet rank who would oversee communications policy. He would head up two Committees, a Home and an Overseas Information Services Committee which, in conjunction with two Official (civil service) committees, would help to coordinate policy. Responsibility for overseas information services would return to the Foreign Office. Herbert Morrison volunteered himself for the post of Minister in charge of information policy.

The intention behind Morrison's recommendation was idealistic. The plan, however, was clearly influenced by political circumstance. To understand the reasons behind Morrison's decision, and how he was able to make it so quickly and with so little consultation, one has to look back to the war years. Only by doing this can one see that Morrison believed he was reflecting a growing progressive consensus but that some of his decisions were made on highly misleading assumptions.

Government communications machinery – from pariah to progressive consensus

When the Ministry of Information was established in 1939, it was done so on the proviso that it be disbanded at the end of the war. Prior to 1939 there had been deep suspicion of government communications machinery. It was considered at best unnecessary and at worst frighteningly sinister. Most people associated government communications machinery with the Nazis and the Soviets. So entrenched was this suspicion that government held back from creating a Ministry of Information until the outbreak of war itself. Eventually, when Chamberlain announced its formation he made sure to promise that it would be wound up as soon as the conflict was over.[14]

The experience of the first two years of the MOI appeared to bear out people's previous suspicions. It was bungling and inefficient and was even lampooned in contemporary novels like Evelyn Waugh's *Put Out*

More Flags. But, over the course of the war, as the MOI gradually became more effective, some people began to rethink their attitude towards its continuation and to see it as an increasingly useful asset of modern government.

Unsurprisingly, one of these was its Director General, Sir Cyril Radcliffe. 'One of the outstanding intelligences of his generation', Radcliffe had joined the MOI shortly after the outbreak of the war, having already had a successful career at the Bar.[15] By 1941 he was appointed DG. He and the Minister of Information, Brendan Bracken, worked very well together, and by 1943 the two of them had managed to make the Ministry efficient and uncontroversial, if not loved.

But in November 1943 Radcliffe broke sharply with Bracken. 'I believe these activities [information services] have been beneficial' he wrote to his Minister, 'and I would not be surprised to find that the balance of popular approval was in favour of their continuance. I also believe that no Government after the war will either be able or expected to abandon the use of publicity in its approach to its own citizens'.[16]

Radcliffe must have known that Bracken would not agree with his new perspective. Bracken had always been implacably opposed to keeping what he saw as an 'army of public relations officers and publicity men at home and abroad'.[17] He did not approve of Radcliffe's change of heart.

But it so happened that Sir Alan Barlow, the veteran Treasury mandarin, was at the time already reviewing the machinery of modern government. Radcliffe asked if he could add the MOI to his list. Though initially sceptical, having examined the issue, Sir Alan came round to Radcliffe's position. 'We started our study', he wrote, 'on the assumption that a Ministry of Information would not in any event be retained as part of the permanent machinery of Government. In the course of it, however, we have been driven to the view... that, purely on the grounds of organizational efficiency, there is a strong case for retaining a permanent Ministry'.[18] It was no coincidence that Radcliffe himself had been one of the witnesses to the study. His testimony was critical.[19]

Vested interests undoubtedly also played a part in the recommendation. By 1944 the MOI and departmental press offices employed nearly 4,000 people on home information services.[20] There were another 1,661 people working within Britain on overseas information services.[21] These public relations advisors were naturally keen to hold onto their jobs and had no trouble justifying government information services. One civil servant felt it necessary to report to the Treasury (anonymously) that there was 'active "jockeying" for permanent positions... among various PROs [Public Relations Officers]'.[22]

Officials began to murmur about the growing public need for information and how that could only be satisfied by the continuation of the government's information services. A Treasury Study group wrote in 1944, the 'experience of war-time conditions has shown the need for much more extensive and continuous information'.[23] Officials made sure they told their Ministers the same. 'We feel it necessary', Barlow wrote to Radcliffe, 'to impress the value of M. of I. work pretty strongly on ministers'.[24]

Barlow's Official Committee passed its findings on to its Ministerial counterpart in the summer of 1944, on which sat the then Home Secretary, Herbert Morrison. Morrison agreed with its essentials. 'The war', he wrote after having read the official report, 'has shown the need for it [communication] and pointed the way to its proper development in peace'.[25]

Over the course of 1944 and into 1945 Morrison then had time to reflect on information's 'proper development in peace'. As ever, he surrounded himself with clever people who helped him do this. Clem Leslie was one of them. Leslie was a smart, if prickly, Australian Christian Scientist who had first come to Britain as a Rhodes Scholar in the early 1920s. After lecturing briefly in philosophy he moved into business and found he had a real talent for marketing. He joined the London Press Exchange and in 1935 met Morrison. The two of them 'immediately became very attached to each other'.[26] Leslie then volunteered to work with Morrison on his 1937 London County Council publicity campaigns, recruiting and chairing a team of advertisers, public relations men and journalists. The partnership was very successful. When the war started Leslie joined the Ministry of Supply as the Director of Public Relations. Within a year Morrison had poached him to head up his own PR team at the Home Office, paying him a generous salary which raised the prestige of public relations and set a precedent across government.[27] Leslie remained at the Home Office until 1943 after which time he became Morrison's Principal Private Secretary (PPS).

In late 1944 and early 1945, while still PPS in Morrison's office, Leslie chaired a Political and Economic Planning group researching the future of government information services. The broadsheet the group published in February 1945 was much longer and more substantial than the piece PEP wrote in 1933 (already referred to in the introduction).[28]

It was also speaking from a concrete rather than a conceptual basis. Information services existed in 1945, they had not in 1933. The broadsheet set out the rationale for the services and a plan for their continuation. Government communication 'has emerged from the test and opportunity of war' PEP said, and 'has come to stay'.[29]

Even if Morrison did not have a hand in writing this broadsheet, then it certainly reflected his thinking and fed into his plan for the information services later that year.[30] The arguments within the broadsheet, even in their minutiae, reflect this. For example, the broadsheet is uncomfortable with the term 'Public Relations' and recommends that it be abolished in favour of 'Information'. Morrison tried to institute this change consistently throughout the late 1940s, even though quite a number of departments objected. Similarly, the broadsheet constantly emphasises rights, both those of the government, which has the 'right to make its purposes and methods effectively known', and those of the people; 'it is high time, in consonance with democratic principle, that fuller and simpler explanations be given to the great majority of people, who have a right to know'. Both these 'rights' are also referred to by Morrison in his plan.[31] Neither Morrison nor PEP addressed the question of whether people wanted to know.

Morrison had extensive links with PEP. Max Nicholson, the founder of PEP and 'a man of mercurial intelligence', was also the head of Morrison's office.[32] Michael Young, a frequent contributor to PEP, wrote the Labour manifesto for the 1945 election with Morrison. A series of PEP reports on the press in 1938 formed the basis of the research done by the Royal Commission on the Press formed by Morrison in 1947. And, PEP Planning Broadsheets are dotted throughout the Lord President's files throughout the mid to late 1940s.[33]

Though the idea that communication was the responsibility of modern democratic government may have become more accepted during the war, there were considerable differences of opinion as to what this meant in practice. Some saw no need for any communications machinery or specialised personnel and still associated both with authoritarian regimes.

Harry Crookshank, for example, the irascible Coalition Postmaster-General, after seeing the Barlow report in June 1944 said that the machinery proposed by the Committee would give the government far too much power over public opinion and set it on 'the road all the dictators have travelled'. For him it smacked far too much of Goebbels and government sponsored propaganda. He recommended that after the war the information services be cut back not by the 'pruning hook' but by 'the axe'. By this he meant restoring 'Public Relations Departments to their pre-war scale' and closing down the MOI entirely. There was not even any need for departmental press offices, except 'in departments with something to sell'.[34] Crookshank's view was widely shared, particularly on the Conservative benches.

The press were similarly against continuing the central machinery of information. When news leaked out about the government discussions on the MOI on 17 September 1945 it immediately led to articles accusing Labour of trying to create a totalitarian style propaganda machine. Newspapers speculated that Cabinet was conspiring to keep the MOI and pointed to Morrison as the 'leader of the survivalist group'.[35] The *Daily Express* said that 'if the Ministry is not wound up there is sure to be a first class rumpus. The Opposition will insist that it is improper for Party Government to use for propaganda a Ministry financed by public money'.[36]

Even amongst those who thought some communications machinery and personnel were necessary, most believed departmental press offices would suffice. Brendan Bracken, the Minister of Information from 1941, expressed this view throughout the war, and as late as March 1945 Winston Churchill said that the MOI would be dissolved as soon as the conflict with Japan was over, and each department 'cut to the bone', although he conceded some technical functions might remain.[37] Even some of those within the Labour Cabinet, such as Aneurin Bevan, thought the same in 1945.[38] Morrison was one of only a limited number who believed that both departmental offices and a central office were now necessary aspects of government.

Information as a mechanical task

Part of the reason Morrison believed both were necessary was because of his conviction that government communication was simply a mechanical task, like the provision of water, and could be provided in much the same way. The state just had to set up central facilities through which departments could pass information, on its way to a (supposedly) receptive public. Far from being a sinister tool of authoritarian regimes, information services were like a tap, which, once installed, could simply be turned on.

This misleading perception had once again been conceived and nurtured during the war. So effective had the MOI become after 1941 that the belief had grown up that it was 'little more than a convenient funnel through which news and publicity was passed to the Press and the public'.[39] This analogy of a 'convenient funnel' was particularly attractive to those worried that the public might see the Ministry, or its successor, as an instrument of propaganda, equivalent to Nazi Germany's Ministry of Popular Enlightenment and Propaganda.

In keeping with this view, Radcliffe and others convinced themselves that communication could be handled by a small technical office. In 1944 Radcliffe told Barlow's committee that after the war 'a small central organization with projections in each of the Departments' would be adequate to channel information to the public. News could be distributed to the press, for example, 'by a small Government office in Fleet Street, connected by teleprinter with Government Departments'. The need for other wartime aspects of information services, such as home intelligence (public opinion testing and the Social Survey), would, Radcliffe thought, be 'extremely limited'.[40] As it turned out, he could hardly have been more mistaken.

Barlow's committee followed Radcliffe's lead and suggested that the peacetime job of communication was essentially mechanical, representing simply a 'dissemination of facts'. The MOI could therefore be replaced by a 'common service unit' which would fulfil all the production functions on behalf of the departments.[41] This should, they hoped, also make it more politically acceptable to its many critics.

Morrison read the Barlow report and bought into the mechanical idea. Although he saw the peacetime job as 'more difficult and delicate' it was, he now said, 'a largely technical one'. The primary function of the machinery would simply be to 'convey to the public the facts, pleasant or unpleasant, which are necessary for the understanding of operative Government policy'.[42] The tricky questions of which facts and how they should be conveyed that so exercised subsequent governments did not arise. Neither did the even more apposite question of whether the public would take any notice.

Morrison's conviction that communication could be mechanical was borne out by his plan for restructuring the information services. He could 'see no justification for it [the new central information office] being under the charge of a separate Minister'.[43] He felt 'it should be kept on a light rein, free from over meticulous Ministerial control'. He thought the Opposition would also find it much more difficult to attack the information services without a clear Ministerial target to aim at. Morrison made it clear that it was the responsibility of the departments to initiate campaigns, not the central office. The limited amount of attention Morrison subsequently gave to the information services in 1946, despite being head of both Ministerial Committees to oversee them, indicates that he was convinced that the process of communication was relatively straightforward.[44] The Prime Minister's statement to the House regarding the formation of a new central information service, which was drawn up by Morrison's office, stated unequivocally, 'this is merely a technical organisation'.[45]

But there were a number of people who questioned the premise that communication was such a straightforward task. Clem Leslie, after reading the Barlow report in May 1944, was shocked at how much it downplayed the rapidly growing significance of communication. He wrote to the chairman to tell him that after the war information would be much more important than the Committee realised.[46] He objected to 'this limited come-and-go approach to public relations'.[47] Far from being easy, communication was an extensive and complex task that required attention and direction.

The Committee sympathised with Leslie's position but thought he exaggerated the situation. They regarded him as too much of an 'enthusiast with no inhibitions'.[48] In a telling aside, however, they acknowledged that Leslie was probably right but that the political context made it impossible to say so: 'Though it may tactically be wise to hasten rather slowly along the road towards Leslieism, it is probable that we shall get there in the end and be all the better for it'.[49]

Ted Williams, the Minister of Information, also questioned the premise, believing that without a Minister the new information service would lack unity and coherence and would be unable to attract good recruits. Morrison assuaged Williams, 'As you know', he told him 'I have a great deal of sympathy with your point of view and I am anxious that, so far as is practicable, we shall continue to secure that unity in British publicity policy which is so clearly desirable'.[50] But privately Morrison dismissed the charges, agreeing with his Private Secretary that Williams' 'real quarrel is with the basic assumptions which have already been decided against him'.[51]

Others suggested that far from simply being mechanical, information machinery could be a positive force for political change. Dr. Stephen Taylor was one of these. Taylor had been head of Home Intelligence at the MOI and championed the cause of public opinion surveys after the war. He was elected to Parliament in 1945 and later became Morrison's Parliamentary Private Secretary. In his 1945 Fabian Quarterly article, 'The Future of Government Information Services', he tried to offer comfort to those who feared information services would be used as they had been in the fascist states.[52] Information machinery was just a tool of government, he said. If the government was fascist then it would promote fascism, if democratic then it would promote democracy. He argued this was a natural development emerging from the growth of mass communication and commercial advertising, 'Sooner or later it was inevitable that those with ideas to sell, rather than toothpaste, would enter the field'. This connection of politics and commercial advertising appeared to cause him no concern. 'The war', Taylor argued, 'has provided a large scale demonstration that the ideas and ideals of democracy can be successfully handled in the same way'.[53]

Morrison ignored Williams' advice and baulked at Taylor's zeal. The Lord President was well aware of the political sensitivities surrounding propaganda. As well as being a pragmatic politician, Morrison was also a very savvy one.[54] Francis Williams, in 1945 the public relations advisor to the Prime Minister, said Morrison had that 'instinctive awareness of the political consequences of unpolitical events which is the mark of the genuine man of politics'.[55] He wanted to play down the political significance of the new information services, not highlight them.

Morrison predicted the new information services would attract far less hostility without a Minister, and said as much to Attlee: 'There would be the advantage under this scheme that, having abolished the Minister of Information, you would not have to say that you had appointed another Minister to give whole time attention to Government information work'.[56]

Similarly, he knew that home information services were far more controversial than overseas ones, and made sure it was the overseas services which were emphasised in the Prime Minister's statement to the House on 7 March (which his office drafted).[57] Kenneth Grubb, from the MOI, put this clearly to his Minister the previous September: 'It comes to this. We cannot justify the Ministry solely by reference to its past work as a central agency of home publicity. The case rests on arguments in favour of greater activity and initiative on the fringe of political controversy. These arguments are the crux of the whole issue and are debatable'. Grubb then summed up with refreshing candour, 'But we are spared this stormy passage if our craft has already reached permanent moorings through the calmer waters of overseas publicity'.[58]

This sensitivity to political controversy also helps to explain why Morrison excised public opinion testing from the final version of his plans. He well remembered the furore surrounding 'Cooper's Snoopers', the door to door researchers sent out by the Minister of Information Duff Cooper to check on morale in the early stages of the war. He had no wish for a rerun of that. Therefore, despite his own belief in it, he removed it from the original remit of the COI.[59]

The role of ideology

Unlike his colleagues, Morrison was very good at scraping the ideological coating from his policies and presenting them as plain common sense. There were, however, important ideological factors informing his decision to establish the government information services.

Labour's plans in 1945 presupposed a much more extended and extensive relationship between the government and the citizen. Once nationalisation and the provision of a welfare state were implemented then everyone would have greater and more frequent contact with the State. Attlee spelt out the implications of this at the Scarborough conference in 1948. 'Socialism is a way of life, not just an economic theory' he said, 'and in the process of achieving Socialism we have got to be good citizens of the Socialist state. Socialism demands a higher standard of civic virtue than capitalism. It demands a conscious and active participation in public affairs'.[60]

With this extended relationship would come a much greater need for information. If people were to understand their relationship with the State and take advantage of the welfare provided for them they would have to be told what the government was doing. 'It is clear' Stephen Taylor wrote to *The Times* in October 1945, 'that in the next five years the calls which the Government will make on the ordinary citizen are going to increase. If he is to know what Parliament has done in his name, and what part he has in the post war social structure, he must be told and told repeatedly in language he can understand. This is not Socialist propaganda, but simply a condition of the survival of democracy'.[61]

Morrison fully subscribed to this vision. Speaking to the Fabian society in the autumn of 1945 he described how he saw 'the people, the Party, the electorate... steadily reasoning out the Government programme as it goes along, in partnership so to speak with Parliament and Government itself. That' Morrison said, 'would be true democracy'.[62]

Since this was the first Labour majority government, it was the first opportunity Labour had to explain its policies to the people from an authoritative position. Once the people had heard and understood Labour intentions, Morrison thought, they would embrace them. In an interview after Morrison's death, his Parliamentary Private Secretary in 1945, Christopher Mayhew, said that 'He [Morrison] had a simple trust and belief that if one put the facts in a reasoned way, in a common sense way, the people would come round'.[63]

Morrison was a great believer in the power of communication and media. He had always been fascinated by press and publicity, dating from his job with the Labour run *Daily Citizen* in 1912. In the 1920s, as Mayor of Hackney he had begun cultivating editors and journalists. In the 1930s he 'pioneered Labour's use of volunteers from the professional advertising world' for his London County Council (LCC) campaigns.[64] Part of this fascination was, of course, about promoting his candidacy and winning elections, but Morrison also genuinely believed that people needed to be informed in order to participate in government. 'He was in advance of his time in his awareness that Governments of the 20th century must communicate to the people and that public relations had become an essential instrument of modern mass politics'.[65]

Morrison's plan for the information services

Morrison's eventual plan reflected this mix of idealism and pragmatism. It reflected his own expertise in publicity coupled with his ambition to create an informed electorate. Moreover, it reflected his awareness of the uses to which propaganda had so recently been put and the public's anxieties about it. These conflicting pressures meant that there were significant contradictions in the eventual plan that emerged.

Morrison had removed the Minister of Information only to replace him with two Ministerial policy-making Committees and a Minister of Cabinet rank to oversee them. He wanted the Central Office of Information to be a purely technical agency servicing the needs of the departments but he also wanted it be an 'instrument for infusing vitality into the Government's information services as a whole', staffed by people 'of lively imagination' – in other words, a creative agency.[66] He was determined that the government should project a 'common line' so that 'publicity at home is consistent and overlapping and conflicts are avoided'.[67] Yet the departments were supposed to commission their publicity independently and there was only limited machinery to coordinate action. He thought that the service would be limited and controllable and even called for 'drastic cuts in expenditure'.[68] But then in the first committee meeting used open-ended language to encourage its use by everyone. 'Ministers and Departments' he said 'should feel that it [the COI] belonged to all of them and should make the fullest possible use of its officers and the help they could give'.[69]

Despite its internal contradictions, Morrison's plan was presented to Cabinet on 6 December 1945 virtually unchanged.[70] Ted Williams was the only Minister to object to it, arguing again that the department needed a Minister. The Prime Minister replied briskly that 'it seemed to him politically dangerous that there should be a minister with no other responsibility but the conduct of publicity'.[71] The rest of the Cabinet ratified the plan and Morrison was invited to organise a committee of officials to work out the details of a new central organisation.

Tucked in the pre-Christmas Parliamentary lull, on 17 December, Attlee read Morrison's text to the House, concentrating on the less controversial overseas information services.[72] Two days later Barlow met with his new official Committee that would draw up the structure of the new Central Office that would replace it – based on Morrison's plan.[73] By 11 February most of the Ministries had responded to Barlow's draft proposals. There were criticisms, for example from the Department of Labour and National Service, that 'semi-detached departments always land the Government in trouble', but the Cabinet still approved the plans almost unchanged.[74] At the end of March 1946 the MOI was dissolved. On the first of April the Central Office of Information (COI) took over.

A function in need of direction

In 1946 the government approached communication with a blithe sense of assurance. It assumed that it could still act as though it were a Coalition government during wartime and enjoy the same benefits. It thought that the means and ends of communication were straightforward. It believed that it could create messages that were consensual and apolitical. It assumed that it could continue to distribute information through a compliant media which would then be welcomed by a grateful public. Moreover, it thought that people would continue to consume government information to the same degree as in wartime. A confident Morrison said in a speech in January 1946, 'I think the years immediately ahead will see a great increase in public interest in our national economy, and an enlivened public opinion which will insist on having the facts'.[75] The government was set for a rude awakening.

Even before the Central Office was set up the Labour government had embarked on a major programme of information and publicity. Much of this was overflow from the war. Most of the domestic controls, like rationing, still existed in 1945. While these survived the Ministries saw no reason to curtail information about them. Also, the end of the war led to an enormous dislocation of the population.[76] Information was seen as a means by which to reorient people and help them settle back into peacetime life.

The war had convinced civil servants of the continuing need for extensive publicity. Government had grown to such a size, and society had become so complex, that it could not operate without government sponsored information, they believed. This attitude was apparent in a Treasury report to civil servants written in 1944: '...in the past there was insufficient attempt except on the political side to sweeten the pill of Government. The war has meant that the pill has swollen to something very large, and, unless care is taken, difficult to swallow. This in turn has made it clear that the public must not only be told what to do, but also why and how'.[77]

Most departments were hungry for the chance of more publicity. Thomas Fife Clark, the Public Relations Officer (PRO) for the Ministry of Health, was a young and eager information officer. Aged 38 in 1945, the Yorkshire born Fife Clark had joined the Ministry of Health in 1939. He had witnessed the rapid but haphazard growth of information provision and now he saw the chance for a fresh start.

Hardly had his Minister, Aneurin Bevan, taken office then Fife Clark sent him a letter, telling him that 'The full and proper presentation of news and policy to the general public must be an essential factor in administration during the post war period. It was never so important to have a good publicity organisation'.[78] This was, he said, a new start. Although there had been an office since 1935, 'to the beginning of the war very little was done in the way of mass publicity on health education, apart from a single and abortive campaign'.[79] Even during the war 'we have had to deal with health education in a piecemeal way'. Only now, he suggested, was there an opportunity for 'a much more planned and long term approach'.[80]

Other departments followed Fife Clark's lead and launched into campaigns with gusto. The Ministry of Food continued to publish regular 'Food Facts' giving advice and recipes for rationed food.[81] The National Savings Committee placed ads urging people to save.[82] The Ministry of War Transport still earnestly asked people to 'Remember, a second spent in looking is worth weeks in hospital' to promote road safety.[83] Many other departments maintained or increased their wartime communication.

By the time the COI was set up they had been already been commissioning their own information for eight months. They were very loath to concede any of their autonomy to the new central office and before it was even launched ten departments tried to claim 'special treatment' to avoid using the service. There were certain functions, they wrote to Barlow, which they thought 'could better be performed by them'.[84] They took exception on 32 specific issues, and followed these with another 11 'suggestions that may require further consideration' in the relationship between departments and the central office.[85] Morrison's hopes for easy cooperation and a unified message proved illusory.

There is little evidence that departments had a plan or any long term approach to information policy in 1946. Even once they started using the central service they pelted it with campaigns and campaign ideas without any regard for overall strategy. The COI was quickly overwhelmed. The Official Committee on Home Information Services (IH(O)) was supposed to oversee publicity and arbitrate when disagreements arose. The minutes of its first meeting look more like those of a media buying company than a Committee on government communication. The 23 attendees spent most of it arguing over the distribution of advertising space in the national press.[86] By the third meeting they were trying desperately to secure some additional space, a gap in the newspaper advertising programme that could be saved for emergency information or fast turnaround campaigns.[87] But Sir Eric Bamford, the acting head of the COI said 'the demands of Government advertising were so much greater than the space available that it was impossible to leave a margin for contingencies'.[88]

In an attempt to create some sort of order the Official Committee started setting up sub-committees and working parties. These too proliferated quickly. By the spring of 1947 there were 27 of them coordinating inter-departmental publicity, plus a further 11 ad hoc groups that met irregularly.[89]

It was quickly becoming apparent that not everything could be communicated at once. Yet each department found it difficult to accept that its own information was less important than that of another. The COI lacked the authority to distinguish between them. This led to increasing demands for more Ministerial management and direction.

What to tell the people: the limits of communication

As the departments were busy pursuing their own publicity agendas it was also becoming clear that not only did these need some coordination, but they required some guidelines. For example, how to communicate new legislation. One of the original objectives of the post-war information services was that legislation should be popularised in order to make it comprehensible to the masses.[90]

Morrison reiterated this at the end of 1946. He 'thought it might be useful to issue a series of pamphlets explaining important new Acts of Parliament so soon as these received the Royal Assent'. But this raised a number of questions, including which acts should be defined as 'important', and how they should be popularised. The COI tried to define some criteria to limit its involvement by restricting this to major legislation or 'wherever there is need for a practiced editorial technique, for popularising through the simplification of the text and the use of visual material, and generally for investing the pamphlet with "sales appeal" and "reader interest" by an active editorial approach'.[91]

But this still left many questions unanswered. The Ministry of National Insurance, for example, wanted to know how access to information altered a citizen's responsibilities. In the past it had been assumed, the Ministry wrote, that '"Ignorance of the law is no excuse" but, in a democracy, during an intensive legislation period, can the onus be said to shift to Government?'. Similarly, how far does the government's commitment extend, 'Is a piece of legislation which affects the whole adult population to be explained in a publication that costs money?'. If so, then surely the audience will be restricted; 'Is the group' he wrote 'represented by these purchasers likely to be the group most in need of enlightenment?'.[92] The poor, less well educated would almost certainly be the last to find out.

Equally, it was not clear why the government should stop at legislation. What about the other roles and responsibilities of the government and the citizen? In January 1947, for example, the head of the COI, Robert Fraser, remembered a request from Morrison 'that something should be done to explain the social purpose of taxation. He thought that an effective approach to the problem could be made in the form of a 15-minute cartoon type film'.[93]

The Committee eventually fudged the issue by agreeing 'that information officers should automatically consider the publication of an explanatory memorandum or a pamphlet whenever their Department was involved in legislation leading to the passing of an act'.[94] But their discussions illustrated that only once the government had committed itself to communication did the consequences of this commitment become apparent.

Explaining policy: the need to simplify

It was clear, from the early information campaigns attempted, that the post-war government was being over-ambitious. It had alarmingly elevated expectations of the population's engagement with the process of government. Keynesian economic theory turned out to have limited popular appeal and the government was forced to curtail its aims and consider new ways to reach the people.

The Prosperity Campaign of 1946–7 is a good example of how its approach began to change. Morrison, as head of economic planning, had become seriously alarmed by calculations of a manpower shortage of 1.3 million people by the end of 1946. The effects on production might be disastrous and he wanted to appeal to industry to increase output.[95] If people could be moved more quickly out of the Services back to industry and encouraged to put in extra effort now, then, the idea was, they could be assured 'employment for all' and 'fair shares for all'.[96]

Francis Williams, Attlee's Public Relations Advisor, was asked to head a committee to translate this appeal into action. Williams was a tremendous optimist. In many ways he symbolises the early attitudes of the government towards communication. A good natured socialist idealist, Williams worked as a journalist and editor to the age of 37. During the war he then ran the MOI's Press and Censorship division. The experience led him to believe the public had both an appetite for government information and the common sense to comprehend it.

Williams decided that the Prosperity Campaign should be based on a 'simple presentation of the facts' without exhortation.[97] 'The only thing that seriously upset the British people', Williams wrote in 1945, 'was to withhold facts from them'. His committee therefore settled on a slogan they believed was free from political sensitivity and because 'it had not the character of an exhortation'; *Extra Effort Now Means Better Living Sooner.*[98]

Consistent with the optimistic view of the public's attention span, the campaign was due to run in long phases. The first phase, running from March to October 1946, would include Ministerial speeches, national production conferences and a 'large scale approach to the masses' (the publicity was not to be targeted yet).[99] The second stage would see the campaign broaden out to a regional level with local meetings and discussions in factories. The Committee believed it was key to keep it factual and be meticulously consensual. 'Let us all be quite clear' Robert Fraser wrote, 'that we are concerned to present the successive stages of progress factually as steps forward in a national effort, not politically as feathers in the Government's cap'.[100]

It might have been non-controversial, and, as an observer wrote to Williams 'It can hardly be faulted by the economists, the statisticians or the historians who are always ready to pounce if the Government puts a comma out of place'. But, the same writer continued, 'oh! It's cold!.... cold and impersonal... Cannot there be found something warmer, more human, more tangible to offer?'.[101]

On top of its remoteness, the campaign had perilously high hopes of the electorate. For its second stage, due to start in October, the Committee had grand visions of 'a campaign for economic literacy'. 'This is a very large order', the members wrote on 1 October, 'involving in the first place mass education in elementary mid-20th century economics'.[102] The ambition, it would appear, was to teach the population Keynesian economic theory, since, in the Committee memorandum's words, 'the mass of the nation suffers from a mixture of economic illiteracy and a litter of economic half-truths'.[103]

The memorandum went on to define in more precise terms the Committee's thoughts on national re-education. It need not be over-complicated, it argued, the government 'can merely hammer in the salient points such as:

1. the dependence of standards of living on production;
2. the need to export in order to import;
3. the need to adjust industrial practice to the prospect of full employment and to sweep away restrictionist attitudes and arrangements both on the employers and trade union side;
4. the need to maintain controls where shortages of supplies persist or fair shares are essential;
5. the need for relating wage policy to the required distribution of manpower; and
6. the need for balancing consumption against investment'.[104]

It is remarkable that the Committee members did not see this plan as over-ambitious and patently political. It only seems explicable if we accept Paul Addison's thesis that there was an unquestioned Keynesian economic consensus after the war, especially within Whitehall.[105]

It took an outsider to suggest that the Committee might be being unrealistic. Clem Leslie, who was now working for the Council of Industrial Design, found out about the Committee's plans (probably through his friend Robert Fraser who supported Leslie's observations).

He wrote a memorandum diplomatically suggesting that the government 'must be on guard against over-intellectualising the problem'.[106] He felt a long term programme of adult education was 'unfeasible'. Referring back to the war he cited the National Savings Committee's 'Save to Buy Guns' campaign which, while not sound economically, got its point across without requiring any knowledge of supply side economics. Leslie's appeal to limit ambitions would soon be reinforced by surveys indicating persistently low levels of economic understanding amongst the people.[107] Officials were starting to learn that making information available was only the first step.

Reaching the people: the problems of distribution

Only once the administration had committed itself to producing information did it begin to grapple with the consequent problems of distribution. During the war it had made agreements with the newspapers to provide advertising space, with the cinemas to screen government films, with the BBC to allow the government airtime, and with industry to appeal to factory workers via posters, exhibitions, speakers and films.[108] Though these agreements had no specific end date, the justification for them ended with the war. The production of government information, however, continued.

Without help or direction from senior Ministers, officials tended to cling on to any channels that remained available to them and prolong whatever agreements they could.[109] Their retention did not, therefore, represent a considered policy, but an attempt to retain the privileges negotiated during the recent conflict. Though at the time their resolution often did not seem overly consequential, some had a fundamental impact on the subsequent practice of government communication.

News distribution is a good illustration of this. During the war each of the newspapers and the agencies had kept reporters at distribution points to collect government news announcements. Once the war was over they were unwilling to make this commitment since they did not feel it was 'economic or worthwhile'.[110] Rather than revert to the haphazard pre-war method when each of the departments had been wholly responsible for issuing their own news to whichever media outlets they wanted, Robert Fraser thought 'we could consider… whether some new system might not work more satisfactorily from the point of view of the user and from the point of view of the issuer than either the pre-war or wartime systems'.[111] He suggested that all departments send their news to a central news distribution unit which would then, having made sure there was no duplication, send it to the newspapers. This was agreed and put in place. Forty years later it was still going, being referred to as the 'celebrated "COI Run"', by 1984, 'known to all journalists for its transfusion of Government announcements, processed and packaged in story form by the press officers of the Government Information Services. For most newspapers and broadcasters it forms the spine of each day's news agenda'.[112]

'A large and dashing administrative event'

By the autumn of 1946 senior officials were becoming increasingly aware that government communication was not as straightforward as it had been in the war and that the provision of information, as a separate function of government, was a genuinely new departure that required reflection and attention.

In 1938–9 the government had spent £495,045 on home information services.[113] This was already a huge increase on the previous decade.[114] By the end of the war the government was spending £4,889,848.[115] Despite Morrison's calls for cuts this figure remained stubbornly over £4.5m.[116] There were over 1,600 people working at the COI in 1946 and about another 800 working on communication within the departments, the vast majority of whom had only been employed since 1936.[117] And yet, there had been remarkably little discussion about their role and responsibilities.

The man most aware of the problem was the Director General of the COI, Robert Fraser. Fraser, like Leslie, was an Australian with extensive experience in media and communications. He originally came to England in the late 1920s to study at the LSE but quickly became more interested in socialism than studying. He was befriended by Hugh Dalton and Harold Laski and left the LSE to become a leader writer for the *Daily Herald*. In 1935 he stood, unsuccessfully, as a Labour candidate and then went into advertising. Whilst at the London Press Exchange he met and became friends with Clem Leslie. It was Fraser who recommended Leslie as the man best suited to help Morrison in his 1937 LCC re-election campaign.[118] Along with Francis Williams, Fraser joined the MOI during the war, heading up its Publications division.

In September 1946 Fraser was concerned enough about the situation to write directly to the Treasury. 'When you come to think of it', Fraser wrote, 'the growth of the Government information services, even leaving the Ministry and the Central Office of Information out of the picture, is a large and dashing administrative event. In 1936 they hardly existed. Now all of the departments have information divisions, some of them 60–70 strong, with a total membership, it seems, of some 800. In less than ten years that is, the Government has acquired and accepted a new function, and the Civil Service a new branch'. And yet, Fraser pointed out, 'we are without anything that any of us, I think would care to call a policy'.[119]

In addition to failing to define information policy, Labour Ministers had not properly considered the significance of the adoption of communication as a separate function of the State. If anyone was to blame for this it was Morrison, and Fraser wrote to the Lord President, as Minister responsible for information, about his concerns, hoping to organise a regular weekly meeting to overcome what Fraser thought was a dangerous drift in information policy and to come to terms with this major extension of government. 'War as a simple non-controversial subject, and the political cover of the coalition are both gone' Fraser wrote, 'Our topics are drawn from domestic problems and some of them are subject to controversy... I don't believe any Government in the world is attempting something similar'.[120]

But Morrison did not have time to think about the COI. He was busy navigating the government's massive legislative programme through Parliament. As far as he was concerned the machinery of information had been established and should be able to run itself. Anyway, he was more concerned about the failings of one of the existing means of mass communication, the press. At the time Fraser's letters arrived Morrison was trying to push an inquiry into the press through Cabinet.

Other Ministers were even less interested in communication than Morrison. Indeed Attlee frequently suggested that his Cabinet be careful of the media. In a number of Cabinet directives he recommended that 'Ministerial broadcasts should be kept to a minimum', and that articles should only be written 'in order to supplement the means already used for enlightening the public in regard to measures before Parliament and other administrative questions affecting the work of their Departments'.[121]

Attlee's own uncommunicative nature was infamous. When he asked Williams to be his public relations advisor he said, '"As you know, Francis, I am allergic to the Press".[122] It was not just modesty either Williams himself wrote that 'Attlee is one of the most difficult men in the world to publicize and possesses fewer of the political arts of self-presentation than any public man I know'.[123] For other Ministers the new information services were a means of avoiding the media rather than communicating through it.

Therefore throughout 1946, though there was a significant amount of publicity emerging from the COI, it lacked cohesion, organisation, or focus. Where, one newspaper asked, 'is that co-ordination and toning up of press facilities that was looked for by the appointment of Francis Williams to be PRO adviser at 10 Downing Street? And, further, what balanced coordination obtains between Downing Street, the other departments interested and the newly-fledged COI?'.[124]

Meanwhile, the Opposition maintained its ideological attacks on the information machinery. Churchill questioned the whole premise for the new services. 'Is it not a fact' he asked, 'that during the war we had a national coalition Government, officially representing all parties, and that the use of publicity in those days was for the essential purpose of national survival? Now that we have a two party system again it is very questionable how far public funds and public money [interrupted]... it is a different situation altogether'.[125]

Even the government's own supporters started to lambaste Labour's lack of information policy. They complained that the administration was not nearly vocal enough, and J.B. Usher (Department of Education) thought the government positively supine in the face of growing criticism of Labour policies. Usher offered his own diagnosis: 'Permit me to indulge in teaching my grandmother how to make daisy chains. I know that between the Party in the House, the bright boys at Transport House and the Fabians, you can muster a fair opinion on public psychology but it does seem to me the Labour Government is missing one terrific thing: <u>it is not telling the people about itself and its work</u>' (his underlining).[126]

This rising buzz of criticism eventually reached Morrison's office. His officials had played a major part in drawing up the plans for the information services and they were uncomfortably aware of the growing censure. They began discussing ways in which to make the new services much more effective, ways that would precipitate the government's gradual move away from its original, idealistic intentions towards information.

2
Expedient Outcomes: Communication Proves Harder than Expected

A review of the government approach to communication

Morrison's office on Great George Street was behind Storey's gate, overlooking St. James' Park. Behind it was the Treasury behemoth and next door the Foreign Office. Within his limited space Morrison collected a small but very able team including Max Nicholson, John Pimlott, and P.H. 'Puck' Boon. These worked closely with Morrison's committees and particularly with Robert Fraser and, from 1947, Clem Leslie. 'In calibre it [Morrison's office] was very high'.[1]

Following the criticisms of government communication, in November 1946, John Pimlott wrote a fascinating and prescient draft Cabinet memorandum on behalf of Morrison trying to address the problems. It would later be widely circulated. There had, Pimlott pointed out, 'been a good deal of criticism in Parliament and outside' of the way in which the government had presented its policy. His assessment was that 'There is not a sufficiently close link between policy and publicity'. The memo then went on, in considerable detail, to describe the way in which the government should approach both departmental and government wide publicity.[2]

Success in the presentation of policies relied, it said, 'upon the publicity aspect being kept in mind from the earliest practicable stage in their formulation'. This included 'steps which may not seem directly related to publicity'. But the initial announcement itself was critical: 'the way it is handled by the press and the BBC at the very start may make all the difference to the reaction upon the public and to subsequent publicity'. This meant the information division had to be integral to the process. The Minister should work with them on timing, ('in relation, for example, to the desirability or otherwise of the first appearance of the news in the evening papers'), date, ('What, too, is the most advantageous date of publication?), explanation ('Should there be a summary for the press?'), delivery ('Should there be a press conference? If so, should the Minister take it personally, and who should be invited?), and support material ('Should the announcement be printed as a leaflet?'). Equally they should have asked the same questions of themselves about the follow-up. Particularly if they wanted to make a film or use other publicity that required significant lead time.[3]

The memorandum put particular emphasis on relations with the established mass media. 'I attach special importance to Press relations' Pimlott (as Morrison) said, 'Too much care can hardly be given to the establishment of good contacts with Fleet Street and Broadcasting House'. The Chief Information Officer as well as the Press Officer should be alive to this relationship, and should ask the advice and help of the Number 10 PR advisor if necessary.

The memorandum recognised that one of the continuing frustrations of Morrison and his team was 'how to get over to the public the general background against which the activities of the various Departments should be seen and a picture of Government policy as an integrated whole'. The individual, they believed, could not understand his or her role without a sense of the national situation. This was however, very difficult given that most publicity policy emerged from the departments. Though the memorandum encouraged departments 'not to be shy about throwing up ideas for general Government publicity' it did not propose a solution. That would have to wait for a few months.[4]

Pimlott sent the memorandum to Nicholson and copied it to Boon. Both agreed with his sentiments and even extended them. Boon re-emphasised the need to draw out the wider picture, saying to Pimlott 'you are shooting at too small game. What the public needs is more of the wide general picture. If people are given a simple and easily understood explanation of what the Government is aiming at as a whole I think they will quite readily fit into the general picture domestic and departmental events'.[5] With minor adjustments it was then sent on to Morrison, Robert Fraser and Francis Williams. Fraser accepted that there was 'a certain deadness in the relations between the Government and the people' at the moment, but argued this was the fault of Ministers, not machinery.[6] His response implied that Ministers had abdicated their responsibility for communication, expecting the new systems to do their job for them.

At the same time as Pimlott was adapting the draft to reflect Morrison and Fraser's thoughts, circumstances were conspiring to propel the change in attitudes towards communication. The economic situation was worsening. Immediately before Christmas Morrison had received the 1947 Economic Survey and the draft White Paper. They made depressing reading. To make sure the government remained stable he believed it would have to convince people that there was a plan to see them through their current hardship. The idea of giving people a sense of the broader perspective and using communication as a deliberate weapon in the government arsenal seemed even more necessary.[7]

An article printed in *The Observer* shortly after Christmas substantiated this link between positive communication and the success of Labour policies. The article caught Morrison's attention for this reason and he sent it to the Prosperity Campaign Committee 'to consider and report on the problems raised'.[8] The article, by Charles Davy, argued that there was a malaise, and that there were genuine national anxieties with the way things were going. Planning and social welfare encouraged passivity, he suggested. 'If they are not to lead to the Servile State they require the counterbalance of positive steps to foster initiative and responsibility among the workers – bolder steps than Socialist doctrine usually admits'. Davy asserted that there was an aspect of the Labour programme which had not yet been addressed. 'So far' he wrote, 'the Labour Government has paid much more attention to the technique of planning than to its psychology'.[9]

The article confirmed for Morrison the urgency of his communications memorandum. He quickly had it drafted in order to send it to Ministers and officials on the Information Services Committees. 'Some Observations on Information Policy', dated 10 January 1947, was an explicit appeal to Ministers and their departments to renew their information policies. The move towards a new attitude had begun.

But on 12 January Morrison fell ill with a blood clot in his left calf. When his condition worsened the following week he was admitted to hospital. He continued to deteriorate throughout January and February. By March he was finally beginning to improve but was still not allowed to do work and in April was dispatched for a fortnight to the south of France to recuperate. He did not return to government until the end of that month.[10] While he was away 'his Department came to a standstill'.[11] Stafford Cripps, the Secretary of the Board of Trade, took over information and publicity while the Lord President was ill.

The timing of Morrison's illness was unfortunate for the government. As his health declined, so did the country's. Coal supplies were fast running out. Despite a robust show of confidence in 1946, Emmanuel Shinwell, the Minister for Fuel and Power, had failed to secure enough coal to last the winter. Then, on the night of 23rd January 1947, 'the cold weather and the fuel crisis fused in a cruelly malign fashion'.[12] Snow started to fall and for the next four weeks Britain was caught in one of its worst winters on record, with little heat or power.

The fuel crisis as catalyst for a change in attitudes to information

The fuel crisis seemed to make a mockery of the idea of government planning – how could a government whose rhetoric centred on forecasting the nation's health have failed to prepare for such an obvious emergency. The newspapers leapt on the government's failure with alacrity. A.J. Cummings wrote in the *News Chronicle*, 'Ordinary people blame, not the hostile weather, but the Government in general and the Minister of Fuel in Particular. They think they have been misled, or kept in the dark, and (rightly or wrongly) that reasonable foresight would have mitigated, if not entirely avert [sic], the crisis'.[13]

The *Daily Mail* was even more critical about the government's lack of communication: 'Now they [the Labour Party] are in office, and those who won through to the high places by means of their silver tongues have nothing to say. The so-called "People's Government" are further away from the mass of the people than any administration of modern times'.[14]

But the most painful censure came from the *Daily Herald*, the Labour supporting newspaper which had stood by the Party up till then. It called for the government 'to attend to its duty of informing the public about the difficulties which confront the nation'.[15]

A member of the Home Information Services Official Committee, IH(O), looked at the headlines and commented prophetically, 'The national calamity – for it was a calamity – would erupt violently into the pattern of publicity in the forthcoming year'.[16] Even Attlee was quoted as admitting his administration currently had 'no sense of public relations' and that there is 'something wrong with our publicity'.[17]

Attlee's comments were reinforced by the findings of a Mass-Observation survey the following week. The survey assessed the degree to which people understood the economic situation, as explained by the government's 1947 Economic Survey and its popular version, 'The Battle for Output'. It concluded that both were incomprehensible to the average citizen and that there was 'a wide gulf still existing between the languages of leadership and of the general public'. There were also indications, according to Mass-Observation, 'that the language – indeed much of the approach – of politics is somewhat out of gear with modern mass mentality'.[18]

The pressure for radical change in government communication was mounting, particularly amongst the government's own supporters. One of these, Ritchie Calder, was so convinced of the need that he wrote a lengthy memorandum in April, titled 'The Place of Information in Democratic Planning'.[19] This fed into the government's plans and helped accelerate change. Calder was a close friend of Francis Williams, having worked with him at the *Daily Herald* in the 1930s. It was Calder's scathing article in the *Herald* about the administration of London in the blitz that was said to have sparked the dismissal of Anderson as Home Secretary and his replacement by Herbert Morrison.[20] Though now a journalist at the *News Chronicle* Calder had worked in the Political Warfare Executive during the war, planning subversive propaganda against enemy forces in Europe.[21] His memorandum is particularly useful since its diagnosis and recommendations closely corresponded to the government's subsequent actions.

Calder started by directly linking democratic planning with communication. If Labour wanted to be successful, he wrote, 'it means not only the endorsement of the electorate of the need for planning... but the rational and imaginative realization by the individual worker, the housewife and so on of his or her part in the scheme of things'. Like many others at the time Calder then criticised current government communication. There was a 'lack of consistency' and no 'coherent policy' amongst departments. He proposed that the administration should make the information services much more integral to government. At the moment 'they have usually been left to explain things once they have happened. They have not had... any effective say in the development of plans, or any influence on Departmental policy'. Therefore 'we have a static information service in a dynamic situation'.

For this reason he called for a 'drastic re-evaluation of its [the government's] information policy.' His model of comparison was the European Service of the BBC during the war which, though 'no-one could doubt its veracity... was much the servant of the Chiefs of Staff'. Its effectiveness, he claimed, was based on two important elements – intelligent use of the facts, and a detailed understanding of the audience. The BBC insisted on facts, but 'facts were marshalled to ensure the right response'. And the '"Stimmung", or the atmosphere, mood and circumstances of the recipient, was as important as the facts delivered'.

This, he believed, was directly applicable to the current situation: '…in a fast moving peace-time situation fraught with opportunity as well as difficulty, facts can be made to "work for their living"'. Not that Calder was recommending manipulation, 'It is a question of discretion and never of suppression'. Depending on which audience you were addressing, 'the presentation and the selection is different'. This, he ended, 'is the human aspect of "Democratic Planning" aimed at making the individual a willing party and active participant in the plans'.

This was clearly in radical contrast to the previous idea that a literal translation of the facts to the whole population would enable them to come to rational decisions. Calder's approach did not suggest involving people in shared decisions but directing them towards the government's objectives through the selective use of information.

There was further pressure to adopt a more dynamic approach to communication at the 46th Annual Conference in Margate in May 1947. Labour MPs, searching for a reason why the crisis came with such suddenness, came round to the view that it was not the government's fault for not having *planned*, it was the government's fault for not having *explained* the situation, and for not putting it in the context of the 'Government successes' of the past two years. It was the surprise more than anything that they took issue with. In future, the government had to take the people into its confidence and reconcile them to the situation.

E. Castle (Hornsey, DLP), who had brought forward a motion to 'tell the people the facts', knew where the blame lay and suggested a simple solution: 'In these last 22 months things have gone pretty badly with the public relations machinery of the Government. What we are asking for from the Government is not Socialist propaganda – that is the job of the Party – but a recital of the facts of what the Government has done'.[22]

And yet the government thought this had been what it was trying to do since it took office. That was part of the problem. Maurice Webb, chairman of the Parliamentary Labour Party and a friend of Morrison, was much more astute and tapped into the views already expressed by the Morrison memorandum: 'What is important is that our debate today should lead to one definite and clear conclusion, the conclusion that adequate instruction in the meaning and purpose and consequences and applications of public policy is an indispensable part of democratic Government. It is important that it should be understood by us and by the Government that the presentation of policy is just as important as the content'.[23] This is a startlingly modern statement. Webb then went on to advocate a more flexible attitude towards information, 'We cannot coerce in a democracy, we cannot direct: we have to persuade and coax and win co-operation'.[24]

The ideological link between communication and 'democratic planning' was reiterated by a PEP document published in July 1947. 'The Plan and the Public' criticised the haphazard use of the phrase 'Democratic planning' – 'an important ideological term that should not just roll off the tongue', and said that to be effective this must consist of three elements: consultation, communication, and execution. Consultation, the equivalent of Calder's detailed understanding of the audience, had, according to PEP, been formalised and expanded during World War One, and confirmed as a recognised and essential instrument of government in World War Two. But in peace time its use was still improvised rather than integral to government. Communication, PEP believed, meant situating the individual in the larger plans of the government. This too was like Calder, who recommended making the workers realise their 'part in the scheme of things'.

The Broadsheet recommended the government use information and communication in a more sophisticated way to help the people understand what to do. To engage in ' ... a sustained and intensive attempt over a period of time, with a clearly thought out strategy, to raise the level of public understanding and to change the attitude of ordinary people towards their social and economic responsibilities'. This was the nub of the socialist endeavour. And, in PEP's view, it was the responsibility of the government information services to 'work out a comprehensive policy of public information in light of the facts of the situation and the Government plan'.[25]

The authors of this PEP Broadsheet are not known but it must have reflected thinking within government because Robert Fraser distributed it to all the members of his Home Production meeting of 8 August 1947.[26] Moreover, the actions of the government at this time show that the recommendations were taken to heart.

A new approach to information – the formation of the Economic Information Unit

Calder brought home to the government their previous naïveté. Combined with the Morrison memorandum, the criticisms of Labour's own supporters, and enhanced by the prevailing sense of emergency, it helped effect a sea change in the government's approach to communication. From now on the administration would seek to integrate communication with policy-making and use information in a much more dynamic way. Essential to this change was the formation of a small, central Economic Information Unit (EIU) explicitly dedicated to considering, coordinating and commissioning economic publicity.

The creation of this unit followed the reorganisation of the central economic planning machinery. The fuel crisis had finally convinced the Cabinet that the current machinery was inadequate. In early March Attlee had therefore endorsed Sir Edward Bridges' proposals to enhance it.[27] A fortnight later Francis Williams, Sir Stafford Cripps and Robert Fraser agreed that to make this more effective the machinery of economic publicity also needed to be overhauled. They suggested to Attlee that the solution may be the formation of a new inter-departmental unit.[28] The Prime Minister endorsed their plan at the end of March.[29]

The new unit was established over the following three months. It was to work within the office of the Lord President (subsequently shifted to the Treasury) and alongside the enhanced Central Economic Planning Section. It would be small, high-powered, and staffed by communications professionals (from journalism, advertising, and other departmental press offices). Morrison drafted in Clem Leslie, at a salary 50 per cent higher than the DG of the COI, to run it.[30] It would be directed by an Economic Information Committee (IH(O)(E)), also run by Leslie, and comprising many of the familiar names from the Home Information Services Committee.[31] Though technically a sub-committee to the IH(O) this Committee acted in concert with, and often led, its official parent. It was empowered to plan and coordinate economic publicity, and to commission its own publicity for themes 'beyond departmental limits'.[32] In practice Leslie and Robert Fraser worked closely to ensure the primacy of economic themes. Its objective would be to make people understand the seriousness of Britain's economic situation and persuade them to take action to alleviate it.

Like Calder, Leslie immediately drew on the experiences of the war to inform the new approach. In a note to Morrison at the end of June he wrote that 'the work of economic information is in many ways like "psychological warfare" when this is conducted on a basis of truth. In each the task is to project, and win acceptance for, news information and ideas about a complex and changing situation'.[33] The 'basis of truth' idea represented a new willingness to separate policy from presentation and to use the basic aspects of policy simply as a foundation, from which the Unit could build persuasive arguments and direct their distribution through the mass media.

The EIU also sought to gain a much greater understanding of public attitudes than currently existed in order to target audiences more effectively. The current means of intelligence was, Leslie complained, sparse and inaccurate. 'The time honoured tradition of hearing the people through the "feeling of the House" has', he said, 'within fairly recent memory shown itself capable of wide divergence from the feeling of the country'. By comparison, the newspaper press 'holds up to the mind of the nation a series of mirrors that may be concave, convex, tinted or partially blacked out' and therefore unreliable. But Leslie saved his most scathing words for the senior civil servants who based their ideas on 'their own and their neighbours' wives and conversations in first class carriages from the outer suburbs'. Therefore there was 'an increasingly opaque barrier between the mind of the centre of government and the mind of the mass of the people'.[34]

Leslie intended to rectify this by overhauling the government intelligence service: 'The proposal which I wish to put forward is for a continuous systematic survey of public opinion about economic affairs, with monthly reports'.[35] This was approved by Ministers at the end of July and from December 1947 the COI began doing extensive monthly surveys into public attitudes towards economic affairs.[36] These continued throughout 1948 before becoming bi-monthly in 1949. The surveys were especially useful for identifying who was resistant to economic policies and for what reasons. The EIU could then tailor the message to those groups through the media in the way most effective for overcoming that resistance.

This was particularly useful for targeting women. Leslie believed that a different approach was required for women. This perception was consistently supported by the economic surveys which suggested that women were much less well informed than men.[37] The EIU therefore developed a communications strategy directed at women. It prepared talks and discussions for women's groups, and worked with the editors of women's magazines.[38,39] It produced 'Report to the Women of Britain', an information advertisement that was carried in most of the national press and other relevant journals. The information contained in these reports, and the manner in which the information was presented, was aimed to appeal specifically to women. 'I'd give anything for more clothing coupons', report No. 9 read, 'But would you? Of course you're tired of having to manage on four coupons a month – we all are. But would you be willing to give up your own food, or your children's, to get more?'.[40]

As well as measuring public attitudes, the EIU started to collate and distil intelligence for Ministers to use in set pieces or to add substance to their arguments in the media. For this reason the EIU set up a 'briefing section', according to Leslie one of the most important parts of the Unit. The section accumulated information from official sources, government economic studies and 'a good deal of material from outside sources'.[41] It soon had 'a continual stream of information of every kind' which was organised by a 'librarian' or 'intelligence officer' and then passed on to a 'briefer'. The briefer would then use this material to prepare briefs for Ministerial speeches, broadcasts, press conferences, for an economic and industrial bulletin for opinion formers, and ad hoc briefs for publicity.

By October the EIU was preparing a fortnightly economic *Bulletin* 'designed solely to help Ministers in their speechmaking by providing material and suggesting topics'.[42] It organised an economic press conference twice a month with press packs for the media containing the Minister's speech and statistics to help them in their reports.

So effective was the briefing section that it soon became a model for other departments.[43] This was important because it was this section which was able to reverse the natural dynamic and influence the preparation of policy as well as its presentation. In a memorandum reviewing the work of the briefing section in 1949, Leslie said that it 'safeguards the Unit against the risk of becoming a passive recipient or routine transmitter of information, enabling it to deal constructively with its material, and to take initiatives with its own Department on a basis of some mutual understanding of function and aim'.[44]

The EIU was also supposed to coordinate the release of economic information. This meant controlling its timing and choosing its outlet. It was particularly concerned that unpopular information was timed so as not to damage the government. For example, when considering the economic information film programme the EIU suggested that 'in regard to the films on the National Health Service and National Insurance it was felt that these films should be produced as explanatory films against the time when pay packets were docked for these services'.[45]

Morrison re-emphasised this issue to Ministers in 1948. He wrote that 'when a Minister had an unpopular announcement to make he [Morrison] thought it important that the Minister should consider carefully and, if necessary, consult his colleagues about both the timing and terms of such an announcement'. As a rule he suggested that when a Minister was seeking authority for a particular course of action 'he should, as a regular practice, give some indication of how the publicity would be handled... bear in mind the publicity value and, where appropriate, to consult with their publicity experts'.[46]

This consciousness of context illustrates a growing awareness of the media agenda. For example, the EIU emphasised the importance of 'all public utterances by all ministers, senior and junior', especially speeches and broadcasts. These were, the EIU told ministers, 'the most powerful single method of reaching and influencing the public, and they have powerful secondary effects in their influence upon the scale of news values adopted by the press'.[47] This concept of establishing news values was not present in the earlier advice of the information services and indicates an increasing appreciation of how news management could assist the acceptance of government policies.

Though some of the functions carried out by the EIU had been done before, the difference was the degree of autonomy the EIU was given, its development of information management (timing of announcements, selective use of facts, etc.), its systematic use of intelligence to inform publicity (via its briefing section), its speed, and the explicit use of information to persuade rather than simply to inform. Due to the economic circumstances, it felt it was justified in taking radical action. Working during a crisis constantly compared to a war situation which called for a revival of the 'Dunkirk spirit', the Unit had the authority to initiate publicity campaigns, to work with any department, and to report directly to the Minister for Economic Affairs and Cabinet Committees. It was also, for the first time, trying to plan and execute publicity policy in the light of public opinion surveys. It was, in Calder's words, trying to gauge the 'mood and circumstances of the recipient' before it decided which facts to deliver and how. And, it was targeting its message at specific audience groups, like women, and trying to consider its content and tone in respect to that audience.

The EIU was very ahead of its time, as the American Government Administrator Mr Hoffman told Morrison in 1949, 'I thought I knew something about informational activities. I want to say that having spent the morning with the Economic Information Unit, having learned something of their plans to try and impress all the people of Great Britain with the importance of productivity, I think, to a certain extent, we in America are amateurs. In other words, when it comes to resourcefulness and ingenuity, I take off my hat to ... his [Morrison's] organisation'.[48] It was so advanced that many of its methods did not initially gain acceptance and it was hampered by the less highly developed attitudes of most Ministers.

The EIU was the most visible, but certainly not the only way in which the government began to use communication in a more deliberate and calculated fashion. Also in 1947 the government decided to try to raise awareness of, and increase national confidence in, the British Empire. The Empire Publicity Committee (EPC) had been set up in October 1946, but it was not until the following year that Ministers instructed it to 'consider ways and means of overcoming the prevailing ignorance at home and overseas about the Commonwealth and Empire and to initiate energetic action for the achievement of this purpose'.[49] A small unit, the Empire Advisory Unit (EAU), was set up to act on behalf of the committee.

In contrast to the EIU the EPC decided to focus its attention on convincing younger minds, particularly through schools course material.[50] Children needed to be told, the Committee said, 'that this free company of nations is no self–centred and self–seeking society but a positive force for peace and a vital element in the solution of economic problems affecting Europe and the world today' and that 'The peaceful evolution of the Colonial Dependencies towards full nationhood provides an outstanding example of the progress of the human race towards maturity along democratic lines'.[51] It might be argued the material was slightly premature.

Even less visible, but arguably more influential, was the Information Research Department (IRD), set up by Christopher Mayhew, ex-PPS of Morrison, at the beginning of 1948. The purpose of this secret unit was to 'selectively gather, package and publicize facts about the Soviet Union and its friends that would lead to a negative conceptual framework at home and abroad, which would support British foreign policy'.[52] There is already an extensive literature on the IRD but of particular interest here is the timing of its launch, immediately subsequent to the EIU, and that Leslie was corresponding with its originators even before the unit had officially started work.[53] On 8 January Leslie congratulated C.F.A. Warner on his new position (as head of the IRD) and wrote that we must 'meet some time soon to exchange background information about our work and to explore possibilities of mutual help'.[54] Discussing the IRD with the Chancellor the previous day Leslie wrote that, 'So far as the unit requires data about economic and industrial achievement at home, some provision should perhaps be made for proper liaison from the outset with the EIU'.[55] In mid-1948 Morrison recommended that Warner attend meetings of the information services committee.[56]

Given the astonishing problems that Britain faced in 1947 it is not surprising that the government sought to cope as best it could.

Domestically, the fuel crisis and subsequent currency crisis threatened to undermine any credibility the government had for managing the economy. Internationally, relations with the Soviet Union were deteriorating quickly and in the autumn the newly established Cominform began to target propaganda against Britain. This was combined with the fissiparous tendencies already latent within the British Empire. India gained its independence in 1947, Burma and Palestine in 1948.

To deal with these problems the government chose to try to adapt the machinery of communication and use it much more effectively in order to persuade people of the need to work harder, of the evils of communism, of the benefits of social democracy, and of the magnanimity of the government's policies towards the colonies. This represented a major shift from the original intentions behind the establishment of the information services and a transformation in attitudes towards information within government. The EIU was at the forefront of that change.

However, there were problems associated with coordination and centralisation. First, the departments had information agendas of their own and were not happy to see them sacrificed on behalf of a small, non-departmental unit. Second, centralisation and coordination created higher profile campaigns and attracted the criticism of the Opposition and the press. Third, in the context of the Cold War, when repressive socialist governments were monopolising media outlets, promoting a single message across all media began to make Labour look dangerously authoritarian.

Centralisation and the departmental reaction

Robert Fraser approved of the 1947 shift to bigger campaigns and broader themes. He believed these had a greater impact on 'public enlightenment' and on morale. However, he was also conscious that this required the COI Divisions to turn down the smaller requests of departments. He encouraged the Division heads to do this. 'The only way of counteracting an inordinate number of trivial requests' he told them, 'was by filling the divisional programme with big projects'.[57]

This suppression of smaller projects in favour of larger ones did not make the COI popular. By the end of 1947 the departments were angry enough to take revenge. One of them (or possibly more than one) spoke to Frank England, an investigative journalist from the *World's Press News*, and offered to give him an exclusive scoop on the inner workings of the government's information services.[58] It resulted in a five part exposé run in weekly instalments from 4 December 1947 to 8 January 1948. The main purpose of the articles was to rubbish the COI. England accused it of being 'the refuge of third class brains', 'home of delays', 'duplication', 'extravagance of useless material'.[59] This was particularly serious, he felt, because Britain needed inspiration and encouragement to help pull it out of its dire economic situation. But, with an interesting twist of logic, England also accused the Central Office of a sinister policy of 'expansion by infiltration' and 'excessive and increasing centralization' such that 'if carried to its logical conclusion, must result in the complete "Goebbelisation" of the Government's information services'.[60] The 'suspiciously powerful' EIU was evidence both of this dangerous centralisation and this creeping infiltration.[61]

England maintained this contradictory dualism throughout the articles. On the one hand the COI was a bureaucratic mess that had 'allowed the MOI machine to go rusty' and caused 'interminable delays' to government information and publicity. Yet on the other hand it was over-powerful and bent on national domination. 'There is an increasing feeling' England wrote on 1 January, 'that the ground is being prepared, willy-nilly, for the day when a still more weakened Press, faced by a more centralized and strengthened Government pro-paganda machine, will tempt some Government to carry the process to its logical conclusion and "Goebbelisation" will become a fact'.[62]

The articles fuelled the paranoid fears of those on the right that Britain was building towards a Nazi or Soviet superstate with an Orwellian propaganda machine. Yet at the same time they managed to criticise the British machine for not being any good. England's answer was to dissolve the COI and redistribute responsibility amongst the departments. This tidy solution was not the only clue as to the source of England's articles. They also contained information that was only known to those within Whitehall. For example, England knew that the Ministerial Committees on information services had not met often.[63] And, he made uncannily accurate estimates of the cost of the Central Office, its number of employees, and the membership of its Com-mittees. Morrison had no doubt that the source was internal: 'It is quite clear that (a) the articles could not have been written without access to documents which could not properly be shown to anyone outside Government information services, and (b) that glosses on these documents unfavourable to the COI have been supplied by someone with intimate knowledge of the current workings of the information machine'.[64]

Though they were overly melodramatic, England's articles still contained elements of truth. The COI was producing a lot of material, much of it going unread. The process of producing and distributing information was lengthy and bureaucratic. The COI was expanding into all areas of government.

But each of these elements was consistent with the principles of providing information established in 1945. The COI was not supposed to censor and prioritise. If the departments wanted enormous amounts of material produced then it was not the job of the COI to question the innate value of that material or the likelihood that it would have any effect. If the process was fraught with delays that was because the COI did not have the executive authority to prioritise. If its role was expanding, that was not by infiltration but by demand. Departments had accepted the idea of communication and were trying to integrate it to the process of democratic governance.

Frank England simply highlighted the problem that Morrison and others had already become conscious of; that communication was not a straightforward, functional task. The new information machinery was not like a tap which, once set up, could just be turned on and left to soak the people with information. The production and distribution of information required thought, selection, prioritisation, management, and execution.

1947 showed that the system did not work without direction. The government found itself in consecutive crises for which the people had not been prepared, nor for which the government had an adequate subsequent explanation. Given the circumstances the government was therefore willing to forego some of its original ideals about communication. Rather than produce neutral information across government and let it accrete gradually in citizens' minds, it decided it had to select information, target specific people with specific messages, and use information as a means of persuasion. Experience, in other words, led it away from its former purist vision towards a more pragmatic realism.

The EIU was one consequence of this shift. It was supposed to co-ordinate the provision of economic information across government. Though it was not a department, it had, in conjunction with the Economic Information Committee, the authority to commission media – films, advertising, publications etc. It adapted some of the methods developed during the war so that they could be used in peace.

The perceived success of the EIU meant that it then acted as a precedent. As the government's problems persisted and multiplied, so did the new approach to communication. The disintegration of the

Empire, the descent into Cold War, the continuing financial debacles each prompted the government to consider how it could use information as an aspect of policy. 1947 was therefore the year the government lost its innocence towards information and embraced a new approach.

Morrison was convinced of the need for such a new approach. He was conscious of the criticisms that had been made about information policy. He wanted there to be greater Ministerial attention and direction of information. In early 1948 he told his colleagues that 'Energetic action by ministers was required to remove the cause of these criticisms'.[65] As part of this change he decided that the division between home and overseas information policy was unnecessary. In December 1947 he wrote to the Prime Minister recommending the two Ministerial committees currently overseeing each should be amalgamated.

This was important because, up to this point, it had always been accepted that, whereas overseas information services had an explicit propaganda purpose, this had not been the case at home. Now, Morrison accepted that 'that the two fields do, to a great extent, overlap' and could learn from one another.[66]

The Foreign Secretary, Ernest Bevin, objected to the amalgamation. Not out of principle but because he was determined not to let Morrison muscle in on the territory of the Foreign Office. But this was not Morrison's intention. Morrison wanted to make communication at home more effective and develop a workable framework within which information policy could develop. 'One of the objects of the amalgamation', the Lord President said, 'was to create a corporate spirit amongst Ministers and to evolve a body of doctrine or bible of public relations in the same sort of way as his S.I.(M) Committee had done in the sphere of nationalized industries'.[67] A framework, in other words, for the future.

It is no coincidence that at just this time Christopher Mayhew, Morrison's old Parliamentary Private Secretary, was setting up the IRD at the Foreign Office, a body which specialised in the production and distribution of anti-communist information. Rather it was symptomatic of the new approach to communication.

At the beginning of December 1947, Francis Williams stepped down from his position at Downing Street to take up a job as *The Observer's* Washington correspondent. Williams remained idealistic about the provision of information within a democracy and very much against its selection or manipulation. Just after leaving Williams wrote an article in the *Evening Standard* spelling out his concerns: 'When do

Government information services become dangerous to a democracy?' he asked, 'Only when they become a monopoly'.[68]

Williams was replaced by Philip Jordan. Jordan was less overtly idealistic than Williams. Like Leslie he had spent part of the 1930s working in advertising, for J. Walter Thompson. From there he moved to journalism, but unlike Williams, left Fleet Street and became a correspondent, going to Spain to report on the civil war for the *News Chronicle*. Jordan's dispatches were such a success that after 1939 he became the paper's chief war correspondent, reporting from Europe, Africa, the Soviet Union and Asia. He died suddenly before turning 50 in June 1951, having been at Downing Street for less than four years.[69]

1947 not only showed that information required direction, it showed that government communication was complex and problematic. Choosing what information to communicate, in what form to present it, working out how to distribute it, making sure it was seen by the right people, and trying to ensure it was acted upon, all had to be considered and determined.

The EIU was important, but it was certainly not the only part of government going through the heady experience of creating government mass information for the first time. All departments and the COI were now using mass media to communicate with the public, and many of them were having similar problems. As they did so their initial confidence shifted first to frustration, and then towards experimentation and finally towards pragmatic solutions. The next chapter illustrates how the government went through this painful but instructive experience with film.

3
Slipping towards Spin: The Film-Making Experiment

The film opens with an alarm clock running backwards. Richard Massingham, the endearing clown of government information films, climbs out of bed, shaves, dresses and then heads downstairs for breakfast. His wife is already standing by the table and spends the meal complaining to him about rationing and the parlous state of the country. Indeed everyone Massingham meets that day complains about the economic situation. By the evening Massingham is so depressed that he and a friend try to drown themselves. But when they leap from their rowing boat with weights round their necks they find they're standing in only three feet of water. Bursting out laughing they decide life is not that bad after all and head to the pub in time for last orders.

This oddball film, *What a Life*, was one of over 500 that the Attlee government made between 1945–51. In six years this administration produced more films for home consumption than any British peace-time government before or since.[1] From 1946 to 1949 alone the Central Office of Information made 433 films.[2] In 1949 Robert Fraser wrote that at any one time the government was overseeing the development, production or distribution of approximately 150 films.[3] These ranged from films to boost morale, like *What a Life*, to animated shorts about the country's economic situation, to feature length fiction films about nursing.

A huge number of people saw these films. Many of them were screened as part of the support programme in cinemas which, in 1946, were at the peak of their popularity. There were approximately 1,585 million admissions per year.[4] This equates to over 30 million viewers a week, out of a population of approximately 49 million. Forty per cent of those who went to the cinema went more than once a week.[5]

Anyone who did not see a government film at the cinema almost certainly saw one somewhere else. The COI had a fleet of mobile film projectors. It used them to screen films during lunch breaks in factory canteens, in town halls, in schools, and at local clubs and societies. Every year between 1945 and 1950 between three and seven million people saw government films screened by mobile film units.[6]

This remarkable output could be described as the British government's Great Film-Making Experiment. The experiment was, however, short-lived. In 1949 the film budget of the COI was cut back. After 1951 the Conservatives hacked it down even further and closed the State run Crown Film Unit. No subsequent government has since tried to repeat the experiment, although they have been willing to invest in overseas films.

Why did the Attlee government make so many films? It is not a question that has been asked or answered. Nor why the government retreated from film making in 1949. And yet it makes for a fascinating case study. The experiment vividly illustrates why it is so difficult for any democratic government to produce its own media, especially media as complex as films, and why, in the end, they find it is so much easier to channel information, overtly or covertly, through existing media rather than create their own.

Government film-making up to 1945

The government first became properly involved in film production during the First World War. It produced two minute 'advertisement' films known as 'film tags', factual films, newsreels, and even invested in *Hearts of the World*, a large scale dramatic film.[7] Production virtually stopped when the Ministry of Information was disbanded at the end of the war.

Some government departments used film sporadically in the 1920s but neither widely nor consistently.[8] Even Sir Stephen Tallents, Secretary of the newly formed Empire Marketing Board, who in 1926 decided to use film as a means of promoting the Empire overseas, saw it as only one of a number of methods available.[9] But Tallents employed John Grierson who, on the strength of his first film, *Drifters*, created a film unit.

Grierson went on to use this unit as the basis of his 'documentary movement' which, along with Grierson himself, then become infamous. It produced a series of films for the government in the 1930s (first with the Empire Marketing Board, then as the General Post Office film unit), including the popular and critically acclaimed documentaries *Song of Ceylon, Night Mail* and *North Sea.* Grierson himself was brilliant, arrogant, and very sharp tongued. By 1947 his fame had reached 21st century proportions, *The Observer* referring rather breathlessly to his 'almost legendary celebrity'.[10]

Like Lenin, Grierson was a great evangelist of the use of film by the State. He saw it as an essential instrument of social education and per- suasion. 'The documentary idea was not basically a film idea at all', Grierson wrote in 1942, 'and the film treatment it inspired only an incidental aspect of it... The idea itself... was a new idea for public edu- cation, its underlying concept that the world was in a phase of drastic change affecting every manner of thought and practice, and the public comprehension of the nature of that change vital'.[11] Soviet propaganda films of the 1920s were a strong primary influence on the development of his documentaries.[12]

But despite the reams written about the documentary movement, the government only sponsored a limited number of their films before the Second World War.[13] It was only once the war broke out that the government began producing films in earnest, and then it did not restrict itself to documentaries. Between 1939 and 1945 the govern- ment made 726 films.[14] Many of these were made by the government's own film production arm, the Crown Film Unit; films like *Target for Tonight* and *Fires Were Started*. The wartime Coalition also invested in and facilitated the production of a host of feature films, including *49th Parallel, Millions Like Us* and Olivier's *Henry V.*

It was no use making so many films if they could not be seen by the public. So the government worked out four different ways in which to distribute these films. The first was non-theatrical distribution. This involved regional film officers from the MOI screening films from mobile projectors to audiences in factories, schools, village halls, women's societies etc.[15] In 1946 there were 144 such mobile units.[16] The second was through a Central Film Library and regional film libraries. In these the government held a number of copies of its films which it would lend out, free of charge, to local organisations to screen themselves. The third was through a theatrical distribution deal with the Cinema Exhibitors Association (CEA), which represented a large proportion of the cinemas in Britain.[17] Through this deal, first agreed in 1940, the government was able to screen a number of its short films in the cinema as well as government trailers or 'flashes' – essentially government advertisements of under one minute in length. After 1943 this was fixed at 12 government short films a year, or one a month, and 25–30 trailers.[18] The fourth and final means of distribution was commercial. The government could, just like a private film distributor, try to secure commercial deals with cinemas. Only a limited number of government films managed to find commercial distribution.[19] By the end of the war the government was making, on average, more than ten films a month, or about 20 reels.[20]

Expectations of change at the end of the war

Given that the government's involvement with film before the war was limited and that film production and distribution was very costly, it might have seemed reasonable to expect that the government would revert to such limited involvement at the war's end. This was certainly the expectation if the Conservatives won the election. The documentary makers were particularly anxious, as Irmgarde Schemke wrote in 1948, that had the Tories gained power 'it had been feared that the end of the war might see the end of regular government support to the Documentary units'.[21]

If the government did continue to make films many people assumed that it would reduce its wartime output. A memorandum sent by the MOI to departments in February 1945 on the 'Post War Film Needs of Govt Departments' told them to assume, for example, that at the end of the war the CEA deal 'will probably cease'.[22] That, though a few 'general' films may continue to be made, 'only comparatively few Government films of exceptional merit which are likely to secure extensive paid showing' would be shown in cinemas. And, that the main outlet for government films would therefore be through non-theatrical distribution.

However, even while the future of the COI remained unclear, between the end of the war and early 1946, there was hardly a lull in government film making. Production persisted, and then increased. In 1945–6 there were 143 reels made and in 1946–7, 148.[23] Indeed by February 1947 the COI was having to turn down twice as many films as it accepted, demand from departments was so high.[24] In addition, the government not only maintained its non-theatrical distribution, it maintained its distribution with the CEA (and Rank and ABC), and its option to distribute films commercially.

The documentarists like to claim the credit for the government's continuing use of films after the war.[25] But from his actions it seems clear that Morrison just saw film as another means of communication. Having been given the brief to decide the future of the information services Morrison met the heads of the Ministry of Information on

15 October 1945. He was obviously aware of the MOI's film production.[26] But in his report on the Government Information Services he did not refer to films outside a very general context.[27] HG Welch, an official at the MOI, commented on this lack of clarity in a note to Bernard Sendall in October saying that whilst it was still unclear what was going to happen to films, it had to be assumed their future was wrapped up in the general question of Government Information Services.[28]

Morrison was certainly conscious of the nature of film as a means of information and propaganda. The use to which the fascist governments had put film prior to and during the war was well known and documented. Moreover, Morrison was aware of John Grierson's ideas about the importance of using films as a progressive force. Morrison even received a note from the founder of the British documentary movement in late November on 'The Nature and Form of a Government Information Service'.[29] 'A Government Information Service may be, if it is so willed, a powerful instrument of national and international progress' Grierson wrote. 'Its form will reflect the degree of progressive or reactionary will which inspires it'. It continued in the same vein, outlining how an information service should be structured to persuade, direct and inform. Sir Stafford Cripps, who also received a copy, was so impressed that he suggested Morrison send the note to the Prime Minister.[30] Morrison forwarded it, but also advised Attlee that Grierson's proposed scheme would be difficult to set up and lead to problems in Parliament.[31]

Morrison was not comfortable with the executive control of the information process in Grierson's scheme. The Lord President's plan for the process by which films were made was designed to be consistent with the government's intention to use films simply as a channel through which to pass information from the state to the citizen. This process was supposed to be as politically neutral as possible. A department would decide it had information which would best be communicated through film. It would approach the COI Films Division to discuss the idea and then together they would choose a film unit from which to commission the work.[32] The film unit, presuming it accepted the commission, would draw up a treatment which would then be signed off by the COI and the department. Once the Treasury had then agreed the funding, the unit would produce the film.[33] Grierson's proposals involved too much calculation and conscious persuasion.

All this suggests that, as with other aspects of information policy, the Labour government was committed to communication through film in principle. As an editorial in the *Documentary News Letter* said in spring 1947, 'That the present Government realizes this [the importance of public communication] in theory is obvious from the fact that the Central Office of Information exists (the Tories might well have dispensed with it)'.[34] But it also suggests that it wanted to restrict its use to the passive transfer of information from state to citizen. Film was simply another means by which to facilitate this transfer.

The production of 'Information' films proves unsustainable

Over the next 18 months it became clear that there were serious problems associated with the process of producing neutral government information films. The first was that, without some criteria by which to rank the films, it was very difficult to prioritise one over another. Not only did this make the job of the COI very difficult (particularly in negotiating with departments), it meant decision making and film making took a long time.[35] Sometimes the process would take so long that government policy had moved on before a film was started. The film 'International Trade', for example, commissioned by the Prime Minister's office in 1946, was supposed to 'explain and praise multilateral trading' but had to be dropped by the Board of Trade when Britain was forced back onto bilateral trading in 1947.[36]

There was also no underlying plan or strategy (although this was again consistent with the production of purely informational films). This meant the COI and the film makers lacked purpose and focus.[37] John Grierson, once again writing advice to the Lord President's Office, said in August 1947 that 'They [the documentary makers] say they have lost the conception of a total driving plan for the use of the documentary film in the urgent service of the nation'.[38]

Even more important, this neutral process of film-making tended to lead to the production of tedious films. For example, two of the theatrical monthly releases for 1946 and 1947 were *Getting on with It* (Merlin and Films of Fact compilation for COI 1946) and *Introduction to Aircraft Recognition* (CFU for War Office 1947), both of which were intended for a general audience. The first film was made up of three short film packages, the second titled 'Photo-Elastic Technique in Industrial Research'. The subtitle, 'The Research Department makes a modification to the cylinder head of the Sabre Aero engine' quite accurately describes what the package contained.[39] It is unlikely it sent pulses racing.

Straight information films such as this could be said to be consistent with the theoretical principle of informing the public but were inconsistent with successful film-making. Not only were ambitious documentary makers losing enthusiasm for making such films, distributors were not keen to try to rent them. *Cumberland Story*, a four reel second feature, which was produced for commercial distribution, was turned down by all distributors 'because too political and too dull a subject'.[40] Similarly *The World is Rich*, 'a grim and harrowing piece full of social conscience, having been rejected by all the major renters, has just now found a potential dealer who strongly recommends heavy cuts and the removal of "some of all that misery"'.[41] Exhibitors were equally loath to show information-led and over-worthy films for fear of alienating the audience.

Though the government was able to make and distribute its neutral 'information films' for a brief period after the war, by 1947 the situation was becoming increasingly untenable. The documentary makers were becoming very frustrated and highly critical. The distributors and exhibitors were becoming unhappy. But it was the fuel crisis which highlighted the unsustainability of the situation and triggered a significant change in direction.

1947: The government changes its approach

Following the fuel crisis of 1947 the government reviewed its approach to communications. As outlined in the previous chapter the government came to believe that, up to this point, it had failed to communicate its position adequately to the electorate. As part of this review it began to change its approach towards films. It sought to make the films more topical and immediate. It created a central unit, the Economic Information Unit, which, amongst its other roles, was to co-ordinate and commission films on economic themes. It also looked for ways to enhance links with the newsreel companies, and started to develop its own 'official' newsreel. And, it established an informal inquiry to study the causes of the breakdown between the COI Films Division and the film makers.

This Economic Information Committee (EIC), whose origins are discussed in chapter two, was responsible not only for the coordination of economic information but also for commissioning films and other information media. Clem Leslie, head of the EIU and chair of the EIC, already had experience, in the 1930s, of commissioning films for the Gas Coke & Light company.[42] Leslie was conscious that part of his remit included adding urgency to the communication of government information. He immediately began considering how films could fulfil this.

In only the second meeting he chaired, in June 1947, his committee discussed how it could make current films more topical.[43] It wanted to give films an immediacy they currently lacked, and develop morale-boosting pictures that gave context to the various crises that people in Britain were facing. Robert Fraser, writing to Bernard Sendall, head of production at the COI, after the meeting, described how they wanted films to imbue the current economic battle with the status and urgency of the epic battles of the war. The people of Britain, Fraser wrote, 'are waging a battle for coal, a battle for food, clothes and houses, and a battle for exports'. '...while the struggle lasts,' he asked 'cannot a film be made to chronicle regularly the successes and setbacks, the human details and the national purposes?'.[44]

Amongst other proposals the committee thought about what to do with an industrial film currently being made for non-theatrical distribution, called *Britain Can Make It*. This was a conscientious, unambitious cine-magazine usually made up of three separate stories, one scientific, one industrial and one social. The EIC wanted to change this into a newsreel. This would not only make it feel more immediate and topical but 'had the additional advantage of providing the Central Office with ready-made material for possible supply to the commercial newsreel companies'.[45]

As the summer wore on the committee's ambitions for this 'factory newsreel' increased. Until mid-September 1947 the intention was to keep it for non-theatrical distribution. But on the 19th Fraser told the committee that there was a chance of getting the film distributed to cinemas nationwide via the CEA. This would transform the size of its potential audience. Moreover, Fraser said it could still be distributed non-theatrically and the theatrical release would not 'impede the flow of material to the newsreel companies'.[46]

If the newsreel was to reach this many people, then it had to have compelling stories. The same month an advisory briefing committee was therefore formed in order to start 'systematically supplying the COI with material for the factory newsreel, and planning the overall policy'.[47] Even before the new newsreel was produced, this committee began passing stories on to the existing newsreel companies. By October Leslie was already able to report to the Economic Planning Board that 'a method of liaison is now in operation which enables the newsreels to draw fairly widely on official suggestions about material and enables departments and the Economic Information Unit to put their proposals forward effectively. In one week recently the newsreels contained eight different items on industrial and economic subjects, all originating from departments'.[48]

Throughout the autumn the committee discussed how to make the official newsreel effective by presenting economic material in a striking way. The EIC wanted to show people the dramatic and heroic nature of the struggle ahead, 'Above all there must always be present a sense of urgency and a feeling of activity'.[49] But at the same time the newsreel must remain credible. The committee stressed that though the main emphasis should be on good news and success stories the newsreel 'must be more than ready to produce bad news for its audiences, not only so that they may know the real position, but also because the presentation of bad news increases the credibility of the rest of the material'.[50] It is difficult not to see this selectiveness as persuasion rather than information.

So excited were they about the potential of the newsreel that though the committee considered substituting the current monthly government film release with the new official newsreel they decided that it would be more effective to have both.[51]

This newsreel, and the other proposals being considered by the EIC, were already moving rapidly away from the neutral information films envisioned by the government when it decided to set up the COI in 1945. Two people at the COI Films Division were very conscious of this move; Ronald Tritton, head of the Division, and Helen de Mouilpied, Chief Production Officer. Since the move first became explicit, in June 1947, they had both been considering the implications for government policy. 'It has been suggested', Tritton then wrote, 'that the Films Division could do more to inform the public on the situation in the country and should be making films planned to lift morale by means of an appeal to the emotions comparable to that which was achieved by some wartime films'.[52]

Tritton was uncomfortable with the shift in policy, feeling that the government was not taking into account the difference between the end of the war and now. During the war the policy line had been 'clear and straight'. Now, 'The themes are themselves intensely complex. They are confused by politics. They are unpalatable to the audience because they have no heroic stature in themselves'.[53] Helen de Mouilpied agreed, writing that 'Warfare is rich documentary material, ("the dramatic interpretation of reality"). White papers are not'.[54]

Tritton also felt the government underestimated the level of opposition to its policies. 'The whole country is not behind the present methods of tackling the aftermath of war problems. Perhaps only half agree with the policies and a further large proportion are totally uninterested. The result is that every audience has a large proportion of cynics, doubters, the bored and the frankly antagonistic. This makes a pretty formidable core of audience resistance'.[55] The government would have to change the current factual films considerably to overcome such resistance, and maybe even expand into non-factual features as well.

De Mouilpied reiterated Tritton's point, indeed assumed that the government realised that its new ambitions could only be achieved if it expanded from short information films into producing fictional feature films. 'In making these recommendations' she wrote, 'it is assumed that Government film making is not necessarily documentary film making, that although documentaries will still have their place, the main effort of present Government propaganda can only be made through "feature" films of from 10 minutes to 90 minutes in length'.[56] De Mouilpied seemed already to be assuming that these films should be classified as 'propaganda'.

Morale films did not fit the original, politically neutral intention of COI film making. They were likely to be more general than departmental. They required argument and persuasion rather than straight information. They were unlikely to be aimed at a single, specific, direct reaction. These issues were brought home to the committee when, in early September, the Treasury refused to approve funding for *The Changing Face of Britain*. This film, though sponsored by Town & Country planning, was supposed to have a more general appeal, to 'lift people's eyes from the fish queues' and give them some hope for the future.[57] The Treasury did not think the film was consistent with the remit of government films.

Until the autumn of 1947 the change in approach to films and newsreels had mainly been due to the pragmatic reaction of the EIC to circumstances. A more fundamental shift in government approach required backing from senior government ministers. This only came after the Paymaster General delivered the results of his film inquiry in October 1947.

The findings and the repercussions of the Marquand Inquiry

In the summer of 1947 Herbert Morrison set up an informal inquiry into the relationship between the COI and the documentary film units, to be led by the Paymaster General, Hilary Marquand. The inquiry had been triggered by the deterioration of this relationship. Marquand collected information from the COI, and interviewed COI officials,

Treasury officials and documentary film makers.[58] He split the conclusions of his inquiry into 'process' and 'purpose'. Regarding process he concluded that though the film makers were justified in feeling frustrated by the various interruptions and cancellations, their problems were just as much caused by the natural decrease in demand for documentaries after the war coupled with the glut of documentary companies searching for work.[59]

Regarding 'purpose', Marquand's most serious allegation, and one which was to lead to a more fundamental rethink in the government's use of film, was that 'in dealing with the most creative and artistic of all media of information, the film, we are <u>tending</u> – I say no more – to limit ourselves too closely to mere information. Somehow – perhaps not in every film – we must get more inspiration. The creative spirit should blow more freely' [his underlining].[60] Marquand believed that this focus on 'mere information' was leading to a slump in motivation amongst the film makers and the consequent production of uninspiring films. John Grierson (writing from his position at UNESCO in Paris) had already made a similar complaint that government films were not 'firing the public will'.[61]

The importance of Marquand's allegation, and his recommendation deriving from it, has to be emphasised. Until 1947 the intention behind government communication had been to provide information. Marquand believed this was simply not enough.

Government reaction to the problems and to the Marquand Report

Government Ministers and officials could have reacted in a number of ways. They could have accepted that it was difficult to make straight information films and focused on other means of communication. They could have conceded that the government could not continue to press information films on a general cinema audience and reverted to specialised audiences and non-theatrical distribution. Or they could have altered government policy, accepted Marquand's recommendations and not limited themselves to information but let the 'creative spirit blow more freely'. They decided to do the latter.

Robert Fraser, DG of the COI, wrote his reaction to the report on 1 November, 'We all agree most warmly with what we take to be the sense of the main paragraph – that we must make films that change people's moods and attitudes as well as films that just inform... The creative spirit must find an ally in the technique of showmanship, in entertainment value, and in rugged promotion'.[62] On 5 November Marquand spoke to Morrison and the Lord President agreed.[63] In addition Morrison felt the COI should 'take full advantage of the recommendation in paragraph 7c that it should itself initiate the making of films of wider scope... [and] The EIC are rightly already taking a wide view of their functions in the economic field, and I endorse the recommendation in paragraph 8b that they should be encouraged to continue'.[64] Martli Malherbe, a member of Leslie's EIU, endorsed the report but added that it was not just a case of making films more inspirational, they must have a clear persuasive objective. 'COI should appreciate' Malherbe wrote to Leslie on 11 November, 'that the Sponsor department have, or should have, when they commission a film, a definite propaganda purpose in mind'.[65] Malherbe's use of the word 'propaganda' illustrates how acceptable this previously resisted approach to government communication was becoming.

At 5pm on Wednesday 12 November the Ministerial Home Information Services committee met at 11 Downing Street to discuss the Paymaster General's report and Morrison's response.[66] The Ministers not only approved the recommendations of the report but supported an even greater use of film. Harold Wilson, the new President of the Board of Trade, argued that 'In addition to these considerations an increase in the number of documentary films was important from the aspect of public morale, for example it would be helpful if additional films could be produced showing various aspects of food production'. Aneurin Bevan 'welcomed the proposal in the report that the documentary film unit should be encouraged by the Government to embark on the production of film which would stress the achievements of the present Government in various fields. There would for example be room for an impressive film on the results of the housing drive'.[67]

Patrick Gordon Walker, newly appointed as assistant to Morrison on information matters, was keen that Marquand's report be put into action quickly and 'therefore proposed that he should seek from the Lord President a specific remit to follow up the carrying out of the recommendations'.[68] Having been given this remit Gordon Walker set to work with the COI to shift the films policy, to resolve some of the tensions with the Treasury, and to consider how to enhance government film distribution.

There were four important consequences of this shift in 1947. There was an effort by government to force its official factory newsreel into cinemas, alongside the existing commercial newsreels. There was a more conscious attempt to expand the remit of films and move away from 'mere information'. There was a concerted effort to impose a coherent information strategy on the films programme in order to make it a much more effective instrument in the education and persuasion of the electorate. Critical in this effort was the employment of John Grierson as the new head of the films division in 1948. And there was an attempt to maintain and enhance theatrical distribution and to breathe new life into non-theatrical distribution. This was not a government winding down its films operation. Quite the reverse, Labour was now consciously trying to use film as an instrument of policy.

The government's own newsreel

Clem Leslie recognised that the EIC's official newsreel had a much greater chance of being distributed to cinemas across the country after the Ministerial meeting of 12 November 1947. He was keen that this enthusiasm of senior Ministers regarding the influence of film be directed towards this as well as other specific objectives. He therefore wrote to the Chancellor, 'knowing his interest in films in general', to point out that the real issue was with distribution, not with production. He drafted a note for the Chancellor to write to Morrison, suggesting that 'one ten-minute film a month does not take us very far' (Leslie ignored the trailers and commercially distributed films) and that the government should aim to add the factory newsreel to the film programme. He went so far as to write on the Chancellor's behalf that 'Efforts are to be made to persuade the exhibitors to give it [the factory newsreel] general showing once a month in addition to the present free ten minute film'.[69]

On 11 December 1947 the Chancellor signed this note and sent it to Morrison. A few days later Bernard Sendall met up with W.R. Fuller, the General Secretary of the CEA, to discuss the issue. At the meeting Fuller suggested that, were the government to make some concessions on the ration on film stock for the newsreels, the exhibitors might consider taking on another film.[70] Sendall took this up with the Board of Trade, telling them that the inclusion of the official newsreel in cinema programmes had the 'strong personal blessing of the Chancellor of the Exchequer'.[71] The Board of Trade then discussed the issue of film with Kodak. Kodak were reluctant to release any more film stocks since they were 'virtual dollar exports', but it would 'be prepared to act in accordance with whatever decision HMG may come to in this matter'.[72]

The official newsreel appeared to be making significant progress, but up to this point the newsreel companies themselves had not been consulted. It was not until one of their regular meetings with the COI, on 2 February 1948, that Ronald Tritton introduced the idea. It was not well received. Howard Thomas, Chief-in-Production of Pathé Pictures, 'made the point with some vehemence that the exhibiting side of the Industry was getting tired of overmuch propaganda'.[73] Though Tritton tried to assuage them by claiming that the film would be 'a feature rather than a news piece' this did not help.

The newsreel companies were understandably upset. Since the end of the war they had offered their support to the government's campaigns and refrained from criticising government policy. They also 'felt that they had been helpful in giving coverage to subjects of interest to the Advisory Committee' in the past, and they considered the factory newsreel 'to be an invasion of the sphere of private enterprise'.[74] Neither did Thomas change his mind when Tritton took him and Gerald Sanger to one side at the end of the meeting to mention the film stock concession.[75]

The government consequently gave up on the idea of separate theatrical distribution. It did not, however, abandon the plan of producing industrial success stories to raise morale and promote productivity. 'It was suggested', in EIC discussions, 'that the Government might produce 'achievement' items and give them to the newsreels'.[76] This would have the added benefit, if it melded with the rest of the newsreel, of appearing less like government propaganda. The idea was accepted and three months later the Ministry of Supply was able to report that many official films were being made and a good deal of material given to newsreels: 'A constant supply of material is also provided for Newsreels, to draw attention to the assistance given by the Ministry in industry and science and to achievements in industry'.[77] The government had therefore taken another step towards deliberate news management, providing 'news' stories aimed at influencing the perceptions of the audience, without an official tag attached.

Expanding the film remit from 'mere information'

A critical consequence of the Marquand inquiry was the decision to move towards inspiration and entertainment. It was now generally accepted within the COI that films were not the best means of communicating plain information but were good at stimulating feeling. Tritton was very clear about this when responding to a letter from Harold Wilson of 25 November which suggested that films were 'an extremely good way of explaining the factual background of many of the problems that are embarrassing us at the moment to the general public'.[78] Tritton replied that Films Division, 'hold the opposite view. We think that film can be used to arouse an emotional response, but not to present statistics or explain problems'.[79] The need to sublimate information was even plainer when it came to longer films, such as second features. Philip Mackie, Films Division, wrote that 'With possible second feature projects, we have necessarily first to consider the subject, the informational purpose, the "message". But it is clear that the eventual success of each film depends not at all on the informational purpose, but very largely on the interest and entertainment value of the characters and the story'.[80]

Though Films Division had already been trying to move in this direction the reaction to the inquiry allowed them to move faster and gain funding for projects which might not otherwise have gone ahead. In particular this meant the endorsement of the plan to make a number of second feature films. Bernard Sendall was pleased that by late January 1948 'It is relevant to record that our intention to make story documentaries of $3^{1}/_{2}$ to 6 reels is known to Mr Gordon Walker, the President of the Board of Trade and the Lord President, and has been welcomed by them'.[81]

By this time the Crown Film Unit had just finished filming *A Yank Comes Back*. This film shows graphically how government policy was shifting. The project was originally discussed by the EIC in June 1947.[82] Leslie thought that a one-reel documentary film which showed 'what reasonable and sympathetic Dominion nationals and foreigners thought about Britain' would 'stimulate national group feeling'.[83] This morale boosting picture could be released as part of the monthly release schedule in the autumn.

The COI criticised the initial idea as insincere and suggested changes.[84] Helen de Mouilpied remembered that during the war the MOI had made a film called *Welcome to Britain*, starring Burgess Meredith. Why not, they thought, make a post-war sequel.[85] Meredith was willing to do so (for the price of his passage from the US and expenses) as long as he could also script the film.[86] The COI agreed. Having then received a brief about the proposed film Meredith also wanted to change the structure.[87] 'Important drawback' he telegrammed from the US in October, 'impossible my opinion to make point effective one reel stop seems waste and cramps technique'.[88] The 10-minute morale film was subsequently extended to two reels and the budget increased.[89] *A Yank Comes Back* was eventually completed in July 1948. By that time it had become a four-reel scripted second feature, described as a 'serio-comic film about Britain's economic situation'.[90] This is a suitably euphemistic description of a film which is clunky and highly contrived.

This was a short film which became a second feature as the approach to films shifted. Its successors were less ad hoc. In all the COI planned to make five features over the following two years.[91] The topics being considered were Nursing, Local Government, The Farmer's Life, and Mental Health Services. Each would cost between £25–30,000 to produce.[92]

The government also tried to add entertainment values to shorter films. Sir Stafford Cripps commissioned John Halas and Joy Batchelor, who ran an independent film company specialising in animation, to develop an animated character, 'Charley' for use in government shorts.[93] He was designed to be an easy-going, timeless British everyman, who was only able to understand Britain's current difficult situation by experiencing how it got there. In light-hearted historical narratives Charley would learn about what life was like before social security (*Charley's March of Time*), why Britain was so reliant on imports (*Robinson Charley*) and why the price of coal was so high (*Charley's Black Magic*).

The COI commissioned other short films simply to raise morale, such as *What a Life* and *Eye of the Beholder*.[94] By July 1948, John Grierson was able to comment that 'In regard to the form of the films themselves there had lately been a welcome change. The new cartoon series for instance was a precious instrument, and the tendency generally was towards drama and humour'.[95]

Through 1948 and 1949 the government sought to make films whose purpose, though partly to inform, was more importantly to persuade and direct. The EIU wrote in January 1949 that, 'The monthly release programme, that is to say, gives and is intended to give the Government the opportunity of inducing the public to accept ideas, and to take actions, which are of practical importance in the national interest'.[96] And for a period after 1947 the COI was keen to integrate values such as drama and entertainment. The Home Film Programme Committee was convinced that this was successful. 'Evidence is becoming available', the Committee wrote in December 1949, 'that the policy of reserving the monthly release for subjects of first-rank national importance which are capable of arresting and entertaining treatment is producing results...There is some reason to suppose, therefore, that the monthly releases are appreciating in value in the eyes of the leading exhibitors'.[97]

Imposing a coherent strategy on the film programme

A third consequence of the 1947 shift was the attempt to impose a coherent strategy on the film programme. This was now possible since the COI and the Economic Information Committee had been given greater latitude to centralise decision making on film production and distribution.[98] But it was given much more emphasis with the arrival of John Grierson as the new head of the COI Films Division in April 1948.

It is important to recognise the significance of the government's employment of Grierson. Clearly one of the main reasons he was brought in was to heal the rift between the government and the documentary units. But Ministers and officials were also aware of Grierson's beliefs about the use of government information and film as a means of education and reform.[99] For Grierson, state sponsored propaganda was a pre-requisite of a modern social democracy.[100] In his address on 'Education and Total Effort' in 1941 he said the role of the state was not simply to add to the mass of informational material already 'thrown at the head of the benighted citizen'. It was 'to give the citizen a pattern of thought and feeling which will enable him to approach this flood of material in some useful fashion'.[101] And in the letter he wrote to Morrison and Cripps in 1945, Grierson asserted that a government information service 'is the instrument by which the Government secures the cooperation of the people to national and international ends'.[102] In other words, how it engineers consent. The decision to employ Grierson, therefore, was another significant shift away from the neutral transmission of information from state to citizen.

As soon as he arrived in his new position Grierson began putting together a plan 'to impose a pattern upon the future film programme and to weld it gradually into an articulated national service'.[103] In this plan, the government's short films would become part of a small number of series, each with its own identity and targeted at a specific audience. 'The purpose of this pattern' Grierson wrote, 'was to gear production to distribution. Each series would as it were be fitted into a particular jig, and those concerned would know from the start what shape and size and style a film should take and for what type of audience it was intended'.[104] Outside instructional or educational films, Grierson separated the domestic programme into three areas, Spirit of the Nation; Progress of the Nation; Principles and Practices'.[105] This would later be translated into a 'World in Action' series, a 'Report' series, the Charley films, a 'Where do You Come From' series, and a factory magazine.[106] Robert Fraser told departments that they 'should try to fit their individual projects into the pattern proposed... so that official films, instead of being entirely unrelated, should form part of a visible design'.[107]

To oversee this shift Grierson developed a Film Programme sub-committee in September 1948. Fraser later said the committee's creation 'can already be seen as a milestone in the history of Information Service film work'.[108] Its intention was, he said, to 'advise on an identifiable group of films concerned with social progress and achievement'.[109] It also had 'the responsibility for guiding the programme of films for distribution at home excluding those of a purely specialist and instructional nature. This will entail decisions of priority and emphasis, the assumption of sponsorship by the most appropriate department and, in certain instances, by the COI in its own right'.[110] It was therefore explicitly responsible for films with a propaganda purpose. The government was adopting the Griersonian model of state film-making.

A greater awareness of distribution

A fourth and final consequence of the 1947 shift was that Ministers and officials became much more conscious of distribution. After the Marquand inquiry Ministers became more aware that distribution was as much, if not more, of an issue than production. When Harold Wilson wrote to Morrison strongly pushing for the COI to produce more films, for example, the Films Division were grateful for the attention but surprised that the President of the Board of Trade did not realise how many films were already made and not screened.[111] Films Division explained the rudiments of distribution to Leslie who quickly passed these on to Cripps and Gordon Walker.[112] By the middle of December 1947, JA Lidderdale was writing back to Films Division on Gordon Walker's behalf that he and the Chancellor were very conscious that distribution was the problem and not the number of films made.[113]

This was particularly pertinent since there was much more screen time available at this point than there had ever been before. This was thanks to the current dearth of American films. In August 1947 the government had imposed a 75 per cent tax on imports of American films to stem the tide of dollars leaving the country. The American distributors' association, the MPAA, responded immediately by imposing a boycott on American films to the UK. Though British cinemas held enough US feature films to show for a few months, after that they would be reduced to replaying old films or showing new British films. This included the support programmes. Suddenly there seemed to be a gap on British cinema screens that needed filling.[114]

Ministers considered how they could increase the production of British documentaries and shorts and ensure a greater number of government films were screened in cinemas.[115] Gordon Walker thought that the government should, in the new Cinematograph Act which was due for renewal in 1948, set renters and exhibitors a high quota for the screening of British films.[116] He was 'keen to get the Y percentage [for other films and shorts] fixed high enough to provide an incentive for the greater production in this country of documentaries, story documentaries and second features'.[117]

Morrison, talking in a specially convened meeting to discuss the production and distribution of British films for the support programme, said he thought the 75 per cent tax might be an opportunity to reduce the three-hour cinema programme to one main feature and two shorts, one of which would be a documentary.[118]

Though there were problems with these and other suggestions, Wilson took them into account when drawing up the Cinematograph Act. Though the Act itself did not set a percentage it stated that there would be a quota for first features and for the support programme and that the exact figure would wait on discussions with industry.[119] When Wilson announced that it would be 45 per cent British-made for first features and 25 per cent for the support programme the exhibitors were stunned.[120] This was considerably higher than they had expected and they did not think it could be fulfilled. Under significant pressure Wilson later lowered the figure for first features, but not for the support programme.

Even before the opportunities opened by the new Cinematograph Act the government was having more success distributing its films commercially. In February 1948 Fraser was able to boast that 'About twice as many films had been placed with renters in the last twelve months as in any previous year. If the feature-length films made during the war by the Service Departments were excluded, then about four times as many Government films were receiving theatrical showing as in any previous year'.[121] Fraser was quick to ascribe this to the inclusion of more entertainment, telling the Home Information Services Committee that 'the rising figures for the theatrical distribution were an indication that the problem of giving official films a higher entertainment value was being tackled not without some success'.[122] The figure increased further in 1948 and by July Fraser was able to announce that the commercial distribution of government films in 1948 would reach a level 'sensationally higher than any achieved before and five times as great as in war time (if Service made films were excepted)'.[123]

These commercial successes were, of course, in addition to the agreement the government still held with the CEA. This not only guaranteed the distribution of 12 government short films a year and 25–30 trailers in approximately 3000 cinemas, but, unlike advertising in newspapers or on billboards, guaranteed it free of charge. Officials within government were very conscious of how valuable this now was. When the original agreement had been extended in 1946 Mr Plumbley of the Home Information Services (Official) committee calculated that 'the average weekly cinema audience was about 30 millions, which' Plumbley thought 'was an audience worth paying for. It had been computed that the free publicity given to the Government trailers during the war represented a gross value of £3 to £4 millions'.[124] Though the agreement had been intended as a national concession during wartime the government clung to it desperately in its aftermath. In late 1946, when it seemed the deal might be under threat, Fraser and Morrison managed to convince the exhibitors to extend it for another year.[125] In 1947 and 1948 the government further cultivated the CEA to ensure the deal persisted.[126]

Shortly after Grierson became controller of the Films Division, in July 1948, he described the new distribution situation; 'opportunities of the moment were enormous. The theatres were waiting for new films (though the desire for a reduction in Entertainment tax caused the exhibitors to appear hostile), and the latest quota arrangements made the possibilities even greater'.[127]

The government also sought to enhance its non-theatrical distribution programme. In 1947–48 there were 52,244 non-theatrical shows compared to 46,789 in 1946–7.[128] The figure rose further in 1948–9. Particular thought was given to the factory audience who were so difficult to reach by other media.[129] A working party was formed and met twice in 1949 and proposed that 'a determined, planned and fully equipped effort should be made in the coming winter to restore to the factory film show as much as possible of the widespread popularity and influence which it enjoyed during the war'.[130]

Therefore in 1948 the government was increasing the number and exposure of its films through theatrical and non-theatrical distribution. This included everything from 30-second advertisements to short morale films to 45-minute second features. It was doing this by adjusting legislation to help some of its own films gain screen time. It was leveraging its authority to ensure the continuation of a wartime distribution agreement, and it was increasing the number of screenings to non-theatrical (often captive) audiences. Films were now playing a significant role in the promotion of government policy.

Problems encountered as a result of the 1947 shift

The government experienced significant problems as a result of its shift in policy after 1947. These problems are important because not only do they help to explain why the government drew back from its newfound commitment to film, they also help to indicate why film is such a difficult medium for any democratic government to use. There were two main difficulties. First, by trying to make inspirational films the government found itself open to charges of propaganda and to complaints from audiences and exhibitors. Second, by trying to make entertainment features the government was taking on financial and critical risks that were much greater than it initially realised.

Inspirational films or propaganda?

The government soon found itself in difficulty over inspirational films. Documentary shorts whose purpose was to inspire invariably tended to focus on positive stories and achievements, the message behind them being that things were hard but were getting better fast. Yet it was very difficult not to elide the efforts to rebuild Britain with an affirmation of Labour policy. For example the first film the EIC commissioned, *Report on Coal*, talked about the 'formidable task' the NCB took on when it was nationalised but that '8 months later the Coal Board reported progress'. In its first eight months, the film said, there were 30,000 more men employed in the industry, and 4.5 million tonnes more coal was being mined; 'Not a perfect figure, but they show a profit since the country took over, after years of loss'.[131]

Similarly, it was difficult for these 'achievement' films to resist comparing current growth and improvements to the privations of the past. The government's monthly release for August 1950 was about 'building a new country', *From the Ground Up*.[132] As the camera panned over building sites, factories, coal mines and locomotives, the commentator told the viewer that 'Today we're investing one-fifth of all our resources... in the making of a new Britain for our children and ourselves. We're rebuilding, modernising, expanding, the whole vast productive machine by which we live'. This was contrasted with the view of the past. A child was filmed with her face pinned against the glass of a basement flat with bars on the windows. 'What of our cities?' the voiceover asked, 'Can we let our children inherit a legacy of the past like this?'.[133]

These films were also increasingly perceived as government propaganda by the audience, by exhibitors, and by the other political parties. This did not necessarily mean people objected to them. Those who accepted the position of the films tended to condone the propaganda. Those who disagreed with it did not.[134] This was most clearly demonstrated when Films Division commissioned the Social Survey to find out what a preview audience thought about *A Yank Comes Back*.[135] One respondent thought the film 'A very good idea, makes you feel proud of England. Brings back to mind memories we ought to be proud of' (Dentist's assistant, 43). A second had 'Rather mixed feelings about it. Not very good propaganda' (Ironmongery sales manager, 41). And a third 'Didn't think much of it. Propaganda. A waste of time and money' (Housewife, 25).[136]

Some cinemas were also now objecting to screening government films. In June 1948, Ken Jones, the chairman of the Birmingham branch of the CEA, told the *Daily Mirror* that 'We were happy to give screen time during the war, but we feel these films are now political propaganda. We should feel the same if the Tories were in power'.[137]

The Conservatives drew increasing attention to the issue of political propaganda in films in 1948. In March Boyd Carpenter criticised the film *Ours is the Land* for contrasting the current administration's record on housing with the governments of the 1930s. He quoted the commentary which said, 'They promised us houses in 1935. Look at Paisley and Dunfermline. Now they have got them'.[138] And during the lengthy May debate on information services Anthony Marlowe (Conservative) attacked the COI for its plans to spend £30,000 on six animated Charley films 'dealing, I suggest, entirely with Government propaganda'.[139]

Though Ministers strongly denied that films sought to applaud the government's achievements, it was slightly embarrassing when the Labour Party announced, in January 1950, that they would be using some of the COI films as part of their election campaign.[140]

Once exhibitors and audiences objected to these films as government propaganda it was hard for Labour to continue making them. Such tax-funded bias could not be justified for long by a democratic government.

The risks associated with making entertainment films

The government found the integration of entertainment values through the development of second-feature films even more difficult. Using fiction as a means of government communication required much more depth and nuance than a short documentary film made for a specific purpose. Helen de Mouilpied was very clear about this after having read a series of suggestions for second features from the EIU.[141] She told Tritton that the ideas the EIU set out 'suggest a fundamental misunderstanding of what a second-feature film should be. It is <u>not</u> an elongated short propaganda film with a nice moral rammed home at greater length than in the monthly release films. It must be first and foremost a good story in its own right, a story in which characters develop in action. It must entertain. It influences people's opinions only by drawing them into the story and opening their hearts and sympathies, but if it is good in this way then people won't come away with a neat synopsis on their lips'.[142]

De Mouilpied may have been right but this suggested a degree of creativity and experiment generally unsuited to government ministers and officials. Indeed their intermittent attempts to put forward feature ideas show how far many of them were from understanding how a fictional film might best represent government policy. In December 1947, after the Ministerial committee had agreed to push forward with second-features, Gordon Walker wrote to Tritton and Sendall asking 'whether you had thought of the possibilities of the short story as a basis for shorter features, lasting about $3/4$ of an hour. De Maupassant and Kipling might provide material for a new type of short feature which would at the same time make a good deal of use of the documentary tradition'.[143] It is not clear how Gordon Walker thought de Maupassant or Kipling would illuminate the national situation.

The government did not make any films based on these short stories but it did produce a number of others. *Life in her Hands*, starring Kathleen Byron, was a slow-burning drama about a woman who decided to become a nurse after her husband was killed in a car crash. By showing what a rewarding experience nursing could be it was intended to encourage women to go into the profession.[144] *Out of True* was a film devised to show modern methods at mental hospitals to 'to remove public misconceptions'.[145] It also made *Waverley Steps*, a film about Edinburgh, and *Four Men in Prison*, a Home Office feature on the penal system.[146]

However, as many feature films were attempted and abandoned as were made. In May 1949 Fraser asked Philip Mackie to draw up a list charting the history of government feature film making since the end of the Second World War. 'This is one of the most fascinating COI documents I have ever read' he wrote to Grierson when he had received it.[147] Though the record with long documentary films was reasonably good, with the 'big-fiction propaganda film – here the record is simply ghastly – false and feeble and fumbling start after start, wasted money, strained tempers, horrible wasted effort and talent'. 'Surely' he wrote 'there is a great deal to be learnt from all this'.[148] That the government was not well suited, for example, to making fictional films.

In addition, 'the few [non-fiction feature] films that have been completed ("Cumberland" and "Yank") [have been] total distribution flops'. *A Yank Comes Back*, for example, was originally agreed as a £7,000 one reel film for autumn 1947 release. It was eventually completed as a four-reeler in July 1948 at a cost of over £19,000.[149] Despite the protestations of the COI that it had great potential to earn back the expense through commercial distribution, by May 1949 it had only received 22 bookings and receipts of £154.[150]

The problems with *Yank* helped to convince the Treasury that making second features was risky and unpredictable. This was compounded in the case of fiction films by the problems inherent in measuring their success. If they were not 'elongated short propaganda films' as de Mouilpied suggested, than their success could not be measured by the audience's immediate reaction. Yet neither could they be judged solely by their receipts since this would suggest they were competing with commercial entertainment films for profit rather than communicating an important message.

The problem with state sponsored film making

By 1949 the COI was also aware that there were some very practical problems to government film making. For one thing, most of the films took an age to make. By the time one was completed, the political context in which it had been commissioned had often passed. *What a Life*, described earlier, was devised in 1947, when the national mood was very gloomy and pessimistic. But by the time it was screened, in January 1949, the mood had changed such that a film about two old men who consider drowning themselves and then think better of it no longer suited the country's temper.

There were also many opportunities for films to go wrong. Each film required a lengthy gestation, involved significant numbers of people, and was often delayed by tortuous discussions over distribution. Film-making was, therefore, a nightmare for State officials to control. When the COI gave independent film makers the freedom to produce films which were more creative and engaging their grip slipped even further.

Film-making was also expensive. The ten-minute shorts the government made cost between £3,500 to £6,000, on average.[151] Second features cost upwards of £25–30,000.[152] In total £1,186,454 was spent on films in 1948–49 (over 70 per cent on films to be screened in Britain). This equates to over £25 million pounds in 2005 prices. The figure would have been much higher still had the government had to pay to distribute its trailers and shorts in cinemas.

The government could not afford expensive failures in 1949. Stafford Cripps was pressing hard to reduce expenditure through his austerity drive. In this atmosphere socially progressive films without any specific objective looked like a luxury. Ministers decided, for the near future at least, that they should concentrate on 'action publicity', information which elicited a clearly identifiable reaction, rather than more subtle approaches.[153] This included short films, although they had to have a straightforward and measurable purpose.

The Treasury took this as an endorsement of its general scepticism towards film and intervened more frequently in production decisions, refusing funding for new features and diluting the autonomy of the COI. Grierson was forced to make staff cuts and reorganise the process by which films were made. Unhappy about the cutbacks Grierson resigned from the COI the following year.

After his departure the COI introduced a range of controls designed to reduce the costs and the risks of film production. It drew up specifications sheets which required departments to lay out the purpose and function of each film they commissioned.[154] It integrated audience research into film production and distribution. And, it made the consideration of distribution a pre-requisite to each film's production. The process became, in other words, very similar to that of a modern advertising company. A fortnight before the election of October 1951 Niven McNicoll, head of Films Division after Grierson's departure, told Fraser that 'During the past two years, we have revolutionised the process of examining proposals before taking them on as jobs'.[155] Not surprisingly, the controls scared off some of the original documentary movement directors like Stuart Legg.

Though the government was forced to retreat from its larger, Griersonian film-making ambitions, it did not lose its faith in the power of film. 'Once successfully made', Leslie wrote in March 1949, 'their effect will be strong and deep, for they bring to bear upon a large and organised audience emotional forces much more powerful than can be given expression in press advertising or posters'.[156] Films could encourage imitation, conformity and compliance. The government did not want to give up on such a powerful medium.

So instead of making and distributing its own films, the government looked for alternatives. An obvious one was the newsreels. The newsreels were still immensely popular and the newsreel companies normally amenable to working with the government. The COI and departments had collaborated with them in an ad hoc way before but in 1949, just as the government was reducing its commitment to film-making, the COI institutionalised this collaboration. It established a newsreel desk, the explicit purpose of which was to foster good relations with the newsreel companies; suggesting stories, providing access, and giving them government footage when available.[157] Fred Watts, previously Production Manager of Pathé Gazette, was appointed to run the desk.[158]

Evidence from 1950 suggests that it was very successful. Since it was set up 'the newsreel companies have been persuaded not only to cover many events which they would not otherwise have considered but also to include in their newsreels a number of items made up from official material in the course of production for other purposes' the COI told the Treasury. 'The result' it continued, 'has been, broadly, that a great many more items of direct informational value are now getting into the newsreels produced for home circulation'.[159]

The government also looked to the BBC. It was on good terms with the monopoly, publicly funded broadcaster and saw television as another possible outlet for its films. 'Television is now emerging as a highly important method of distribution for information films', the COI wrote to Ministers in 1950, 'and it may well grow one day into the most important of all'.[160] By the final year of the Labour government the COI was able to report that 'Many films had been televised during the past two years, and the medium was now also being used experimentally for the showing of trailers'.[161]

Turning to these less expensive, and often unofficial, alternatives, the government was effectively institutionalising news management techniques. This was a critically important repercussion of this administration's great film-making experiment. The government failed to become another Disney or Warner Brothers but in the process learnt the value of film and how useful it could be as a means of education and persuasion. It came to realise that producing and distributing information could be an expensive, difficult process open to uncomfortable risk. Much better to channel material through existing outlets.

The experience also led those within government towards a different understanding of information. Indeed this was one of the most significant outcomes of the experiment. Ministers and officials came to office with the idea that information was a neutral good and its communication to the public a simple mechanical task. Their experience showed them that it was actually malleable and complex, and its importance depended not on its intrinsic merits but on the objectives to which it was put. It showed them that how information was communicated then determined its interpretation and people's response. The State, therefore, needed to separate information from policy and use information pragmatically as a means of manufacturing consent, rather than simply aiming to make people better informed.

This important and fundamental change was spelt out by none other than the head of the COI himself, Robert Fraser. 'Information' he wrote in April 1949, 'is not a function independent of the purposes of society, and informative or persuasive material derives its significance from the end to which it is directed. It may have its own integrities of truth and imagination, but its purpose is derivative from some national end. Information is not "for its own sake"'.[162]

4
'Information Management' Becomes a New Tool of Governance

Before 1948 the machinery and methods of government information were not set. There was still ongoing ideological opposition to their continuation in Parliament and there were increasing concerns about its cost. However, once these were resolved over the following two years the foundations of government information management – institutional, conceptual and methodological – had been established.

The challenge to the information services in Parliament

Frank England's investigation into government communication helped to spark a public controversy that led to questions in the House throughout January, February and March 1948. This culminated, on 13 May, in the most important debate on information services since the war. This debate was significant for a number of reasons. It represented the high water mark of ideological dissent with the information services. After this point the debate shifted to efficiency and cost reduction. It identified the increasing tendency of government to manage information, for example by selecting facts that supported its objectives. And it highlighted the continual problem inherent to government communication – how a government explains its actions without always creating a rationale and justification for them.

Harold Macmillan, the future Conservative Prime Minister, opened the debate with a strong critique of the inherent partiality of government information. 'I have no doubt' he said, 'that the temporary civil servants in charge of this vast machine try to be objective... Nevertheless, the analysis of a problem, whether positively or negatively, almost invariably tends to be one-sided. The Central Office is a Government agency. It cannot very well attack or criticize the Government it

82

serves. It can make no reference to its failures and it must pass lightly over its lack of foresight. The fuel crisis must be represented not as a failure of the Minister but as an act of God... What happens is that all the facts are emphasised which are favourable to the Government, who are represented as a kind of band of heroes struggling bravely against adverse conditions and events outside their control'.[1]

Though he does not refer to it, it is likely Macmillan had in mind publications like the 'Battle for Output', written in early 1947 by Max Nicholson. This popular version of the Economic Survey began by explaining that it was 'the plain story of Britain's production in the first full year of peace. It is the story of a great beginning towards recovery, against heavy odds'.[2]

The determination of the government to overcome this one-sidedness by only presenting 'the facts' was equally fraught with difficulties (as they had already found). The Conservative John Boyd Carpenter pointed this out: 'The Lord President has talked of factual statements. I am not going to suggest that, on the whole, these statements are not factual, but the question is which facts. No information service in the world can disseminate all the facts about the situation in the world today. Even the Government's present lavish expenditure of paper cannot carry that. So we are driven to the conviction that the officials of this Department have to select between one fact and another'.[3] And the illusion of objectivity was perhaps one of the greatest dangers of the information services since the patina of truth added to their power. This could, Macmillan argued, lead to the 'sapping of individual judgment and substitution of the state machine'.[4]

In a similar way, if the government tried to promote its cause through its machinery, 'as it has every right to do', it necessarily compromised the objectivity of that machinery. The Labour MP S.N. Evans admitted as much when he said, 'Today we are engaged in the greatest experiment of all time; one to abolish want without, at the same time, abolishing liberty... It is in the service of this experiment that the COI has a great part to play'.[5] As Kenneth Lindsay (Independent) commented, 'Implicit behind the whole of the arguments [presented by the government information services] was that a very important change was going on in this country, and it was important that the people here and abroad should know about it. But supposing they do not agree with the change?'.[6]

The Opposition also argued that the information services were leading Ministers to bypass the constitutional route of communication – Parliament – and go directly to the media. 'Ministers are detaching themselves more and more from the House of Commons. They are proceeding far more by method of Press Conferences, broadcasting, and now this Central Office of Information'.[7] The importance of the fortnightly economic press conferences were evidence of this, as was the high number of broadcasts made by Ministers as part of the production drive in 1947.

On the larger point of the justification of information services, Labour had argued that the world was much more complex than it had been in the past, and it was the duty of the government to explain that complexity to its citizens.[8] However, as Kenneth Pickthorn, historian and Cambridge MP, responded, 'the past looks easy only because it is not here, and because, comparatively speaking, we do not know anything about it', hence, 'the notion that things are infinitely more complex now than they used to be is an illusion'.[9]

Unfortunately the Labour responses to some of their counterparts' challenges did not engage with the fundamental difficulties of government communication raised. They were so prepared to counter the charges of Party politics that they did not connect with the overarching dangers of government control of information. 'It is not a question of party politics' as Kenneth Lindsay unsuccessfully tried to make clear, 'We have had too much of party politics here today... Suppose a Conservative Government get into power and they have these creative civil servants, what is the position? ...they would focus its propaganda on the legislation which they were going to put through. That is inherent in a domestic propaganda service'.[10]

But the government benches refused to take on the complexities or nuances of the debate. They told the Conservatives their evidence of Party propaganda was unconvincing or petty (Morrison, Granville and Driberg), that the justification of information services in a democracy was straightforward (Gordon Walker), and that given the level of commercial advertising the government had to shout to get itself heard (Driberg). Their only criticism was that the information services were not powerful enough given the growing communist threat (Woodrow Wyatt).

The single aspect of debate on which the Conservatives could properly engage with Labour was expenditure. This was the original focus of Macmillan's speech. 'Expenditure has grown year on year' he said, and was now 'impressive' and 'extravagant'. His own calculations had given him a figure of £7.5 million on home information services and £9 million abroad. The cost of this 'vast machine of Government information' could easily be cut back, Macmillan said. Frederic Harris

(Conservative) accused it of 'wanton extravagance'.[11] Though Gordon Walker, the deputy information head, defended it, saying it saved as much as it cost thanks to preventative healthcare advice and recruitment campaigns, this was the one aspect of debate that the government took seriously. With Sir Stafford Cripps as Chancellor and Economic Overlord constantly exhorting people to austerity, the government could not be perceived to be spending profligately. Therefore, in the autumn of 1948 the Treasury appointed a Committee of inquiry, headed by Sir Henry French, to examine the costs of the Home Information Services.

Even before its appointment, Morrison had been aware of the rising costs and had started to think about cutting back. He was conscious that after the immediate post-war reductions, costs had been rising since 1946.[12] The estimates for 1948/9 were only 8.5 per cent below the level of 1944/5 (the wartime peak in spending) despite Attlee's assurances in December 1945 and March 1946 that post-war information services would be significantly reduced. For the information services meeting in April, Morrison prepared a memorandum showing the total cost of the information services now amounted to about six shillings per head of the population.[13] This equated to over £13 million, a figure estimated to rise to over £16 million for 1948–49. Even still, Morrison told the Committee he was not looking for large scale cuts, just for more care in departmental spending.

However, in his memorandum Morrison also outlined three major reasons why information had now become so critical to government. The reasons indicate the importance of the change in the nature of governance and the significance of this change happening while this particular government was in power. 'Before the war', Morrison wrote, 'the Government Information Services were in their infancy. During the war Departments learned the value of publicity and information work. They are now great believers in its efficacy and importance'. There had also been, since the end of the conflict, a 'great flow of post-war social and economic legislation' which needed to be explained to the public. Finally, there was 'the continuation, and indeed intensification, of the nation's economic difficulties' which meant the information services had the task 'not only of persuading the public to act in a certain way' but also explaining the reasons for the economic difficulties.[14] Information was now a necessary corollary of democratic administration.

After the Supply debate in May the government sought to make further cuts in the budget for the information services. In October the

Chancellor told Cabinet that any expenditure on new services or increase in existing services had to be taken from the existing budget.[15] In December Morrison wrote that 'the time has come to call a halt' in rising costs, and, if possible, try to reduce the estimates for 1949–50 below the total figure of £16.7 million.[16]

But the reduction in spending and consequent cancellation of many of the government's campaigns disguised the most important aspect of the debate and its aftermath. The principle of government information had been upheld. After 1948, the arguments against information services dwindled. The government had successfully defended the practice of communication and the machinery that went with it. And it continued to develop its techniques of communication. By May the following year (1949) Robert Fraser was able to write to Morrison, 'I do not think this [the need for information services] is seriously questioned now. Among the newspapers it is only the Express Group that occasionally clamours for abolition' and Boyd Carpenter was now the sole voice in the Commons.[17]

The French Committee confirmed this the same month: 'The justification for some Government information services is beyond question. The citizen has a right to be told, and the Government has a plain duty to tell him, what it is doing in his name and with his money, and why'.[18] Though the French Committee identified areas in which the government could make savings on the cost of the home information services, most notably press and poster advertising, they also ratified the responsibility of the government to use information services to communicate with the people.

Institutional framework

Therefore by 1949 the institutional framework of government information was in place. The Central Office of Information, an entirely new feature of British government, was established and exists to this day. This included the Social Survey and machinery for measuring the public's response not just to government policy but to government publicity (French emphasised the importance of measuring the effects of publicity in his report).

At the same time the Treasury finally accepted the findings of the Crombie Committee, which had been set up in 1946 following Fraser's concerns that the government had not taken account of its new communications role. By the end of 1949, the Treasury established information professionals permanently within the government. This meant the formalisation of civil service positions, remuneration and recruitment criteria, and career paths for information officers.[19]

The position of the PR advisor to the Prime Minister was also, by this time, established. Its responsibilities, of briefing the Parliamentary Lobby every day, coordinating departmental communication, and leading the government's information personnel, were set by Francis Williams and enhanced by Philip Jordan. When Winston Churchill returned to Number 10 in 1951 he initially tried to return to the days without a Downing Street press secretary, but found he could not do without. The uber-efficient Thomas Fife Clark effectively took up that position in 1952.

Conceptual framework

More important even than the physical framework was the radically new conceptual framework of information management which had emerged by 1949. As described in the last chapter, the government had, over the course of four long years, become convinced not only that information was a critical aspect of modern democratic government, but that it was much more complex than they had first thought. Presentation did not emerge naturally from policy. It had to be considered separately. Information was simply a starting point from which one had to decide on direction, method, speed, style and, of course, where to finish.

This represented a radically new conceptual understanding of information, embraced by both Ministers and civil servants. Most integrated it, almost subconsciously, into their thinking and actions. Some did so more explicitly. Patrick Gordon Walker, a Minister from October 1947, and John Pimlott, Morrison's private secretary, even wrote books about it.

Gordon Walker became Morrison's deputy on information policy towards the end of 1947. Tall, willowy, with thinning hair and a pipe, Gordon Walker was young, only just 40, with an owlish patrician air. Politics was his fourth career, having already taught at Oxford in the 1920s, written for the *Daily Telegraph* from Nazi Germany in the 1930s, and broadcast for the BBC European Service during the war (famously broadcasting from Belsen in 1945). His political career was later marred when, as Foreign Secretary apparent, he very publicly lost his Parliamentary seat in the 1964 election.

Gordon Walker's observations of government information policy after the war had a profound effect on him. So much so that he wrote a book, published in 1951, called *Restatement of Liberty*. This was a theoretical tract on how to achieve the 'better society' through practical government. Communication and propaganda were fundamental to Gordon Walker's vision. Indeed they were one of the state's 'chief necessary functions'.[20]

He saw propaganda and information as a means to avoid coercion and direct people towards the greater good. 'Persuasion', he wrote, 'is particularly necessary to help achieve the sorts of natural behaviour that the new State is almost wholly debarred from bringing about by the use of its direct powers'. This 'new State' needed to use propaganda 'to help to change human nature' and 'to clarify and disabuse the minds of members of society' from their natural errors.[21] For fear of this sounding too authoritarian, Gordon Walker explicitly tried to differentiate this type of propaganda from that of fascist or communist states.

Gordon Walker's political philosophy had been inspired by developments in Britain in the late 1940s. He believed Britain only survived the post-war economic crises thanks to the information campaigns of 1946–8: '...because the people through State propaganda had an infinitely better understanding than before of what was happening, they remained infinitely more steadfast, calm and energetic than in 1929–31'.[22]

The particular relevance of Gordon Walker's political theory is in confirming the wholesale shift in government attitude. From an assumption that communication was a simple, mechanical task of an administration to a realisation that not only was it much more complex, but that its direction had to be determined and ideologically justified. For Gordon Walker it was an ideological imperative of a socialist government if it was to create a better society.

John Pimlott also wrote about this change. His book makes for a fascinating parallel with Gordon Walker's since it shows this conceptual shift extended much broader than just Party. John Pimlott, who had written the influential memorandum of 1946 on government communication, was so struck by the emerging importance of communications and public relations that he took a sabbatical in 1947–8 to go to America and research it further. In his book Pimlott argued that communication was now an important and inevitable aspect of democratic administration. 'Modern techniques of mass information and persuasion are powerful tools,' he wrote, 'and all who seek to acquire or maintain power in a democracy must make use of them'.[23]

Pimlott also argued that information now had to be presented in such a way as to have mass appeal and convince people to take action. To do this governments might have 'to select facts which are most likely to interest the audience; to state them in the language of a mass circulation magazine; to repeat them; to use other media than the printed word such as broadcasts, motion pictures, comic strips; and to follow up with personal contacts'.[24] Or, put another way, to manage information.

These two, the Minister and the civil servant, represent a new consciousness within government. They illustrate the new conceptual understanding which would soon come to typify all the departments and frame the future parameters of government communication.

Methodological framework

When it first came to office the government did not give too much thought to the methods of communication. It assumed that transferring information to the public was a straightforward task. Though interested parties, like the documentary film makers, stressed the value of one medium over another, Morrison chose not to distinguish them but to let departments and the COI decide on the best method of transferral.

Experience quickly showed that the method was extremely important. Some media were good for some things and awful for others. Films are an obvious case in point. Though potentially very powerful, they were also time consuming, expensive and risky. Other methods, like newspaper advertising, were much less risky but lacked the emotional impact. Deciding which media to use, and how to use it was complex, protracted, and liable to lead to lively debate.

Since Labour had signally failed to comprehend the size and scope of its original ambition, it found itself developing communications policy on the hoof. When crises hit, Ministers and officials reacted to them as best they could. If the methods they adopted were effective, they stuck. The lessons learned then became precedents. This was the case both with the process by which the government responded, and the media which the government used.

The decentralised process first established in 1946, for example, was quickly found wanting. It was re-engineered in 1947 to deal with the fuel and the currency crises. Once the new process, of coordinating the commissioning and release of economic information, proved successful it was copied by other areas of government.

Similarly, departments, the COI, and the Economic Information Unit (EIU) experimented with different media in order to find the best method of communicating with the public. The EIU was particularly innovative and pioneered methods which then became common practice. Clem Leslie was conscious they were doing something very new. 'We know well that we are not finished practitioners, but experimenters' he told the Institute of Public Administration in 1949. 'It is not usually given to those who have to explore new territory to find the best route at the first attempt and go straight to their objective. We have to feel our way toward the best methods, and to content ourselves meantime with a good deal less than complete achievement'.[25] Trial and error therefore helped to determine both the process by which the government communicated and the media it chose to use.

But there were two other factors which were critical in shaping the methodological framework. One was the public's response to government communication. The government learnt, through market research, that despite its best efforts much of the public did not notice, did not digest, and did not respond to government communication. This had a significant impact on subsequent campaigns and publicity.

Market research had not even been included in the original plan for the COI, because of widespread suspicion of it. Morrison snuck it through after the Central Office had been established. Even once established it was initially ignored by most departments (some Ministers being as suspicious of public opinion research as the people). But over time they began to find it more and more useful. This was especially true when it came to preparing for, then measuring the results of, information campaigns.

The surveys were enlightening. They revealed how little people knew about government policy and how disinterested many were in learning more. 'Large sections of the population are ignorant of or have only very hazy ideas about many aspects of our national economy' the economic survey of May 1948 discovered. 'Our educational system in the past has not provided them with a balanced picture of how the nation's economic affairs are managed'.[26] People were similarly ignorant about Britain's empire. 'The population as a whole lacks fundamental geographic knowledge of the Commonwealth', the Colonial Affairs survey of 1948 found. Less than half the respondents could name even one colony correctly. Three per cent thought the United States was still a British colony.[27]

The government's initial response was to try to educate people. But it soon found that however much information it provided, a lot of people took no notice. This came across most vividly in some research done on behalf of the Economic Information Committee by Dr Mark Abrams company, Research Services Ltd. in 1947. Abrams had been asked to test the public reaction to *Report to the Nation* – a series of government information advertisements placed in the national press. In October 1947 his company interviewed readers of the *Daily Mail* and the *Daily Mirror*. The readers were asked whether they had read the recent Report to the Nation advertisement completely, had read it partly, had only glanced at it, or had missed it entirely. Forty-five per cent of *Daily Mail* readers said they had read the ad completely whilst only 18 per cent had missed it entirely. By comparison, not one *Daily Mirror* reader had read the ad completely. Eighty-four per cent had missed it entirely.[28]

The government responded by retreating from its broader ambition to educate the nation. Instead, it decided to provide information for those who would understand it, and for the rest, to simplify the message and use information to trigger action rather than to inform. 'Economic information should be addressed to the minority who were capable of grasping the facts of the problem', Littlewood from the Treasury concluded. 'Action publicity should be directed to those who never would understand them but could nevertheless do much to help'.[29]

By 1949 the surveys appeared to confirm that the government had made the right decision. According to the COI the research showed 'with what difficulty anything like a coherent argument is followed by the average subject'. If the government wanted people to respond, it was better to appeal to their emotions than their reason. 'Emotional appeals are more effective than rational' the surveys showed.[30] The COI therefore encouraged the 'present tendency towards greater simplicity of presentation in Government advertisements'. Advertising messages, it said, 'must be brief and to the point', and, in an early recognition of the values of branding, it recommended they keep to a consistent artistic style in order to enhance recognition and interpretation.[31]

The second crucial factor in the development of a methodological framework was austerity. Austerity had two important effects. First, it meant that departments had to reduce their use of paid publicity and, when they did use it, target it towards specific, identifiable ends. However, by this time departments were converts to the perpetual use of information to secure consent. Moreover, they now had the machinery and personnel in place to produce, direct and control the flow of this communication. The second effect, therefore, was to lead departments and the COI to search for less expensive channels through which to

guide their information. Inevitably, this meant working with the existing media to try to incorporate information into their output.

For those who had not worked this out for themselves, Morrison
made it more explicit. Information officers should show more initiative
in accessing free media to get their message across. 'It seems to me' the
Lord President said to the Information Services Committee in 1950
'...that we should give further thought to methods of economizing in
Government publicity without detriment to its effectiveness. Indeed in
some cases it may be possible to get better results by cheaper methods'.
He was thinking particularly of the mass media – press, newsreels and
the BBC. 'This form of publicity is all the more effective' he said
'because it does not come from official agencies'.[32]

The EIU had already been using 'free' media whenever it could.
Indeed its briefing unit was 'the main basis on which effective exploita-
tion of "free" media rested'.[33] Leslie's team listed many of its methods
and outlets to the French Committee. They included the preparation of
briefs as background material for Ministers, the press and the BBC;
special feature material for popular magazines; stories for newsreels;
BBC broadcasts and the development of commercial advertising
themes.[34] Other departments were now encouraged to do the same. At
the end of January 1949 the Economic Information Committee agreed
that 'one of the most important means of publicizing economic information was through news and the presentation of it in such a way
as to influence editorial comment'.[35]

Getting information out via the 'free media' may have been less
expensive, and potentially more effective, but it also required greater
thought and management. The free media had an awkward way of
altering or even rejecting government information. Ministers and
officials therefore found themselves thinking more carefully about the
best way in which to present it, the best time to release it, and the best
outlets through which to communicate it. This equated to information
and news management.

The framework in action

By 1950 a working framework of information management existed. Of
course it continued to develop after that time, but the structural lines
had been drawn. The central and departmental offices were established, as were their personnel. Civil servants and politicians had a new
understanding of information as a function separate from policy. And
the government had, through trial and error, developed a range of sys-

tematic methods by which to persuade the people. When a new crisis arose, at the end of 1950, the government almost immediately adopted this framework in order to deal with it. This is what happened with the rearmament re-education campaign of 1950–51.

On 18 December 1950 the Prime Minister announced to Cabinet that he would be raising the rearmament budget to £4,700 million over the next three years. This was in response to the deterioration of the military situation in Korea and escalation of the conflict. Attlee recognized that this was a significant increase and would not just have meant economic but also major social and political ramifications at home. It could mean sacrificing some of the universal benefits Labour had only just established – like free dental and eye care. It might mean maintaining and even increasing rationing. Some of the controls that Harold Wilson had so publicly 'burned' might have to be re-instituted.

Morrison was not sure the British people would accept this. He immediately got in contact with Leslie (still head of the re-named EIU) to discuss how they should present it.[36] In a note to the Prime Minister Morrison wrote, 'two aspects have to be taken into account, the education of the Government and the education of the people. The Labour movement has also to be considered, as an important part of the people'.[37] A flurry of letters then flowed between Philip Jordan in the PM's office, Max Nicholson, Sir Edwin Plowden (head of the Economic Planning Board) and Morrison. They agreed that education would be necessary to convince people of the need to rearm.[38]

Informally Morrison talked further with his own office advisors to come up with a re-education plan. On the evening of Sunday 14 January he saw Attlee who approved his basic proposal.[39] Morrison would use all the information machinery available to convince the people, and the government, of three things: the aggressive imperialism of the Russians, the independence of Britain from the US, and the need for rearmament and its economic consequences.

That Wednesday he met with the departmental Chief Information Officers. The meeting had been arranged more than two months previous but he used the opportunity to tell them that 'during the coming year special attention will have to be directed to two main subjects: the economic consequences of rearmament and the status of Britain in the democratic life of the world.'[40] For this and their other tasks they should use some of the initiative they had shown in recent years, particularly in gaining free media attention. 'Greater use might with advantage be made of unpaid non-official media... it was up to all Information Officers to use their ingenuity to get stories of news value into the press, on the wireless, and into other media such as newsreels'. The Central Office could help, particularly at a regional level, and so could 'unofficial organisations'.[41] Morrison also suggested they prod their Ministers into radio broadcasts. 'Information divisions should not overlook the possibility of suggesting broadcasts by Ministers when they had something to say which would be suitable for this medium'.[42]

Shortly after the Prime Minister's December statement Clem Leslie had begun gathering data on public opinion to feed back to Ministers. On the 23rd he sent his first findings to Morrison, Jordan et al. These added to their anxiety. 'All the evidence I can find is that the country is full of doubt and confusion about increased rearmament... While people were shaken by the invasion of Korea into realization that a measure of rearmament was necessary, their moral [sic] and resolution have since grown less'.[43]

But Leslie was unsure how far the situation justified a significant increase in media management. To what extent, for example, could they direct action at the BBC? 'In wartime the BBC has within a certain field to accept guidance from Whitehall departments. In peacetime, apart from certain high level directives, it is pretty well free to go its own way. Is that state of affairs appropriate to a lukewarm war period which affects the home front in ways increasingly reminiscent of the war, or should some partial return towards wartime arrangements be considered?'.[44]

He was also hoping that he could test 'public opinion much more rapidly and frequently than is possible under the Social Survey', in other words 'a partial return to the wartime "home intelligence" arrangements'.[45] Presumably this meant 'Cooper's Snoopers'. Leslie's statement provides a compelling insight into the way in which the government rationalised its actions. It compares directly to 1947 when the government talked about an 'economic Dunkirk'.

Morrison and his team also sought to use the information and knowledge of the covert Foreign Office information unit, the Information Research Department (IRD). It was supposed to be for overseas publicity only but its material was also occasionally used at home.[46] It was normally sent, unmarked and with strict instructions for the user not to give the source any attribution, to journalists, academics and other opinion formers. In 1949 Morrison and other Ministers had baulked when Gladwyn Jebb of the F.O. had proposed using it to inform an official propaganda campaign against British communism.[47]

But when Morrison decided to embark on this re-education campaign he decided that they should be involved. Ralph Murray, the head of the IRD at this time, attended the early meetings to prepare the strategy. Murray explained that 'the F.O. had machinery for collecting a wide range of information on Communism which they [already] fed to Ministers, the political parties, leaders of thought, the BBC, etc.'. Morrison 'emphasised the need to make the maximum use of material already available in the F.O.'.[48] Murray also wrote the notes for the anti-communist speech which Morrison delivered in Cambridge on 28 January.[49]

One of the first things Morrison's publicity planning team decided was to form an information unit – something 'rather along the lines of the briefing section in the Treasury Information Division [previously the EIU], might be a suitable instrument for this purpose'.[50] It should collate material on four areas: the international reasons for disarmament, the nature of the defence programme, the economic and social impact of rearmament, and communism in the UK. It would also 'collect information on the public reaction to increased defence measures'. It could then process this 'to supply material for use through Ministerial speeches and other straight information channels'.[51] This established important precedents for both process and method.

At the centre of the plan, as in 1947, were Ministerial speeches and broadcasts. Each Minister was supposed to speak about the issues from the perspective of his department. For example, the Minister for Labour would speak about living standards in the USSR compared to Britain, the Minister for Pensions would speak about trade unionism. As Leslie, Fraser and others had emphasised before, these speeches were not only reported themselves but could set news values in the media.

It was extremely important that these speeches put forward a common line. For this reason Nicholson introduced a paper that had originally been written by Patrick Gordon Walker in 1948. Titled 'The Use of Words in Propaganda' it went into considerable depth on the words that should be used to describe the Soviet Union and its impact on the outside world. The word 'Kremlin' for example, 'is the best way of fixing in people's minds the cruel, backward, tyrannical and centralizing aspects of the Communist movement as now organised'. 'Stalinist' and 'Stalinism' should be reserved for more intellectual audiences. The word 'communist', on the other hand, 'was not suitable, because it was too vague and internationalist, and possessed an attraction for too many people'.[52]

Gordon Walker went on to explain how to secure their use. 'At first we shall ourselves have to use the words deliberately, and with conscious effort'. For example, he suggested building 'up the name of one or two well-known camps until they are as familiar as Nazi ones. Karaganda... is considered the most promising name to use'. Then, 'for a month or two, or more, we should go out of our way to use the words often, and to seek means of making their meaning clear'.[53]

In addition to Ministerial speeches Morrison intended to utilise the COI speakers who had been used so extensively since the war to explain the economic situation.[54] The plan was for there to be a total of 3,000 talks from April 1951 to April 1952. Their primary purpose was 'to make people aware of the why and the how of the defence programme'.[55] This meant explaining that Britain was re-arming in response to Soviet imperialism, not because of any aggressive intentions of its own and not due to American pressure. However, since these speakers were not connected to the government they were supposed to steer clear of political topics. It would be difficult to talk about Soviet belligerence without becoming political.

For this reason they were asked to speak about 'National Defence'. They should refer to Soviet expansion, although not too much to their policies since 1945. The speakers should emphasise how crucial it was that Britain be able to defend herself, and they should promote America as an ally. As some of them said at a conference of lecturers on 30 March, this would be very tricky. It proved harder still when the IRD began feeding them facts and figures about Soviet iniquities. The speakers were told they could use them as long as they made no attribution as to where their information came from, and did not leave the material lying around anywhere.[56] These were clearly political speeches, whether or not they were party political seems beside the point.

The freshly formed Briefing Group on Rearmament also drew up a bulletin intended for widespread distribution which was supposed to 'become the foundation of a highly successful campaign'.[57] This 'Defence Digest' was first printed in September 1951 and sent to Ministers, senior civil servants at home, UK diplomats and high commissioners abroad.[58]

Throughout the rearmament drive 1947 was frequently mentioned as a precedent. When the official paper for the information campaign eventually went to Cabinet in June 1951, Gordon Walker justified it by saying 'In 1947 a successful campaign of this sort was carried out... very considerable success was achieved in informing the public mind about the rather complex problems of exports and imports, the balance of trade and the true nature of the then danger of inflation'.[59] Whether the 1947 campaign had been a resounding success or not, it was perceived to have been in retrospect, and this was important in the development of government communication.

Similarly, the lessons learnt, in terms of briefing, opinion polling, the pursuit of the 'common line', the malleability of information, were re-used in 1951. Also, 1951 shows the migration of ideas from the overseas information offices to the domestic. There was never going to be a Chinese wall between the two (especially after Morrison amalgamated the Home and Overseas Ministerial Committees in 1948) but until 1951 they had made a conscious effort to keep their methods and approach separate. The 'luke warm war period' of 1951 drew them together.

But by the summer of 1951 the campaign was dissolving. As Leslie had originally noted, it was the government as much as the people who needed 'educating'. Nye Bevan in particular objected to rearmament from the start because of the consequent effects on the social services. And the government would have to overcome the anti-Americanism of the Cabinet before they could realistically convince the country. Most importantly, circumstances intervened. In April 1951 Attlee finally shifted Bevin away from the Foreign Office because of his health and replaced him with Morrison. Morrison passed on his position as Information Supremo to his assistant, Patrick Gordon Walker. Since February the UN forces had succeeded in pushing back the North Koreans and by April, with the removal of General MacArthur from UN command, an escalation of the conflict looked unlikely. With Morrison gone and Korea cooling the energy left the campaign.

But the campaign showed that communication was now part and parcel of government thinking and that the framework within which it would be managed had been established. This is not to say it would not change and mutate over the following 50 years, but the idea was embedded, the basic machinery had been created, and formative methods adopted.

Once the Ministers and officials overcame their initial reticence about using the new methods of communication they began to integrate them to their thinking. Public opinion research is a good example of this. In 1944 Sir Cyril Radcliffe told Alan Barlow that the need for such research would be 'extremely limited'. Indeed, the Social Survey (the area of the MOI responsible for such research) was almost disbanded after the war, and even when saved departments had to be coaxed into using it. And yet, within three years the Social Survey had more work than it could handle.

'Government departments are queueing up to have surveys made of you and me' the Sunday Express reported in June 1950. The article described how government surveying had grown rapidly since its inception during the war in 1941 to the point at which 'most of our administrators now appear scared to make a major decision without first asking for a survey of their problem'.[60]

As with much journalism, this article had a basis of truth but also a number of inaccuracies. One of the most significant, ironically, was that despite the *Express's* emphasis of the excessive nature of surveying (the article's title was 'Sixty Thousand Pounds a Year!') the paper had significantly underestimated the amount being spent on the Social Survey by this time.[61] But it was accurate in suggesting that surveying was becoming a vital tool within central government, particularly as a way in which to measure the effectiveness of government communication.

Neither did survey research end when the Conservatives came to office in 1951, despite having been described by Harry Crookshank in 1944 as 'a public menace' which employed the techniques of 'informers, GPU, [and] Gestapo'.[62] After initially cutting the number of full time Social Survey staff from 100 to under 60, and reducing the budget to £89,000 in 1953–54, the government then increased its expenditure consistently and by 1970–71 it stood at £1.2 million. This represented a real terms growth of 580 per cent.[63]

Part II

Government Communication in Practice: the Press

Part II
Government Communication in Practice: the Press

5
Neither Free nor Fair? Government Opinion of the Press

> *The democratic form of society demands of its members an active*
> *and intelligent participation in the affairs of their community... It*
> *assumes they are sufficiently well informed about the issues of the*
> *day to be able to form the broad judgments required by an election,*
> *and to maintain between elections the vigilance necessary in those*
> *whose governors are their servants and not their masters... the*
> *responsibility for fulfilling these needs unavoidably rests in large*
> *measure upon the press.*
>
> Royal Commission on the Press 1947–49 – Report, Cmd.
> Paper 7700, p.101

Amongst the media in 1945, newspapers were the pre-eminent agents of political communication. The BBC still held a monopoly for radio broadcasting and was bound, by its charter, to remain impartial and uncontroversial. Television had yet to be restarted, having been suspended during the war. Plus, since so few people had a television set, it was virtually ineffectual as a means of mass political communication before 1950.[1] Newsreels, though seen by up to 30 million people each week, did not pursue a political agenda because they did not see this as their role. They covered mainly sports, staged events, and royalty. When they did mention politics their relentlessly cheerful commentaries and the background martial music militated against argument or complexity.

Newspapers were, in the words of the editor Wilson Harris, 'the eyes and ears of every man and woman in the land... through the papers they form their estimates of public men, of political issues, of foreign countries'.[2] The press was also about to reach the peak of its popularity in Britain. The total weekday newspaper circulation in 1947 was over

15.5 million for nationals and almost 13 million for provincial dailies (as compared to 12.6 million and 4.6 million in 2004).[3] Moreover, due to paper rationing, each paper would normally be passed around and read by up to three people. As a result, in 1947 an astonishing 87 per cent of the adult population read a daily paper, and 93 per cent read a Sunday paper.[4]

There were 112 daily newspapers published in Britain.[5] Nine of these were general national morning papers. The most popular daily news-paper was the *Daily Express,* selling almost four million copies. It was closely followed by the *Daily Mirror,* then the *Daily Herald* and the *Daily Mail.* The *Daily Telegraph* was the best selling 'class' newspaper (the contemporary term for broadsheet), reaching one million sales in mid-1947, while *The Times,* the newspaper of record, sold approx-imately 270,000.[6] The *Manchester Guardian* was just making the jump from a regional to a national paper.[7] There were six significant national political periodicals: the *Spectator,* the *New Statesman and Nation, Tribune,* the *Economist, Time and Tide,* and *Truth.* Combined, their cir-culations totalled just over 200,000 (compared to the *Radio Times* which, by-mid 1947, was selling over six million copies a week).[8]

So, if a government wanted people to know about what it was doing it was clear it had to rely on the press. The press was simply the most con-venient and accessible means of political communication. Successive government's recognised this and had, as the contemporary editor of the *New Statesman* wrote, 'deliberately left the job of political education to be a by-product of the business of news-selling'.[9] Morrison acknowledged the extent of the newspapers' responsibility during the debate on the press in October 1946, 'in our subtle British way the press of this country is, so to speak, an unofficial part of our Constitution'.[10]

Due to its ideology and programme, this new Labour administration was even more reliant on the press than most. As well as helping people to adjust to the massive dislocation and disruption following the war, it had to communicate an immense legislative and welfare programme, much of which had an immediate and direct bearing on people's lives. The planned nationalisation of the health service, of coal, gas, electricity, transport, civil aviation, cable and wireless, iron and steel, and the introduction of comprehensive National Insurance, all had to be publicised and explained. The press was therefore integral to Labour's plans, yet it was very unclear whether it would willingly conform to this administration's expectations of it.

Some newspapers took their political responsibilities much more ser-iously than others. *The Times* printed by far the most political news and comment, publishing speeches from the House and government statements, often verbatim. In the severely shortened papers of this period *The Times* devoted about 18 per cent of its space to Parliamentary reports and international political news. The *Telegraph* also carried political news, although with fewer direct transcripts and more features.[11]

Of the popular press the *News Chronicle* covered the most political news while the rest of the tabloids had a broader agenda which included politics but also general home news, sports, features, finance and of course photographs and cartoons. The *News of the World* made it very clear that its agenda was not driven by politics. 'We have never claimed to take a very prominent part in the political life of the country' its editor told the Royal Commission in 1948, 'We think that a newspaper will fail (I am looking at it from a circulation point of view) if it does not deal with entertainment'.[12]

'An evil system which is rotten at its base'

Though the new government had a clear need for the press, the Labour Party had always had a difficult relationship with newspapers. Up to the Second World War few papers were sympathetic to the Party. When, in 1924 the *Daily Mail* printed the notorious Zinoviev letter, purporting to show close links between Labour and the Soviet Union, it was widely assumed to be a calculated attempt to undermine support for the Party in the forthcoming election. In the 1931 election only the *Daily Herald*, amongst all the national dailies, aligned itself with Labour.[13] On the eve of election day the *Daily Mirror* went so far as to write that there was 'no shadow of a doubt that a return to Socialism [would] bring about sudden and irreparable anarchy'. The *Mirror* was quite a different paper before the war.[14]

For this reason many left-wing politicians had developed a persecution complex. They believed that the press was institutionally biased against Labour. Their attitude was characterised by Ernest Bevin's comment in 1922 that British newspapers were the product of 'an evil system which is rotten at its base'.[15] This system was, they believed, controlled by a clique of right-wing press barons. In 1922 Bevin was referring to Lords Northcliffe, Rothermere and Beaverbrook. By 1945 Beaverbrook was still there but the others had been replaced by Lords Camrose, Kemsley, and the second Lord Rothermere. The faces might have changed but the system was, as Labour saw it, still dominated by bigoted barons.

Lord Camrose (William Berry), 'industrious, thrifty, sober, serious', owned the *Daily Telegraph*, the *Financial Times* and 80 periodicals.[16] Camrose was a close friend of Winston Churchill and the *Telegraph* was unstintingly loyal to the Conservatives (Berry even threw the biggest Tory party on the night of each election).[17] Camrose was so worried about the cataclysmic financial effects of a Labour victory that in July 1945 he sold the *Financial Times*.[18]

Lord Kemsley (Gomer Berry, Camrose's brother) owned the *Daily Sketch* and *Sunday Graphic*, the *Sunday Times*, two smaller national papers, and seventeen provincial papers.[19] Kemsley enjoyed the trappings of wealth, was outspokenly right-wing, and grew increasingly close to Chamberlain and Halifax prior to the war. His support for appeasement went as far as travelling to Germany six weeks before the outbreak of war to ask Hitler how the British press could promote Anglo-German accord.[20] His *Daily Sketch* was a much shriller, tabloid version of the *Telegraph*.

Lord Rothermere was a more reluctant press Lord.[21] He took over from his father in 1937. Within his newspaper group were the *Daily Mail*, The *Sunday Dispatch* and the *Evening News*, as well as 16 provincial dailies and weeklies.[22] Unlike his father, one of the pioneers of popular newspapers, Esmund Rothermere was polite and accommodating. Partly as a result of his political quietude, and also due to the overbearing influence of his wife, Lady O'Neill, the *Daily Mail* was perceived to have lost much of its political influence after the Second World War.[23] However, it still had a readership of over five million.[24]

Lord Beaverbrook owned the country's biggest selling daily, the *Daily Express*, as well as the *Sunday Express* and the *Evening Standard*. Charismatic, conspiratorial, the inspiration behind Evelyn Waugh's Lord Copper in *Scoop*, Beaverbrook was also the most politically influential of the four because of his previous government positions (he was in the Coalition Cabinet during the war), the circulation of the *Daily Express*, and his close ties to the Tory party.

There were other press barons who cast less imposing shadows: Lord Layton, who in conjunction with members of the Cadbury family, ran the *News Chronicle* and the London evening paper *The Star*. Lord Southwood, who acquired the *Daily Herald* from the Labour party in 1929, increased investment in the paper and ensured there was at least one pro-Labour, pro-Union popular newspaper in Britain. And Colonel J.J. Astor, who bought *The Times* from Lord Northcliffe in 1922. The other national papers had no individual owners but were contained within a larger holding or were part of a trust.[25]

The influence of these right-wing press Lords had been enhanced by the rapid consolidation of the newspaper industry after the First World War. In the 1920s Allied Newspapers, then run by the Berry brothers, competed with Lord Rothermere in a frantic buy-out of national and provincial newspapers. By 1937 the four Lords 'owned nearly one in every two national and local daily papers sold in Britain, as well as one in every three Sunday papers that were sold'.[26] The fear grew, the *Economist* noted in 1943, that 'a handful of newspaper proprietors are themselves able to... impose upon the public the newspapers that they (the proprietors) think they ought to read and to stereotype public opinion in a few primitive and not always very sightly moulds'.[27]

During the same period newspaper circulations rocketed. In the 20 years after 1918 sales of national dailies more than tripled. Part of this increase was due to promotions. Newspapers had found that in pre-welfare days they could attract subscribers by offering accident insurance schemes. Whether or not there was a connection between news consumption and accidents, the offers worked. When, in 1929, even the anti-commercial *Daily Herald* joined in, a circulation war began. Sales increased, and increased again. As sales rose, so did advertising revenue. It was due to this escalation in advertising revenue that the financial structure of the national newspaper changed fundamentally at this time. By the start of the Second World War many national newspapers had come to rely for well over half their revenue on advertising.

This search for circulation and advertising revenue led, some thought, to the sensationalisation of news and the suppression of political and economic coverage. Politics was either being drowned out by non-political, 'human interest' stories designed to boost circulation, or the undiluted voice of Parliament and the government was being replaced by opinion and comment. As the circulation of newspapers grew, it was believed, more and more it was the voice of the individual newspaper people were hearing, not the voice of their political representatives. This compromised the position of MPs as the representative political voice of specific communities, and the position of Parliament as the most important forum for the discussion of politics. Wilson Harris worried about this in his 1943 book *The Daily Press*, arguing that the newspapers had begun to replace Parliament and that since Parliament's proceedings were now 'so inadequately reported... it is in the leader columns and correspondence columns of the press itself that the great debate must be mainly conducted'.[28]

Harris' book was one of a number of independent studies which, in the 1930s and early 1940s, began to question the role of the press within democratic society. PEP wrote the most comprehensive of these in 1938. Three hundred pages long and written over the course of three years, its report set the agenda for debate on the press until a Royal Commission was appointed in 1947.[29] There were others by Wickham Steed, Norman Angell, Lord Camrose, and Ivor Thomas.[30] Each of these studies, and a growing number of articles in weekly journals, examined similar issues: whether the control of the media by a small number of men was inherently detrimental to government, society and democracy; how a government ought to relate to its press and the degree and type of control it ought to exert; whether the shift of the press from a 'calling' to an industry which consciously sought profit and influence should be prevented or at least moderated by government support for minority voices (for example by subsidising minor presses).

By the war these publications reflected a mood of underlying discomfort amongst some influential writers and commentators about the structure and direction of the press. This discomfort was shared by many Labour politicians. Rather than sustaining a healthy democracy, they believed the press might have become an obstacle to one. This belief, coupled with the conviction that the press was institutionally biased against Labour, would come to have critical repercussions over the following decade, and would help lead to the emergence of the phenomenon of modern spin.

A temporary ceasefire

The Second World War acted as a kind of competitive ceasefire for the newspapers. The intense pressures of the inter-war years were suspended. While the war was being fought, the newspapers had no need to worry about circulations (which were constantly rising), they did not have to worry about political allegiance since there was a Coalition; they only had to think about their readership. Compared to the commercialism, constraint and cut-throat competition of the years up to 1939, the war years were, ironically, ones of freedom and release.

The most obvious change was economic. Raw materials freely available before the war suddenly became scarce and costly. Since there was no wood pulp produced in Britain all of it had to be imported – either as raw pulp and then converted to newsprint in British mills, or as finished newsprint. Before the war most of the pulp came from Scandinavia, and the newsprint from the US and Canada.[31] The war cut off the supply of pulp from Scandinavia. British newspapers banded together and formed the Newsprint Supply Company to ensure that they could maintain imports from the US and Canada and keep printing.[32] Though this was expensive, it was also so strictly rationed that the average paper was a sixth of the size of its 1930s predecessor. This meant that proportionately, the cost of raw materials for each newspaper produced was actually lower. Since they were still selling at the same cover price this made each paper sold more profitable. They were made more profitable still by much lower staff costs. In the 1930s, due to the aggressive circulation battles, most papers employed armies of canvassers to knock on people's doors, offering all sorts of gifts and enticements to convince people to subscribe to their newspaper. By 1938, 40 per cent of the staff on a typical national morning newspaper were canvassers.[33] During and immediately after the war the interest in news was so great and the supply of news-papers so limited (in both pagination and circulation due to paper rationing) that almost every national newspaper sold all the news-papers it produced. Plus, since the 'no returns' policy was still in force (ie. the newsagent had to pay for and could not return any of the papers they ordered) all newspapers distributed corresponded to guaranteed income. There was therefore no need for many canvassers. Similarly, it took far fewer journalists to write a four page paper vs. a 24 page paper. Again, this reduced wage bill added to the profitability of the paper.

Advertising revenue could not, however, be maintained at pre-war levels. Even though papers could charge more for space in the much depleted wartime newspapers, the increase could not make up for the enormous reduction in size. Therefore where advertising income made up almost 60 per cent of the revenues of the pre-war paper, by 1943 this had dropped to 31 per cent and stayed low while the newspaps remained so small.[34] However, the other increases in revenue and reduced costs made up for this loss. These changes significantly altered the influence of different forces acting on the newspapers. Commercial pressure was reduced, as was competition with other papers. These abnormal economic conditions persisted in the years immediately following the war.

A lack of infighting gave editors and journalists a chance to peer above the parapet, to take a breath from sales promotions and think about other things. This motivated some editors to look to introduce a broader news agenda at the end of the war. Tom Hopkinson, editor of the *Picture Post*, thought that his readers had been through so much they wanted more realism and coverage of more of 'the subjects people talked about and argued about amongst themselves', like life in a mental hospital or life as a prison officer.[35]

For other newspapers the Second World War was a watershed in the growing autonomy of the daily press and independence from the influence of the proprietor. The *Observer*, for example, wrote a statement of principles in 1942 in which it asserted its editorial independence. It followed this up by converting ownership into a trust after the war.[36] The *Express* Group formed a Policy Committee in 1944, which then met monthly and laid down 'the broad lines of policy' which governed all newspapers in the company – 'Lord Beaverbrook has never made the slightest attempt to override the decisions of the Policy Committee', the General Manager claimed in 1948.[37] Even *The Times*, so profoundly a newspaper of the establishment that abroad it was considered the voice of the government, asserted its individual voice during the war. E.H. Carr, the left-leaning leader writer, promoted the Russian cause and later that of Greek independence against pressure from the Coalition. According to Stephen Koss, by the end of the conflict 'Of the major dailies, only the *Telegraph* adhered to a discernible party position'.[38]

The aspiration to independence was the same for provincial newspapers as for national ones. Shortly after the end of the war more and more regional newspapers were defining themselves as independent. As the Institute of Journalists told the Royal Commission, 76 out of 134 said they were unconnected to any political party.[39]

The election coverage of 1945 illustrated this aspiration. There was a mixture of viewpoints and a reluctance within many newspapers to toe the Party line.[40] Only the *Daily Telegraph* and the *Daily Herald* maintained doctrinaire positions. Others, like *The Times* and *The Observer*, went out of their way to illustrate their independence. And, perhaps more significantly, the coverage of the election was limited due to the quantity of other news at the final stages of the conflict.

If newspapers did move politically during the war, they shifted leftwards. This shift was not party political, but reflective of the national mood and in response to the immensely popular Beveridge plan (Beveridge stole the clothes of the newspapers and offered insurance to everyone). This shift was played out in the growth in popularity of the increasingly left-leaning *Daily Mirror*.

In the main the newspapers felt they had waged a good war. Even Churchill, always highly sensitive of the press, praised it in 1943, 'our vast influential newspaper press has known how to combine independence and liveliness with discretion and patriotism'.[41] The press believed it had, through its conduct between 1939–45, proved its responsibility and should now be trusted. 'The public spirit of the press during the war has been exemplary', William Redfern, president of the Institute of Journalists, said in his annual address in November 1944.[42] In this and in his articles for the industry publication, *The Journal*, he praised the behaviour of the press who played 'no mean part in the mammoth fight for freedom. It [the press] has made its stand for truth, the whole truth, and nothing but the truth'.[43] He looked forward to the end of the war and the quick 'restoration of all our liberties'.[44]

The concerns about the effects of newspaper consolidation and commercialisation had not dissipated. They could still be found simmering in the pages of *The Journalist*, in trade journals and in occasional feature articles.[45] But the political and economic changes caused by the war alleviated some of the pressures on the press and so tempered these concerns.

'A new era in the relations between the Government and the Press'?

Thanks to the changes wrought by the war, and the leftward shift of the press, there seemed a chance, when Labour came to office in August 1945, that it might enjoy a good, working relationship with the newspapers. Despite the vitriol that had characterised aspects of their election coverage, some right-wing papers called a truce and claimed they would judge Labour by its deeds, not its words. 'Let us all give the new team the fairest chance,' the *Sunday Express* wrote, 'a candid criticism, an unstinted approval where and when it is earned, and a firm support for all good causes and courses'.[46]

Less partisan newspapers were still more optimistic about the possibilities inherent in a Labour victory. Some were hopeful that Labour would introduce a new openness to government. *World's Press News*, the trade paper of the British press, felt that since Labour was dependent on popular appeal, 'It is likely therefore that the Labour government will make it its business to see that the electors get a better flow of governmental information on policy and practice than ever before'. Newspapers, it suggested, would be the means by which Labour would transmit this information, which could only have a positive impact on the press: 'we consider it likely that the change of Government will intensify the importance of the press and the regard which the press can establish for itself in the public mind'.[47]

Ernest Jay, shortly to become President of the National Union of Journalists, was brimming with confidence about the effect of the new government. 'I happen to know' he wrote on the front page of *The*

Journalist, 'that the new Government is anxious and ready to introduce a new era in the relations between the Government and the Press, and in return it will expect fair treatment in the presentation of its attempts to implement the policy it was elected to carry out'.[48]

Thanks to the war there was also the machinery in place to facilitate a fuller relationship. As explained earlier, all the government departments now had press offices. The Ministry of Information still existed, although most expected it to disappear soon. In 1944–45 there were still approximately 4,000 people working on home information services, either in the departments or at the MOI.[49] There should therefore be plenty of opportunity for more contact.

There were other reasons to believe the relationship would be constructive. Herbert Morrison had good relations with many of the editors and proprietors. By 1945 he had even reversed some of the damage done by his actions as Home Secretary during the Second World War (when he closed the *Daily Worker* and threatened to close the *Daily Mirror*). Before the election he met and charmed Guy Bartholomew (Editorial Director of the *Mirror*) and used the *Mirror's* cartoonist, Zec, to draw some of Labour's election posters.[50] He befriended Percy Cudlipp, editor of the *Daily Herald*, Maggie Stewart at the *News Chronicle*, and Kingsley Martin at the *New Statesman*, as well as other journalists, editors and all the Parliamentary Lobby correspondents.[51]

This was also a Labour government and Parliament packed with journalists. There were over 40 accredited journalists and editors elected to the House in 1945, 20 of them members of the National Union of Journalists.[52] This included: Michael Foot (Labour), previously editor of the *Evening Standard* and shortly to be editor of *Tribune*; Ernest Thurtle (Labour), regular writer for the *Sunday Express*, Wilson Harris (Independent), editor of the *Spectator*, Gary Allighan (Labour), columnist for the *Daily Mail*, Vernon Bartlett (Independent), Tom Driberg (Labour), Jennie Lee (Labour), Hector McNeill (Labour), and Maurice Webb (Labour). Throughout this period many of these, and other, MPs wrote regularly for the papers.

Moreover, in late September, Attlee appointed Francis Williams as Public Relations advisor to Number 10. This was a significant step. As already mentioned, Williams had considerable journalistic and government communications experience. He had edited *The Daily Herald* between 1936 and 1940, then headed the Ministry of Information's News and Censorship division during the war. In 1945 he acted as the head of public relations for the British delegation at the first conference of the United Nations in San Francisco, with great success. When

Attlee asked him to coordinate Downing Street's political communications, on a salary of £2,000 a year, the Prime Minister sent a signal to the newspapers that media relations were going to be taken seriously.[53]

The importance of Williams' appointment was accentuated by the book which he had just finished writing when he agreed to take the post. *Press, Parliament and People* is an examination of the way in which a modern government can and should communicate with the people. The central problem, he said, is how to secure continuing power to the people given the 'inevitable extension of the authority of central government in economic and social matters'.[54] Williams concluded that 'modern Government increasingly requires the knowledge and understanding of the mass of the people if it is to be effective'.[55] This was especially the case with the current Labour administration which, 'pledged to the kind of policies that the present one is, cannot afford not to use to the full every possible channel of public information and education available to it'.[56] Therefore the new government information services were necessary and justified, and it was imperative that the government use the press as much as it could. At the same time Williams was scrupulously conscious of the freedom of the press and the dangers of government control. It was this dilemma, the need to inform without impinging on press freedom, that Williams raised in his book and sought to resolve in his subsequent two years at Downing Street.

The book was widely reviewed and well received. Kingsley Martin, editor of the *New Statesman*, saw it as recognition of the extended role of the 'positive State'.[57] If government was to take a much more active role in economic and social affairs, it made sense that it should do the same with publicity and information. Wilson Harris, Martin's opposite at the *Spectator*, found the book interesting but disquieting. He worried that in Williams' world, the government would seek to determine the news agenda.[58]

Once in his new position, Williams acted almost immediately to increase the amount of information released to the press and the public. He introduced daily lobby briefings for the first time.[59] He sought to professionalise the public relations officers within each department. And he spoke about opening up government to public scrutiny.[60] 'These decisions mark the end of secrecy and understatement' *World's Press News* wrote, 'and the determination adequately to interpret to the world the plans and purposes of the British people'.[61]

After Labour took office it seemed, therefore, that there was the potential for an extended constructive relationship between the government and the press, and that it was in the interests of both to promote such a relationship. And yet, within ten months, almost a hundred Labour MPs were calling for major investigation into the structure and ownership of the press, members of Cabinet were regularly lambasting the press in public, and much of the press itself was alienated and remote from government.

This collapse in the relationship between the government and the press was important because it led Labour to question the whole role of the newspapers within a democratic society. Herbert Morrison went so far as to appoint a Royal Commission on the Press, the first of its kind, with a wide remit to conduct 'a general review of the place which the press should occupy in a democratic community'.[62] He and other Labour Ministers explored ways to make the press act more 'responsibly', and the government as a whole experimented with alternative channels of communication.

Why did relations collapse?

The reasons for the deterioration of relations in this period can be found partly in the actions of the press and the government and partly due to factors out of their control. These factors included certain practical problems that prevented the free flow of information through the press. The first, and most important, of these was paper rationing.

The continued shortage of newsprint after the war meant that the average popular newspaper was only four pages in length (folded to tabloid size this made eight). The average 'class' newspaper was eight pages. *The Times* was ten. Even if they reduced the size of their font, reduced the number of advertisements, reduced the number of photographs and increased the number of columns per page – all of which the newspapers did – there was only a limited amount of news they could fit inside each issue. Naturally some items had to be covered briefly and some not at all. Parliamentary news was reduced in most papers – although they all continued to print some.[63] The lack of paper also meant that newspaper circulations were pegged. In other words they were not allowed to sell more than a certain number of copies each day (judged by their circulation when rationing was introduced).

A second practical reason was the sheer quantity of news, much of it not directly related to the government. For example, in one week in March 1946, Stalin called Churchill a warmonger for his 'Iron Curtain' speech at the same time as he moved Soviet troops south through Persia, Herman Goering entered the dock at the Nuremberg trials, 33 spectators were crushed to death in the worst disaster in the history of British football, the already striking dockers were joined by many of the motor workers, and a Europe-wide emergency food conference was called as many countries on the continent spiralled towards starvation. At the same time the issues of Indian independence, a Jewish home-land in the Middle East, an American loan, and atomic bomb tests rumbled in the background.[64]

The newspapers' difficulty in covering political news fully was increased by Labour's plans to pass a raft of substantial legislation during 1946. During the 1945–46 Parliamentary session, 106 Bills were introduced and only two not passed.[65] To speed the passage of many of these Morrison, as Leader of the House and Minister in charge of Labour's legislative programme, began to use standing committees which would review Bills in parallel with the House. Both the pace of legislation and these new methods of review made it difficult for news-papers to report Bills thoroughly. This led some of them to accuse the government of deliberately trying to suppress public debate and trying to slip things past the public unnoticed. 'An uninstructed democracy is an unhealthy democracy', the *Daily Telegraph* intoned, 'and a Parlia-ment relegated in practice to semi-secrecy by deficient facilities for publicity abdicates its primary function as the forum of the nation'.[66]

The press shared some responsibility for the worsening relationship with the government. They were naturally enthusiastic about the end of the war and the release of government controls. This led some of them to cover more light, entertaining stories than they had been able to in the last six years. This was not 'an unbridled campaign of scream-ing irresponsibility' as described by James Margach, but a spontaneous release of some of the pent up emotions of the war years.[67] As J.J. Astor, Chairman of *The Times*, explained 'After a war I believe there is always an emotional phase, but that is only transient'.[68] More often than not it tended to lead to exuberant inaccuracy rather than political irrespon-sibility. For example, the theft of some of the Windsor jewels caused an enormous sensation in October 1946 and many of the popular papers, without specific information on the jewels themselves or their value, made ill-judged guesses which later proved wildly off the mark.

The worsening relationship was also due to the more ideologically entrenched positions some of the newspapers took which, contem-poraries argued, influenced their news coverage as well as their com-mentary and opinion pieces. From the late autumn of 1945 onwards, animated by the confrontational language of class war used by front bench Labour Ministers in the House, some of the national press became more and more fixated by the idea that socialism represented a threat to freedom. In November a *Sunday Times* editorial claimed that 'Socialism is not merely economically dangerous, but morally wrong'.[69] The *Daily Sketch*, with its rabidly anti-left commentator 'Candidus', argued that 'Socialism is, by definition, totalitarian'.[70] The *Daily Express* splashed its political policies across the paper on 1 January 1946.[71] These included its faith in freedom for the individual, free industry, and no censorship.

The left-wing journal *Tribune* believed these policies had a direct and detrimental effect on news coverage. From early 1946 it kept a record of stories it believed were inaccurate, were unnecessarily emotive, or were simply excluded for political reasons. On 1 February it suggested that the *Daily Sketch* had deliberately kept information regarding the government's social security scheme off the front page. On 15 February it claimed that the *Daily Express* had tried to create a general food panic by its headline the previous Saturday, 'Rush to Buy Flour – Shops Sell Out'. And on 8 March it claimed that the *Daily Telegraph* misused facts about the housing situation to mislead its readers into believing Labour had under-performed.[72]

Though *Tribune* identified some examples of inaccuracies and might have been right in suggesting the inclusion or exclusion of some stories was politically motivated, it was far from immune from political polemic itself. It called Lord Kemsley's influence on provincial journalism 'profound and deplorable', said the right-wing press was doing its 'despicable worst' to bring down the Labour government and that all of them were 'professional merchants of falsehood'.[73] As objective tools for political communication all the contemporary newspapers had distinct drawbacks.

But the government also had itself to blame for many of its communication problems. Having sought to maintain the machinery of information and having introduced new personnel to coordinate communication policy, it then failed, or forgot, to communicate. There are various possible explanations for this failure. The first is that they were spoilt by the war. Until 1945, with the newspapers almost wholly reliant on government sources of information, and keen to support the war effort, the government could normally count on their support. Ministers became accustomed to power and positive coverage. A second is that civil servants had an ingrained tradition of discretion and reserve which had been nurtured by the wartime culture of secrecy and persisted after its end (despite the principled rhetoric).[74] The final, and most likely, explanation is that many Ministers were too busy and too distracted to focus enough attention on it. The failure is important since it led to a crisis in government–press relations and the fundamental reappraisal referred to earlier.

Food and the politicisation of news

The issue which best illustrates the politicisation of news and the government's inability to control communication is food. Food rationing persisted after the end of the war in Europe. However, there was some hope that, as time went on, rationing would be relaxed and eventually removed entirely. Sir Ben Smith, the unsuitably portly Minister of Food, had given encouraging hints and signs from the end of 1945 that there might be some improvement over the coming months.[75] Therefore it came as a stunning surprise when, on 31 January 1946, with no previous warning, he announced that the government was to end the availability of dried eggs. Though a poor substitute for the real thing, dried eggs had become a staple of most households' diet. 'After six weeks press silence in his [Ben Smith's] department this bombshell is dropped', the *Daily Mail* reported.[76] The press objected less to the stoppage of dried eggs than to the manner in which it was done and the lack of public preparation for it.

Though there is nothing in the Ministry of Food files about this episode, from certain newspaper reports and by the reaction of the Cabinet it is possible to piece together what happened. According to the *World's Press News*, Smith himself was so nervous and unsure about how to deal with the dried eggs announcement, and so doubtful about the abilities of his Public Relations Officer (PRO), that he wrote a press release himself, waited until after 7pm (when his PRO had left), and handed it directly to a press officer for distribution. So not only was there no prior warning, but all the other government information about dried eggs (advertisements for them in the papers, and government pamphlets with dried egg recipes) was not stopped, but was printed and circulated despite the stoppage.[77]

Worse was to follow. The world food situation became more perilous. Britain had barely enough wheat stocks to last the summer and was having terrible trouble importing more. There was a likelihood of famine in India and the Germans in the British zone in Germany were trying to survive on close to 1000 calories a day. At the end of January the Cabinet discussed how they might alleviate the domestic and international situation.[78] Attlee was to set up an emergency food committee, headed by himself. Morrison was to take over the communication of food policy to the British public: 'The Lord President should super-vise the preparation and coordination of this publicity campaign [for food economy]'.[79] To fulfil his responsibility Morrison planned to launch a 'Save Bread' campaign.

The campaign would be centred around Ben Smith. He would begin by making a statement to Parliament on 5 February 1946 outlining the full gravity of the food situation. This would be followed by a press conference which would, from then on, become a weekly staple. The Lord President recognised that food was an emotional issue and the government would have to think carefully about how to communicate its policy: 'We must set in motion long-term as well as short-term pub-licity measures' he wrote, 'It is important that these should give the least possible opening for hostile and partisan criticism'.[80]

Unfortunately, even before these measures could be established, Ben Smith's statement provided just such an opening. The Opposition and the newspapers, appalled that the situation was so grave and the news so sudden, attacked the government for its lack of preparation and foresight.[81] At the next Food Supply Meeting, on 12 February, Morrison assessed the reaction: 'Since WFS(46)6 was circulated, press comment on the food situation has been very heavy'. There were three main lines of criticism: the 'lack of warning and information', an 'unsatisfac-tory treatment of priorities', and 'inconsistency in agricultural policy'. But the Lord President was confident that this initial shock had passed and now 'the country is ready for a full and fair factual review of the whole subject'.[82]

The government tried to give this review in the debate and cor-responding statistical paper of 14 February.[83] But already the issue was heavily politicised, with the Conservatives accusing the government of ignoring the basic needs of the country in the pursuit of an ideological agenda (the debate was held after the Trade Disputes Act had been dis-cussed), and of being unnecessarily and damagingly secretive.[84] These two charges also characterised newspaper coverage and dominated their headlines. 'Mr. Attlee's Government have been prodigal in their measures and beggarly in their explanations' J.L. Garvin wrote in the *Daily Telegraph*, 'If the Prime Minister and his colleagues cannot give us more food, at least let them give us more facts'.[85] The subsequent 'Save Bread' campaign suffered from this politicisation. It also kept the issue of food on the front page, encouraging a constant high pitched discussion that drowned out other political coverage.

For the campaign Morrison adopted the same strategy as the govern-ment had in the early stages of the war – encouraging frugality and discouraging waste. The newspaper advertisement campaign began with an earnest, polite plea signed by the Minister of Food.[86] This restrained message was overwhelmed by negative headlines in much of the press. The campaign was not, Morrison felt, 'having a big immediate impact on public emotions and it was for consideration whether a more dramatic appeal was now required'.[87]

There had been some thought given to making it much more sensational, for example by using 'illustrations as a contrast between a starving woman and child in India or in one of the European countries with a dustbin containing half loaves of bread wasted by the British public'.[88] The type of pictures, in other words, which would later become synonymous with charity advertising. This was too much for Morrison and the Food Supply Committee, however, and they persisted with heavily text based ads imploring the public to 'Join the Crusade Against Bread Waste'.[89] The campaign was supposed to take precedence over some other government campaigns but it still regularly had to compete for space and attention with 'Save more Fuel' (Ministry of Fuel and Power), save more money (National Savings), 'Keep Death Off the Road' (Ministry of War Transport), recruitment for the fire service (Home Office) and 'What Exports Mean to Us' (Board of Trade).[90]

From mid-March the government increased its direct appeals to the people. Letters were sent to women's organisations, to the bakery trade associations, and to divisional food officers.[91] From 15 April there would be posters stuck on about 10,000 sites nationwide. For May and June all letters sent were to be franked by the Post Office with 'Don't Waste Bread – Others Need It'. Food flashes would be screened in cinemas. The BBC agreed to insert references to the Bread Campaign into its talks on food. And five million dustbin labels were prepared.[92]

But despite this escalation of exhortation, the government did not release factual information on the stocks held within Britain as against the available imports. This fuelled the idea that the government was still being too secretive. For the next eight weeks newspapers focused on rationing rumours while leader articles kept calling for 'Food Facts'.[93] The situation was made worse by further media mismanagement by the government. On 21 March, Shelton Smith (no relation to Sir Ben), the hapless P.R.O. in the Food Office, gave a press conference to the food correspondents telling them to expect further cuts in fat rations. But when the headlines broke the next day Sir Ben Smith announced there had been a mistake. There would not be further reductions and his PRO had got it wrong. Needless to say, the following day the papers led with 'Ration Cuts Warning Was Government Blunder'.[94]

To extricate itself the government held another debate and released a more detailed White Paper on 4 April.[95] The aim of the White Paper was 'to set out the facts of the present crisis in the world's food supplies, to show how the crisis developed and to trace the steps taken by the Government in the face of it'. Instead it showed, the Opposition said, that the government knew much more than they admitted in December and January.[96]

By this time Morrison had begun to lose confidence in Sir Ben Smith and in May he decided to travel to Washington himself to negotiate more wheat imports from the Americans. Christopher Mayhew, Morrison's PPS at the time, travelled with him. Though Mayhew says Morrison argued hard with the US he was unable to secure more wheat.[97] Indeed, in exchange for a US concession to help Britain feed the local population in the British zone in Germany and send food to India, Morrison actually had to commit 200,000 more tons of British wheat abroad. In order to avert a food crisis in other countries Morrison was diverting food away from his own. Unsurprisingly, most of the popular press did not emphasise the magnanimity of these actions: 'Morrison Gives Away 200,000 Tons More' yelled the *Daily Express*.[98] Morrison 'has done a worse stroke of business than Smith ever accomplished' the *Daily Mail* reported.[99] To add further to Morrison's embarrassment, a press officer from the US State department then flatly contradicted his earlier statement and claimed the US had made no such commitment to further concessions.[100]

The press coverage of the food situation became more and more vicious, especially whilst the government continued to fail to give out adequate information. Against Sir Arthur Salter's charge that the government was not telling Parliament or the people enough, Sir Ben Smith replied weakly that 'we have been thinking of giving quarterly reviews'.[101] But this and other comments failed to mollify the press, and Smith became the first minister to resign from Attlee's government, at the end of May 1946. He was replaced by the distinctly slimmer Sir John Strachey. The new food Minister then had the unenviable task of announcing to the House, on 27 June, that the government was going to introduce bread rationing the following month.

There was another important reason why the British government did not release more facts and figures regarding the food situation. Economising on food consumption and bread rationing was done partly for negotiating leverage with the Americans rather than to feed directly into export. Since Sir Ben Smith's trip to Washington in January the British had been unable to convince the Americans that the world food situation was not a short-term problem but potentially catastrophic. This is what they believed they had to do in order to make the American government adopt compulsory domestic measures to secure higher quantities of wheat for export. When, in early April, after receiving information that international conditions had significantly worsened, the British food mission was still unable to shift the Americans, the Cabinet sent a telegram to Washington and authorised a press statement which they hoped would prompt action.[102] The statement announced that Britain would be prepared to take the radical step of adopting bread rationing 'in the interests of the peoples of the world who are faced with starvation and famine'.[103] Though the statistics suggested the actual impact of British bread rationing on the world situation would be marginal, the Cabinet hoped the proposal would induce the Americans to act.[104]

The statement did have a profound effect on the American government and people. Lord Halifax wrote from Washington on 13 April, 'The British offer to introduce bread rationing has made a deep impression [on the US] and sharpened the appreciation of the extent of the food shortage in Europe'.[105] Just over a week later the US government agreed to set aside 25 per cent of the domestic millers flour expressly for export. The problem was, having made the gesture, the Americans were very keen that the British see it through. 'I wish you would ask your government if it would regard the institution of this limitation on the domestic consumption of flour to be a comparable step to the one heretofore proposed by your government namely bread rationing' wrote the US Secretary for Agriculture, Clinton Anderson.[106] Though the British government would not have introduced such a radical measure simply under pressure from America, it was a factor in their decision. But since the statistics were ambivalent as to how much effect British rationing would have, it was difficult to justify the proposition to the British people with facts and figures. So the government released some, but not all, the statistics. For its persistent lack of candour, and withholding of facts, the Conservative Opposition and much of the British press continued to attack the government.[107]

It was at this time that the government became more generally concerned about the negative influence of the press. Attlee expressed this concern in his opening speech to the delegates of the Imperial Press Conference at Grosvenor House in June. He called for all those in the media who reported the news to 'do so with a steadfast awareness of the responsibility they bear and of the obligation upon them to place all the facts before the public and not simply those which support one particular case'.[108]

Francis Williams, speaking later in the week, indicated that he was beginning to give up on newspapers as a means of political communication. He warned against the growing commercialisation of papers and their excessive concentration on entertainment value. Due to their excesses they now had, he believed, 'less influence [on politics] than at any time in their history' (ironic since they had just precipitated the resignation of a government Minister). Williams used this argument to justify the increasing use of government information services which would act as an essential bridge 'built on the information world between Government and people'.[109]

Attlee and Williams were expressing diplomatically what other Labour voices were expressing more bluntly. The *Daily Herald* accused the Conservatives and the 'Tory Press' of using food to make political capital. 'Of all the Tory tricks since the General Election... none has been more blatant, more consistently practised and more repugnant to human decency than the attempt to exploit the world food shortage for party ends'.[110] Food had become explicitly political. The unwillingness of the government to release the full official facts about the world and domestic situation led many papers to make their own calculations and rely on stories from abroad about full German bakeries and vast untapped stocks of Argentinian wheat. The *Daily Mail*, under the headline 'Planned Famine', suggested that there was no food shortage and that government rationing was a policy decision to save dollars.[111]

But no-one was more infuriated by the anti-government press than Herbert Morrison. Morrison had always had a certain sensitivity to the newspapers. As outlined earlier in this chapter he cultivated journalists and was highly conscious of positive coverage (of himself as much as the government). But he was also very aware of negative headlines and held grudges, and kept clippings.[112] Since the end of 1945 some of the right-leaning papers had targeted him as the 'evil genius of discord' stage managing Labour policy.[113] After he took over the communication of food policy and returned empty-handed from the US in May, many other papers joined in the attacks against him. The magazine *Truth* sarcastically referred to 'Morrison's Triumph' and most of the national papers emphasised his personal failure to secure more wheat for Britain from the US.[114] Mayhew, who saw both Morrison's actions and the press' response, recalled later that Morrison 'was very sensitive about the press. He read them all, everything about himself and had a cuttings book'.[115]

It is clear that from the spring of 1946 Morrison was becoming seriously concerned by the level of reporting in the press. Shortly after this time he started keeping records of mistakes he found in the papers.[116] We have an idea of the level of accuracy Morrison sought from newspaper coverage by his reaction to an article in the *Daily Herald* in June 1946, reporting on his Party conference speech. Morrison wrote an angry letter to the paper telling them that the headline, 'Herbert Morrison tells Conference Delegates the Government has Gone as Far to the Left as is Wise' was inaccurate and irresponsible. 'I think an apology is due to me... Quotes should be quotes and not sub-editorial revised versions' Morrison wrote rather pompously.[117] Not content with the seven inches the letter took up in the newspaper itself Morrison went round to the *Herald* offices and lectured them on their sloppiness.[118]

Morrison was hurt by the coverage he received in the newspapers. Despite his efforts to befriend journalists and talk to the press he felt he was being misrepresented and insulted. It is not surprising therefore, that as the vitriol of the national press reached its peak, immediately after Strachey announced rationing on 27 June 1946, it was Morrison who helped to revive an idea first raised in Parliament by Tom Driberg a few months earlier, for a Royal Commission on the Press.

6
Can Newspapers Be Made 'More Responsible'?

Tom Driberg was a member of the National Union of Journalists (NUJ) as well as a Labour MP. He had been a successful journalist in the 1930s, writing under the pseudonym of William Hickey for the *Daily Express*. 'An unreliable man of undoubted distinction' in the unusually colourful words of his *Times* obituary, Driberg had been sacked from the paper in June 1943.[1]

At the 1946 conference in Liverpool the NUJ passed a resolution calling for the government to set up an independent commission examining the ownership and control of British newspapers.[2] The journalists within the union believed the owners wielded excessive influence. Driberg sent a copy of the NUJ's resolution to Clement Attlee and, on 30 April 1946, asked the Prime Minister in the House whether he would consider setting up a Royal Commission to study the issue.[3] Attlee said he would not: 'I have given careful consideration to this matter' he said, 'which, however, I do not see my way to adopt'.[4]

Morrison had advised Attlee to respond in this way.[5] But by early July, after the personal attacks on him in the papers, Morrison was having second thoughts. On the second of the month he received a note from Clement Bundock, General Secretary of the NUJ, repeating the proposal for an investigation of the press within a more 'general inquiry into the channels of public information'.[6] His Private Secretary and personal assistant, John Pimlott, suggested Morrison advise the PM to say just what he said in April. But Morrison scribbled a note at the bottom of Pimlott's memo saying, 'I'm not sure. I wd like him [the P.M.] to say that he will consider the idea in relation to any enquiry abt the BBC'.[7] So instead, the Lord President wrote to Attlee saying that there was now strong support for a press inquiry both from within the

Party and from the NUJ and that it might be wise for the government to reconsider.[8]

This was an important change of heart for Morrison. The Lord President had enough experience of dealing with the press, and enough respect for its political influence, to realise that to appoint such a commission would cause a serious rift, not just between the press and the Labour Party, but between the press and Herbert Morrison. He could not have taken such a decision lightly. By picking a serious fight with the newspapers Labour could once again be presented as recklessly anti-establishment. This could destabilise Labour's middle class vote, so recently won and so highly prized by the Lord President.

Therefore even if his decision to push for a Royal Commission was triggered by personal pique, Morrison must have convinced himself that the press as currently constituted had become a major obstacle to the democratic process. Moreover, that the threat had reached such a state that it could only be remedied by a major reassessment of the role of newspapers within British society.

In case there was any confusion as to how Morrison felt about the state of the press, he resolved it in a speech in Lewisham on 8 July. 'The great Tory newspaper combines have been seen at their worst' he said, 'Suppressions, misrepresentations, inventions: these things happen day by day and constitute a disgrace to journalism'. He was particularly critical of the 'Kemsley gramophone chain' where he believed the irresponsible voice of the proprietor was projected throughout his group of over 20 newspapers.[9]

Three days later 91 Labour MPs, led by Haydn Davies and Michael Foot, tabled an Early Day motion in Parliament for a Royal Commission on the Press. It is hard, given Morrison's actions over the previous ten days, not to conclude that the Lord President did not play a part in encouraging the motion. As John Gordon, editor of the *Sunday Express*, wrote in an editorial on 21 July, 'By an odd coincidence, just at the moment when Mr. Morrison is so deeply concerned about the newspapers, up jump 90 MPs like rabbits out of a conjurer's hat, to demand the very thing Mr. Morrison is trying to think of – a Royal Commission'. Morrison's involvement seems even more likely since at dinner on the night of the 11th, he and his PPS, Christopher Mayhew, were putting together a shortlist of names that might serve on the Commission.[10]

From that point on Morrison championed the idea of a Commission until, in a free debate on 29 October 1946, Parliament voted in favour of an investigation. In Cabinet on 15 July he told other Cabinet members that he 'thought that some sort of enquiry on the lines suggested in the Motion might well be useful'.[11] The following day in the Broadcasting debate (on BBC Charter renewal and whether there should be an inquiry into the Corporation) Morrison deliberately broadened the question from broadcasting to the press and suggested to the House that 'All great channels for the dissemination of information to the public – all of them – would, the government believes, benefit from having their state of health examined by independent inquiry, and I don't exclude the Press from that consideration'.[12]

After meeting with a deputation of the National Union of Journalists (NUJ) on 22 July, Morrison submitted a memorandum to Cabinet in which he personally recommended a Royal Commission on the Press be set up.[13] He was even pressing for the Commission to be announced before the summer break but was held back by a note from Attlee and by the reservations in Cabinet of Stafford Cripps.[14] What, Cripps asked Morrison, would such an inquiry achieve? If it was supposed to lead to legislation, what kind of legislation? And how would you get credible evidence from journalists and editors about their proprietors? Morrison was unperturbed. If nothing else, he said, an inquiry would 'serve a useful purpose in bringing to light undesirable practices which would cease as soon as the light of publicity had been directed onto them'.[15] Morrison was using the opportunity provided by the NUJ's resolution to address his own concerns about the state of the press, and those of other Labour politicians.

The summer break did not quell his ardour. He brought a revised proposal to Cabinet on 3 October again encouraging them to appoint a Commission. But some of his colleagues were still unconvinced.[16] They felt that the chances of finding hard evidence were low. If none were found the report would then look like a whitewash. Even if abuses were found, it would be difficult to deal with them and would reflect poorly on the government that they existed in the first place. 'Was it not preferable' they asked, 'to seek a practical remedy for the present state of affairs by improving the presentation of the government's case through those newspapers which were independent and through other methods of publicity?'.[17] But Morrison was adamant. An inquiry would have the time to consider new ways in which to regulate the press and maintain its independence, he thought. Some of his comments indicate that he had a retaliatory motive. For example, 'The exposure of the facts in an authoritative report would in itself educate the public to a truer judgment of the reliance to be placed on statements appearing in the

Press'.[18] He also made an addition to the Commons motion, adding 'accuracy' to the list of issues that needed to be investigated. He had not forgotten the *Herald* headline in June. However, the two camps in Cabinet could not be reconciled. After they argued once again on 17 October Morrison agreed to give time to the proposal through a debate in the House, after which a free vote would determine whether the Commission went ahead.

Morrison's role in reviving and championing an investigation into the press was, therefore, critical. But it would be wrong to think that he drove the investigation through government and Parliament single-handed. He had strong support from some other members of the Cabinet. Hartley Shawcross for example, the Attorney General, spoke publicly against the press twice in July, condemning their 'selection or misrepresentation of facts to suit opinions'. Shawcross did not, however, think their behaviour 'can be stopped by law'.[19] There was also sympathy from many within the Party and their supporters. The left-wing *Tribune* had waged a campaign against the calumnies of its right-wing counterparts since the beginning of 1946. And there was also, as has been discussed above, a latent anxiety about the state of the press and political communication in general. But it was very difficult to focus this anxiety and pinpoint its cause. Morrison tried to do this through the proposal he brought up for debate in the House on 29 October 1946.

The Parliamentary Debate on the Royal Commission, 29 October 1946

The debate, which lasted six and a half hours, was interesting for two main reasons. It illustrated how difficult it would be to prove who influenced the press and with what effect. And, even if it were possible to identify the source and the extent of influence, how hard it would be to do anything about it.

The arguments fell along quite clear Party lines.[20] The left were convinced that the press was no longer free or fair. The press barons were responsible for this; they had bought up independent newspapers and created chains in which opinions were dictated from above and policy driven purely by commercial interest (for circulation and advertising). 'The process of monopoly is not receding. It is getting worse' Michael Foot said, 'During the war newspapers made huge profits. They have built up great financial resources. They have undertaken large advertising campaigns... if no action is taken following this Royal Commission inquiry, these financial resources are going to be unloosed on the newspaper market'.[21] However, it was not obvious what action could be taken. Patrick Gordon Walker thought, like Morrison, that the light of publicity would rectify abuses. Bill Mallalieu was in favour of legislation to restrict ownership and advertising. No-one had damning evidence of newspaper vices. Tom Driberg suggested the influence of advertisers was constant but tacit.

The right were obsessed with understanding the motivation for the Commission. They saw Morrison as the driving force behind the motion, pushing forward the investigation due to his own 'wounded vanity' and in reaction to press criticism of government policy.[22] They could not see what an investigation would achieve and thought it was based solely on socialist self interest. 'What is really wanted, and what is behind this Motion, is not freedom of expression at all; hon. Members want to saddle the country with a number of papers of their own way of thinking' Maxwell Fyfe argued for the Conservatives.[23]

Most of the speakers had personal experience of working for the press. This might, logically, have added substance to their arguments. It did not. They each talked about their own experience and elevated it to an indictment or exoneration of the whole industry. Michael Foot had been a young editor of the *Evening Standard* under Lord Beaverbrook. He talked about the enormous reduction in the power of the editor in favour of the proprietor. Had he worked with Rothermere or Camrose he would almost certainly have had a very different impression. Beverley Baxter, also with the *Express* Group though many years earlier, thought the Motion was 'preposterous'.[24] Only once in his experience as an editor had an advertiser sought to influence him and he had told them where to get off. He assumed his own experience was indicative of the industry as a whole.

Both sides tended to caricature the newspaper world. There was a transparent ideological subtext to the Labour picture of small, independent newspapers and idealistic editors in a desperate struggle against greedy, corrupt magnates. Conversely, the Conservatives saw benign proprietors singled out by a mischievous government bent on revenge. Everything, from the left and the right, was justified as 'securing the freedom of the Press' – freedom from government interference vs. freedom from capitalist proprietors, freedom to say what they like vs. freedom of news from opinion, freedom from advertisers' pressure vs. freedom from state subsidy. The trade paper, the *World's Press News*, was not impressed by the level of debate: 'We imagine that the ultimate verdict of history on those responsible may be a little amusing'.[25] But the debate was not so much amusing as demonstrative of the difficulties to come.

Another nationalised industry?

The motion for a Commission passed by 270 votes to 157. Its passage inaugurated a new phase in the relationship between the government and the press. Now the newspapers were in the dock. They understandably saw the Commission as 'a Grand Jury or Grand Inquest'.[26] And if, as the government had said in the debate, the press was now an industry, what would stop them being nationalised like any other industry? Indeed, less than two weeks after the debate the government announced the nationalisation of railways, ports, inland waterways, and long distance road transport.

This led some people to believe that 'the definite development of the full Socialist State is envisaged'.[27] The *Sunday Times*, Lord Kemsley's flagship which had been at the centre of so much criticism, began a series of editorials about the 'Twilight of Freedom' on 27 October 1946. They described how freedoms won over centuries were now being whittled away. 'The course is plainly being set' the editorials stated, 'towards the one–party system'. The remarkable popular response to the editorials indicated that many people shared the same concern. By 17 November the *Sunday Times* claimed to have received well over 750,000 requests for reprints of the series. By December this had reached a million. For many readers the perceived assault on the press was symptomatic of the growth of state control.

Though some of the papers talked about the threat of newspaper nationalisation in November 1946, there is little evidence that this was Labour's intention at this time. There is, however, substantial evidence to suggest that from mid-1946 to mid-1948 the government did want to change its relationship with the press, and to alter the dynamics of political communication within Britain.

Many within the government and the Labour Party genuinely believed that overly powerful, irresponsible individuals were controlling the newspapers and that this was a serious threat to democracy. Similarly, they thought that the increased commercialism which had characterised the development of the British media in the 1930s was compromising journalists' freedom to write objectively. There is therefore no reason to believe that the government appointed a Royal Commission without the intention of taking some action.

Indeed, the way it acted throughout 1947 suggests it did not need the Commission's consent to flirt with much greater regulation and control. The problems within the wider economy (the dollar drain and fast rising deficit) led Labour to impose stringent regulations which had immediate repercussions on the ability of the press to perform its function. The power that these regulations conferred on the government over the press, an initially unintended consequence, once introduced proved too attractive not to use. Regulatory levers, like paper rationing and control of engagement orders, became an additional means of influence, as will be shown below. The government's simultaneous sustained bullying and belittling of the newspapers suggested that it was creating an environment in which radical change might be possible.

At the same time the government sought to bypass the newspapers as much as possible. If the press could not fulfil its democratic responsibility the government felt it must find alternative means of communicating with the population. As a result it centralised some of its direct communication via the Economic Information Unit, sought to invest more effort in government publications, films and advertising, and explored how it could use other existing media more effectively.

In the two years following 1946 the government tried to transform the nature of democratic communication. Had it not been for a number of serious obstacles, most notably economic constraints and international political developments, it might well have done so.

1947: Government–Press hostility deepens

The fuel crisis of February 1947 not only sparked a wholesale review of government communication (as described in the second chapter), but provoked intense criticism of the government's behaviour by the press. Much of this criticism was focused, as it was the year before regarding food, on the government's failure to keep the public informed. Though understandable, this criticism did not endear the press to the government. Their relationship deteriorated further as a consequence.

The Economist set the tone. After Emmanuel Shinwell made his unscheduled announcement on 7 February about the drastic power cuts the magazine complained that, 'Even in default of inspiration, plain ordinary horse sense should have sufficed to keep the public abreast of the facts about fuel, and almost anything short of imbecility would have broken the news of the power cuts otherwise than late on Friday, at the fag end of a vituperative political speech, in a debate that the government had tried hard to avoid'.[28]

Like *The Economist*, much of the press' criticism was of the manner and amateurishness of the government's communication as much as of the action they took. 'There has not been that cohesion and coordination of policy and interpretation which we expected' The *World's Press News* said.[29] It even put this in a wider political context saying, 'A bigger issue now emerges, the general standard of public relations between the government and press and people'.[30]

Yet the government gave no immediate indication that it wanted to solve this by improving its relationship with the press. In fact, in a public relations blunder, shortly after his announcement on the 7th Shinwell gave instructions that all periodicals, without exception, should stop printing to save fuel and power.[31] This draconian move was an unprecedented curtailment of the modern press in peacetime. Some journals printed part of their contents in daily or weekly papers (at the specific invitation of those newspapers), but most simply followed the instructions and ceased publication for two weeks.[32] As it turned out, they were under no obligation to do so since though the government could have secured legal authority by gaining an Order in Council they had failed to do this.[33] Shinwell also suspended the BBC Third Programme and television.

Though Shinwell's actions are probably best seen (like many of his at this time) as clumsy and misjudged, Philip Noel-Baker, Secretary of State for Air, cast a more sinister light on them when, a short while after the suspension he made a speech in which he told the press if they did not behave then the government could 'close down a newspaper at any time, simply by withholding its newsprint supplies'.[34]

Nor did other ministers seek a reconciliation with the press. Though Attlee admitted in March that he had 'no sense of public relations' and that there is 'something wrong with our publicity' he also pointedly remarked to backbenchers that 'the government was being misrepresented to the country'.[35] The government was clearly not going to resolve its communications problems by trying to ingratiate itself with the newspapers.

The relationship declined still further at the end of March. To the indignation of the House, the MP Will Nally accused MPs of accepting bribes from Lord Beaverbrook in return for news stories. Garry Allighan, another Labour MP and regular columnist, reiterated the claims in the trade press and broadened the accusation: 'Every newspaper in the Street has anything up to half a dozen MPs on its "contacts"' list, he wrote, 'Some of the "contacts" are on a retainer, some get paid for what they produce, some are content to accept "payment in kind" – personal publicity'.[36] Since Allighan had been news editor of the *Daily Mirror*, and wrote regularly for the *Daily Mail*, it could only be assumed that there was some basis to his charges. An investigation was announced immediately and rumbled on till the end of the year. The press snapped up his accusations and used them to suggest that the government's 'pose that they have a monopoly both of political righteousness and of economic know-how' had been severely tarnished.[37]

By the spring of 1947, therefore, Ministers were conscious of the failures in government communication but disenchanted with the press as a means of delivery. As a result they explored alternatives. They looked to other media such as BBC radio, feature films and advertising (their attempts to use these are explored in greater detail in other chapters). Though the government had used many of these already, it used them more extensively and effectively. When it used the press it tried to reduce its distorting influence. For example, with the *Reports to the Nation* which began in October, the EIU booked space in newspapers and filled it with information as and how it wanted. Departments also tried to go directly to the worker, bypassing the press entirely, via industry journals like *ROF News* (for the Royal Ordnance factories) the magazine *Coal* (for the miners), and *Target* for industrial managers.[38]

There were already signs, however, that the government would find direct communication with the people difficult. In March it published its much touted *Economic Survey*, both as a White Paper and in a 'popular version'. This latter version was supposed to raise awareness amongst a wider audience of Britain's dire economic circumstances and the responsibilities of the public. But a different title ('The Battle for Output'), a different cover, and five new charts did not, as *The Times* pointed out, constitute popularisation.[39] By comparison the *Picture Post* published a straightforward, visual exposition of the survey in April, setting out its key points and its implications for the population. Its clarity demonstrated that the government still had a lot to learn in terms of popular communication.[40]

Undermining the ability of the press to do its job

While the government increased its means of communicating directly with the people it reduced the capacity of the newspapers to do the same. Over the course of 1947 it took a whole range of actions which, if looked at separately, were clumsily authoritarian. When looked at cumulatively, they suggest the government was flexing its muscles at the newspapers and undermining their role as the primary means of political communication.

Over the course of the year the government reduced the press's paper ration and pegged each newspaper's circulation. It introduced new economic and distribution controls that gave it increased executive power over the press's means of production. It went on to threaten to make some papers risibly small (two pages). Where possible it avoided the press altogether or formalised its relationship with them to try to limit misrepresentation (with the lobby correspondents, for example). And the whole time it was using rhetoric that seemed calculated to demean newspapers in the eyes of their readers and so make them less credible as tools of political communication.

Since September 1946 some of the wartime controls on newsprint rationing had been relaxed. Penny papers had been allowed to increase to five pages per day, others by a comparable amount, and the basis of rationing had been changed to tonnage rather than circulation (so papers could sell as many copies as they liked, provided they did not exceed their ration). According to Lord Layton this had an immediate impact on political reporting. By his calculations The *Daily Mail* and *Daily Express* increased the space devoted to parliamentary reports by two and a half times.[41]

However, as the dollar drain quickened in June 1947 the government scoured the country's imports to see what it could cut.[42] It quickly decided to reduce newsprint. It says quite a bit about its attitude to newspapers but not much for its commitment to freedom of the press that it did not give a second thought to this reduction, despite its marginal dollar impact and despite the recent long term deals the Newsprint Supply Company had completed with Canadian suppliers. The Cabinet discussions were dominated, instead, by the degree to which food imports would be reduced. In contrast, the discussions about paper were fleeting, consisting of one sentence in the minutes; 'the cut proposed for raw materials was very small but it would involve a return to a four-page newspaper'.[43]

The announcement to the Commons was similarly unapologetic. 'Some restriction(s) of supplies of newsprint is inevitable' Hugh Dalton said, 'which will render it necessary to return temporarily to a four page paper'.[44] He gave no indication that this was a difficult decision to make, or of how long the reduction would last.[45] In the debate following the announcement the government also managed to give the impression that the cut was a deliberate punitive gesture. *The Economist* commented that Ministers seemed 'rather to confirm than to remove the impression that the cut was intended to express displeasure at the use made by the daily newspapers of their occasional extra pages'.[46]

Then, just over two months later, after the currency debacle of July and August, there were even rumours that the government might have to shrink the papers even more, to two pages. The newspapers were stunned. *World's Press News* said that this 'would make a mock of the government's professed desire to maintain a free Press and the democratic way of life'.[47] Though this did not happen, the threat hung over the press for the following nine months.[48]

In September the government introduced the 'Control of Engagement Order' that gave it increased executive power over industries' means of production. This was Cripps' plan for taking control of the economic debacle. From now on the government would direct labour and would issue licenses for the use of raw materials. Any firm which refused to cooperate would have its license revoked. In Parliament Clement Davies immediately saw the possible dangers to the freedom of the press and urged the government to give assurances that it would not use its increased powers to close newspapers or to prevent them printing under the guise of economic measures.[49] Though the government gave these assurances its behaviour suggested otherwise (for example with the journal *Action* which will be described below).

Despite the decrease in newspaper size the government still expected significant advertising space in what was left. Indeed the Economic Information Unit launched the *Report to the Nation* campaign on 12 October, which was 'the largest space allowed to any one advertiser by newspapers for some years'.[50] Some newspapers initially refused to give this space to the government, despite the wartime agreement which still existed. But under pressure they eventually gave way.[51] This seemed particularly unfair when a few weeks later Hugh Dalton announced in his budget that in future only half of all commercial firms' advertising expenses would be deductible from their profit and loss account. The Chancellor also could not resist an ideological dig, saying, 'in these days much of the advertising is a serious waste of money, of labour and of material'.[52] This measure would directly impact the newspaper revenues and might, MPs argued, cause the closure of some of the smaller, provincial papers whose independence the government said it so jealously guarded.

Morrison, Cripps, Bevan and Shinwell maintained this hostility towards the press by regularly attacking it in speeches. In September Bevan and Cripps offered the unwanted advice to newspapers that they could easily make room for more news by cutting reports of certain court cases and stopping serial stories.[53] On 19 October Emmanuel Shinwell called the *Mail* and the *Express* 'scurrilous rags'.[54] The next month, on the 23rd, Bevan said that Britain had the 'most reactionary Press in the world'.[55] It is not surprising then that *World's Press News* felt 'there is at the present time a very definite campaign afoot seeking to belittle and denigrate the influence of the Press'.[56]

The year ended sourly too. Garry Allighan, whose bribery allegations had been investigated by the Privileges Committee, admitted to being paid by the *Evening Standard* through a fictitious company ('Transatlantic Press Agency') to leak information about the Parliamentary Labour Party.[57] Evelyn Walkden confessed to similar charges. As a result, Morrison told the Commons in October that he not only wanted any journalist who tried to bribe an MP for confidential information to be barred from the House, but for every journalist in their group to be barred as well.[58] Scarcely a week after he said this, Hugh Dalton had to resign after leaking information about the budget to a Lobby correspondent immediately before the debate. Dalton had not realised that his comments, made as he was walking into the Chamber, would find their way into the *Star* newspaper before he had completed his announcement. The incident indicates the innocence of contemporary politicians about the mechanics of the press. No Minister would make the same mistake as Dalton again. In each case the behaviour of journalists was strongly condemned, and, though Morrison's intended punishment did not pass the House, he was able to draw up written rules to regulate the government's future relationship with the Lobby.[59]

Government suppression of the journal 'Action'

The press were understandably anxious about the actions of the government. They were worried because not only did the actions themselves compromise the ability of newspapers to communicate, they were taken in a manner as to suggest that the government no longer respected the press as the primary means of political communication and therefore no longer thought it needed careful protection. Though the government frequently said that it was reacting to economic imperatives and would not use its powers to restrict freedom of the press, its behaviour suggested otherwise. A good example of this was its attempted suppression of the fascist newspaper *'Action'*.

Action was the journal of the British Union of Fascists. Though it had been published throughout the 1930s it temporarily stopped printing in May 1940 because most of its contributors were in prison. At the beginning of 1947 it applied for paper to start printing again.[60] Cabinet examined the application on 12 February 1947. Worried about the political difficulties that might accompany the resumption of the journal they discussed whether it might not 'be possible to justify the withholding of facilities to prevent publication'.[61] They asked the Home Secretary, Chuter Ede, and the Lord Chancellor, Lord Jowitt, to look into it.

Ede, who put his memorandum before Cabinet in May, could not see how, short of new legislation, the government could justify suppressing the journal, unpleasant though they might find its politics.[62] This was not the answer the Cabinet had been looking for. It was, in the delicate wording of the Cabinet minutes, 'reluctant to accept the conclusion that nothing could be done'. 'A further attempt should be made' Ministers thought, 'to find means of preventing the publication of this periodical'. Barring all other options, they said, could they not just 'refuse [its] allocation of paper'?[63]

Stafford Cripps looked into it and, in July, thought he had found a way to 'refuse to license the delivery of any paper for the publication of *Action*' through the Paper Control Orders. However, this was not foolproof Cripps said, because it may still be possible for them to secure paper through other means.[64] Another possible answer was to amend the paper Orders to 'make it an offence to publish any periodical unless it had been published before 16 August 1940 and in the month of May 1947'. This slightly absurd suggestion was rejected since it would undoubtedly affect other periodicals which were not politically objectionable. Cabinet had no wish to see *Action* printed but left the issue unresolved.

At almost exactly the same time that Cripps was searching for ways in which to prevent *Action* from appearing by denying it paper he was defending the new round of paper cuts to the House of Commons. The cuts were, he explained, only being made out of financial necessity. 'I hope' he said, 'that [...] the House will realise that this is not an attempt to discriminate against anybody'.[65] *Action* could justifiably have thought otherwise.

Lacking any clear Cabinet direction as to how to proceed Cripps, and his successor Harold Wilson, chose to ignore all correspondence from the periodical between July 1947 and March 1948, therefore not allowing it to acquire a paper license. In March 1948 circumstances compelled them to review the situation again. The journal, now re-titled '*Union*', had started printing, having gathered together enough paper for which a license was not required. In its first issue it accused the government of withholding a license and restricting the freedom of the press. The Cabinet denied that it had prevented the paper's appearance and said they 'would not use paper control as a method of censorship'.[66] Clearly this was not true. Although the reticence amongst a Labour Cabinet to allow the publication of a fascist journal was understandable, it does not excuse the fact that they attempted to use their control of paper to suppress a periodical that was legally allowed to resume printing, using controls they had explicitly said they would not use.

Labour's actions during the course of 1947 strongly suggested it was moving towards a different type of relationship with the press. It looked as though the government was creating an environment in which the press was so ill-thought of by the public, so limited in its ability to communicate (due to its size), and so circumscribed by the executive powers of the government, that it would be possible to introduce significant changes to the way in which it was managed and controlled. It had also appointed a Royal Commission expressly to inquire into these means of management and control.

What was The Royal Commission supposed to do?

The Royal Commission was asked to examine the influence of the press barons and of commercial pressure on newspapers. The motion before the House read:

> That, having regard to the increasing public concern at the growth of monopolistic tendencies in the control of the press, and with the object of furthering the free expression of opinion through the press and the greatest practicable accuracy in the presentation of news, the House considers that a Royal Commission should be appointed to inquire into the control, management and ownership of the press.

The attitude of the government is clearly visible within this motion. It believed there was a serious problem in the 'control, management and ownership of the press'. The motion cites 'increasing public concern' – although what evidence there was of this is unclear, and states that there were 'monopolistic tendencies' – a term vague enough to allow for considerable interpretation. This then elides into the 'object of furthering of free expression of opinion... and the greatest practicable accuracy in the presentation of news', suggesting a causal link between monopolistic tendencies and constraints on opinion or inaccuracy in newspapers.

Senior Labour Ministers were even clearer about their opinion during the debate on the Commission in October 1946. Patrick Gordon Walker claimed that 'the standards of journalism are slipping to the point at which the freedom of the press is endangered'.[67] Morrison asserted that 'Directives come from the back of Gray's Inn Road, in London, to the provincial newspapers, instructing each of the editors on what lines the leading article is to be the next day'.[68]

But, as Cripps' had asked Morrison in July, what was the Commission supposed to achieve? Morrison responded to Cripps' by outlining four possible goals.[69] To begin with, it should rectify many current abuses within the press simply by exposing them to public scrutiny. The continued threat of scrutiny, either by future commissions, a council on the press, or by the standards set by a press institute would then 'be a very potent weapon for keeping the press in order'.[70] Secondly, the Commission would write an 'authoritative survey' of the press which could then be used for 'laying general principles which should govern the conduct and management of the Press'.[71] Researching and writing this survey would also educate the public about the workings of the newspapers to prevent people being too credulous of them in the future. Third, it was hoped that a Commission could work out some way in which to protect the public domain. There was a general anxiety that the public domain was being overtaken by media owners and commercial interests, to the detriment of society and democracy. Therefore, given its 'quasi-constitutional position' Morrison felt that 'a general review of the place which the Press should occupy in a democratic community' was long overdue.[72] Finally, the Commission's supporters thought it might promote accuracy and good conduct by pressing for the formation of a single central organisation (such as the National Union of Journalists).

Patrick Gordon Walker, Morrison's staunch supporter and soon to become his PPS, went so far as to suggest that the Commission should not even be required to make recommendations. The survey, he thought, would be enough to resolve the problems and make it apparent what the government should do.[73]

These objectives were still distinctly vague. This vagueness could be interpreted to mean that the Royal Commission was being given a free hand to make its own judgments. But the leading terms of reference belie this. It seems more likely that they were supposed to give the government carte blanche. If the Commission surveyed the press, confirmed the allegations, and devised some workable alternatives of organising the press, this would justify and rationalise government action to suppress the malign influences and protect the public sphere.

Certain contemporary newspapers and observers thought that this might involve nationalisation. For example the 'Twilight of Freedom' editorials in the *Daily Telegraph* described above. This was always unlikely given the history of the press in Britain. But there were other significant, if less radical, steps considered. Some of these are contained in the initial proposals discussed by the Royal Commission and forwarded to their interviewees. They included: licensing of news groups, a levy to fund experimental publications, the compulsory inclusion of alternative views in each newspaper, or a public corporation newspaper.[74] It is far too easy to dismiss these proposals with hindsight since these and others were dismissed by contemporary newspapers and eventually by the Royal Commission as well. They were all, however, workable suggestions.

For example, the licensing of news groups was an option which was promoted by many contemporaries. Kingsley Martin was the most eloquent advocate of this approach. Martin had been editor of the *New Statesman* since 1931. He would remain editor until 1960. 'Throughout the thirties and most of the forties...' Francis Williams wrote '[Martin] both reflected and shaped the confused emotions of the intellectual Left in a way no other man did'.[75]

Martin outlined his licensing approach in his 1947 book, *The Press the Public Wants*, and in contemporary public lectures.[76] If individuals were not responsible enough to run newspapers, he argued, and if newspapers were becoming commercial concerns which did not 'seek to fulfil the function of systematic truth seeking which the early democrats accorded them' then perhaps each paper should be transferred to a public group – political or social – which could be licensed to run it.[77] 'I do not see that the cause of freedom' Martin wrote, 'need in any way be damaged by insisting that all newspapers should be "public concerns" run by responsible and independent groups, and not by irresponsible individuals'.[78] Something similar had, he said, already been tried in Czechoslovakia and was working. 'In May 1945, a decree was issued by the Czechoslovak government which made it illegal for any individual to own a newspaper'.[79]

A second option considered was 'the compulsory publication in every newspaper of a column of comment by an outside critic or expert' to ensure some degree of political balance. Most newspapers protested against this as a severe infringement of editorial freedom. 'No,' the *Daily Mirror* Group said, 'compulsion prevents freedom'.[80] But, given the nature of the government's regulation of news and political coverage in commercial broadcasting just a few years later, there is no reason to believe that such a proposal was entirely incompatible with newspapers. The Independent Television Authority, when set up by the government in 1954 to oversee commercial television services, had to make sure that its programmes were impartial, balanced and accurate. The Television Bill agreed to allow the new services only if the programmes broadcast by the Authority complied with the following requirements: 'that the programmes maintain a proper balance in their subject-matter and a high general standard of quality', 'that any news given in the programmes (in whatever form) is presented with due accuracy and impartiality', and that for politics, 'no matter designed to serve the interests of any political party is included in the programmes' (unless the programme include discussions or debates which are 'properly balanced').[81] This was much more of an obligation than a single 'column of comment'.

A third option, raising a levy to fund experimental publications, was derided by newspapers as a ridiculous proposal. Why should existing newspapers be asked to pay for new ones, the *Daily Mirror* group asked.[82] 'No other industry has been more fertile of new ideas, more ready to experiment, or prompter to apply the lessons of experience' Kemsley newspapers argued.[83] 'Who is to decide what experimental publications? This would be dangerous and undesirable' the *Manchester Guardian* said.[84] However, again there is a valid comparison between newspapers and broadcasting which suggests the proposal was not quite so ridiculous as they made out. When Channel Four was established by the Broadcasting Act of 1980, the original provisions of the license specified that the channel had 'to encourage innovation and experiment in the form and content of programmes'.[85] Part of this obligation included 'catering for the tastes and outlook' of specific minority groups which were underserved or not served elsewhere.[86] If it was not beyond the realms of government, even in the 1980s, to set up and help fund experimental media, neither was it in the 1940s.

A fourth concept, the 'publication by a body independent of the government of a paper devoted to the objective statement of news and opinion, and possibly of controversial comment supplied or reprinted from the remaining national dailies' amused some newspapers.

Berrow's Provincial Group, for example, thought that 'If it attained true objectivity it would qualify for the title of *Celestial Times*. Its staff would certainly have to be God-like'.[87] While the *Manchester Guardian* thought that if it were too good it 'might kill *The Times*'.[88] Again there is a more recent comparison which suggests the concept was not so absurd. In 1997 the BBC started to publish a text-based version of its news service on the internet, updated regularly. This was, to all intents and purposes, a public corporation newspaper.

The structural differences between broadcasting and the press, especially in terms of content regulation, later became accepted norms. At this point, however, prior to the launch of commercial television and radio, no such norms existed. Therefore while ideas such as Kingsley Martin's for 'lots of BBC's' to replace the contemporary ownership structures of the press may seem unfeasible in retrospect, they were much less so in the environment of the late 1940s.

Morrison, as the head of government information policy and the government's 'socialisation' programme, was well placed to think about alternative means of organisation and ownership for the press.[89] He outlined, in the *Labour Encyclopaedia* of 1948, two criteria that qualified an industry for government intervention.[90] The first qualification was that the industry 'provides a common service for industry generally or is basic in character'. The press was not basic in character but it did provide a 'common service', indeed it was 'quasi-constitutional' in Morrison's words. The second qualification was that 'it is a monopoly, or that owing to its nature or to the muddle into which private ownership has brought it, the public interest can best be served by its becoming a monopoly'. This second criteria would seem to apply directly to the status of newspapers when the Royal Commission was appointed. The terms of reference even cited 'monopolistic tendencies'. Therefore, if Morrison was following his own rules, government intervention was warranted.

Moreover, the Royal Commission found, through its investigations, ample confirmation that the press was not properly informing the population. 'In our opinion', the Commissioners wrote in their report, 'the newspapers, with few exceptions, fail to supply the electorate with adequate materials for sound political judgment'.[91] The popular papers in particular, did not distinguish between what was 'intrinsically important' from what would simply entertain.[92] Moreover, the Commission was able to find evidence that showed that 'the political factor in the selection and presentation of news is apparent in all the national papers'.[93]

Therefore the Commission had both the opportunity and the encouragement to recommend significant changes to the 'control, management and ownership of the press' and to justify government intervention. At the same time the government had created an environment in which such intervention was plausible. It controlled the raw materials of the press and was willing to restrict them, if necessary for political as well as economic reasons. It controlled the movement of labour (through the Control of Engagement Order). It imposed written controls on Parliamentary journalists, and it demeaned the press on many occasions. Newspaper owners and editors could be forgiven for thinking that the government was about to formalise some its powers and introduce regulations which would alter the structure and content of the press. And yet, virtually no reform took place. The next chapter examines why.

7
'Press Freedom' Triumphs; Government Turns to Spin

Despite being set up by the government to confirm its suspicions about the malign effect of press barons and the corrupting influence of commerce and therefore to justify positive action, the Royal Commission ended up doing the exact opposite. Not only did it decide against recommending radical changes to the industry, but when the Commissioners eventually issued their report they had become extremely sceptical about the benefits of any positive action by the government. They came down heavily on the side of maintaining free market mechanisms. 'In our view' they said, 'free enterprise in the production of newspapers is a prerequisite of a free press'.[1]

They went even further than recommending against restrictive legislation (for example, to limit ownership) and recommended against positive interference as well. Of the idea that the government subsidise the capital costs of printing to encourage emergent voices the Commission said, 'We do not think the taxpayer should be asked... to bear part of the cost of starting new enterprises over which he has no control'.[2] It did not recommend the publication of a 'public corporation newspaper' along the lines of a *BBC Times*. Neither did it propose any legal requirements to print certain information since it said this 'in the long run dams the free flow of information and discussion and undermines the independence' of the press.[3] Virtually their only positive recommendation was the establishment of a General Council of the Press, made up of members of the press (plus one-fifth lay members – and even their inclusion caused a rift within the Commission).

The Commission is important because its failure to come up with any means to regulate the press or protect the public space discouraged the government from taking action (there were also other factors acting on the government which are outlined later). But even more so because it indicated to the government that there were no obvious formal mechanisms available to regulate the press. At the same time the press' political influence was such that it could not be ignored. Therefore the government had to resort to informal methods to try to exert control.

The failure of the Commission to recommend any positive changes to the structure of the press was only one of the reasons the government retreated from making major changes to the industry. More important still was the shift in the political climate in 1948. In this year left-wing governments in Eastern Europe began closing Opposition newspapers and imposing restrictions on free speech. Nineteenth century liberal ideals of press freedom suddenly became critical reminders of the difference between democratic and totalitarian regimes. In such an environment it was not possible for Labour to start instituting new government controls.

Unable to force through reform, and unable to develop workable alternative channels, in 1949 the government found itself having to turn back to the existing press as the main agent of political communication. But by this time circumstances had changed. The State had its own communications machinery and personnel in place. Since it had been unable to reform the press, it felt justified in using this machinery to try to influence the way in which its policies were communicated and to manage its news agenda. It was from this point on that the government began constantly, systematically, and self-consciously, to manage the communication of its information through the news media.

How and why did the Commission come to its conclusions?

For two very pragmatic reasons, 1947 was an unfortunate time to appoint a Commission on the press. First, because many of the influences that had motivated the appointment, and had their roots in the developments of the 1930s, were diminished or reversed. Second, because as a result of newsprint rationing the newspapers could not be made responsible for some of the accusations and assertions aimed at them.

The peculiar economic circumstances of the newspaper industry in the 1940s have been described in Chapter Five. Essentially, the papers were insulated from many of the competitive demands that characterised the pre-war period by low costs and virtually guaranteed sales. They were free to include what they wanted without much to fear from substantial drops in circulation, or due to pressure from advertisers. In such an abnormal environment it would be extremely difficult for the Commission to prove that commercial influences were unduly affecting editorial judgment.

Similarly, it would be difficult to prove that the newspapers were deliberately suppressing stories or viewpoints when due to paper rationing, the papers were limited to very few, rather flimsy, pages. Despite their efforts to cram in as much as possible they inevitably had to reduce the breadth and depth of their coverage, and alter the editorial style to make it less verbose and more fact rich. They could, therefore, justifiably claim that any exclusions from their papers were as a result of newsprint shortages, and not made with any harmful intent.[4] This situation was made worse, and the government's case weakened, by the reduction of newsprint that came into effect on 20 July 1947. In the miniaturised newspapers of 1947 it would be hard, if not impossible, for the Commission to pinpoint examples of distortion as a result of commercial influence.

The Commission came to the conclusions it did partly because it was neither strong enough, nor experienced enough, to recommend major changes to the press in Britain. The reason for this was that Morrison appeared intent on appointing members without any direct experience of the newspaper industry. He instructed John Pimlott that 'newspaper proprietors and active full time professional journalists (although I am not quite certain about the latter) should be excluded but, subject to this, knowledge of Fleet Street may be an advantage'.[5]

It is unclear why Morrison adopted this approach although he might have been trying to avoid anyone with any sympathy towards the press. This would also explain why he was so keen to appoint a judge to chair the Commission.[6] But whether Morrison wanted objective observers or simply jurors to indict the press, he found it very difficult to find people who fulfilled his criteria.

The Cabinet vetoed the idea of a judge as chair.[7] It would, the Lord Chancellor said, make it too much like a trial. An academic was sought as an alternative. But few were keen to accept the post.[8] Neither were commission members easy to attract. In all, the government considered at least 17 different chairs and 88 different members.[9] By January 1947, six months after Morrison had begun writing down potential commission members, he had yet to even find a chair.

At this point the Lord President was taken ill and Francis Williams, from the Prime Minister's office, took over. Williams had already expressed his hostility to Morrison's choices. He was appalled by the current members' lack of 'practical journalism and standing in the profession' and wrote to Attlee that he was 'not very happy about the names suggested'.[10] But by January it was too late to reverse Morrison's invitations and instead Williams decided to add a number of names of his own.[11] This increased the experience of the commission but made it large and unwieldy.

Of the Commission's eventual seventeen members only two had extensive knowledge of the press; R.C.K. Ensor ('Scrutator' in *The Sunday Times*) and George Waters (editor of *The Scotsman* from 1922–44). The others included lawyers, accountants, and trade unionists. Opposition MPs were not impressed. 'Who are they?' they shouted when the Commissioners' names were announced in the Commons.[12] The Commission's weaknesses were shown both in its limited ability to conceive of alternative means of press organisation and in its overly deferential cross-examination of major figures like the press barons and the government.

Some of these weaknesses were apparent in the Commission's preparations for the inquiry. The Commissioners were not clear on their objectives and this affected the way in which they approached their investigations.

They started by sending out written questionnaires to all those covered by the terms of reference.[13] These were to be followed up with extensive interviews. The questions within these questionnaires illustrate how unsure the Commission was of its purpose. Some of them were astonishingly academic and went back to first principles (for example, 'In what does the freedom of the press consist?' and 'What is the proper function of a newspaper?'). Others were accusatory and almost predetermined to lead to defensive answers (for example, 'How far are inaccuracy and distortion due to deliberate sensationalism either in the choice or in the presentation of material?'). And though most of them began as open questions they then became very leading (for example, 'What do you regard as a reasonable standard of accuracy? Does it include not merely the correctness of facts stated but also the statement of all relevant facts?'). This made it apparent, to the recipient, what they were 'supposed' to answer. Altogether they added up to a slightly incoherent mishmash, an agenda which, while interesting, was not very focused and not structured to enable direct action.[14]

But even more damaging than the Commission's confused agenda was the lack of preparation by the key prosecution witness, the NUJ. Despite having been confident, ever since it first discussed the idea of an investigation at its annual conference in 1943, that it could prove its allegations about the malign influence of proprietors and of commercialisation, the NUJ failed to produce any damning evidence.

Clement Bundock, the General Secretary of the Union, had written and spoken regularly about this destructive influence. In January 1945, for example, he referred to 'the instructions sent out from the headquarters of a group to the editors of a long chain of newspapers throughout the country telling them whose speeches were not to be reported at all, whose were to be given a good show, whose speeches were to be treated on their news value, and what the leading articles were to be about'.[15]

And yet the NUJ did not even start collecting material evidence of this until after the appointment of a Commission in October 1946. Gordon Walker was shocked when he went to an NUJ committee meeting in early November and saw how little the union had done. 'I am rather disturbed by the lack of preparation of the NUJ' he wrote to Morrison.[16] The Union even resorted to writing to its members requesting information. This was quickly exposed by the *Evening Standard*.[17]

As a consequence, the NUJ's eventual submission was weak and inconclusive. Instead of hard evidence from journalists about blacklists or directives it provided analysis of newspaper coverage (something the Commission were planning to do themselves) and ominous warnings ('There is inherent in those chain newspapers a public danger').[18]

Without substantial evidence from the most important plaintiff and armed with an eclectic and confused agenda, the Commission was going to find it very hard to collate irrefutable proof of wrong-doing that would warrant government action.

When it came to the terms of reference themselves the Commission found that the situation was more complex than the NUJ and Labour MPs had suggested, and that the value laden charges were not supported by sufficient evidence. As a result the Commission felt unable to recommend significant positive action.

Examining whether the number of newspapers was shrinking and whether ownership was becoming more concentrated the Commission found that though this was true, it was neither consistent nor did it necessarily prefigure a 'tendency towards monopoly'. For example, though the number of newspapers had shrunk from 169 in 1921 to 128 in 1948, the highpoint of consolidation was 1929, since which time some holdings had broken apart.[19]

Moreover, some local papers disputed the idea that their independence had been reduced as a result of being members of a newspaper 'chain'. Berrow's newspapers, the publisher of a small range of local newspapers around Worcester told the Commission that 'small ownership is no guarantee of higher principles'.[20]

The Commission also became sceptical about the degree to which individual proprietors had an irresponsible influence on their newspapers. First, because the NUJ was unable to produce any material evidence of the infamous 'directives' (despite Beaverbrook having once given out 147 in a single day[21]). And second, because some of the Commissioners did not believe an individual could direct something as complex and multifaceted as a newspaper via a series of short instructions. They sympathised with Kemsley's complaint that 'The notion that I sit at my desk... giving daily direction as to what features or leading articles are to appear in the respective papers is too fantastic to be entertained by any serious person'.[22]

Regarding the broader question of whether newspaper ownership was having a material effect on the free expression of views the Commission found that it was. The influence was more likely to be indirect than direct but, in the case of many newspapers, it was freely admitted. Lord Kemsley said he had no need to issue directives or dictate policy on the *Sunday Times* because he had employed men 'of sterling character and fine qualities, and men with similar ideas to my own'.[23] The Commission's own analysis corroborated this, showing that the political views within most papers were relatively consistent, and consistently partisan. The coverage of the Gravesend by-election, like that of coal nationalisation and of bread rationing, for example, was found to be biased and characterised by 'a complete absence of objectivity'.[24]

But the Commission found it difficult to indict the newspapers since they were under no obligation to be impartial. As long as there was a broad spectrum of views expressed across the range of newspapers then the individual partisanship of one was not, the commissioners believed, problematic. If 'divergent opinions are of any importance', the Committee concluded, 'their existence will be news and will be reported as such in the newspapers'.[25] The Commissioners assumed any absence of views would eventually be solved by the market. This seems a remarkably complacent judgment from a Commission set up partly to see that such views were nurtured and promoted. Moreover, the Commission did no primary research with the public to ask if they felt the full range of views were expressed.

On the question of the distorting influence of advertising and commercialisation, again the Commission chose to take issue with the charges laid down in the Commons motion. In its conclusions it argued the direct influence of advertisers was negligible and, as regards indirect influence, 'of the various possible sources of income, the sale of their space to advertisers seems to us to be one of the least harmful'.[26]

This was despite having heard evidence to the contrary. It was well documented, for example, that all the popular press had resorted to non-journalistic methods to boost circulation in the 1930s. The respected advertising agency, London Press Exchange, acknowledged that it had colluded with newspapers in the late 1930s to maintain optimism artificially: 'Before the war the vast majority of papers considered, as we did, that it was in the public interest to stimulate the buying of quality goods at reasonable prices, and therefore they took active steps, sometimes of their own accord, sometimes in cooperation with the advertising agents, to produce a frame of mind in the public most likely to achieve this result'.[27] And the Commission also heard evidence that papers would add supplements to increase advertising revenues (particularly on gardening, fashion or books).

However, the situation in 1947 was very different to that of a decade earlier. Due to the enormous drop in advertising space available there was a queue of potential advertisers for every vacant newspaper position. The balance of power, which might have favoured the advertiser in the 1930s, had shifted to each individual newspaper. As the President of the NUJ told the Commission, 'the advertisers are begging for space rather than exercising pressure, as was undoubtedly the case before the war'.[28] And, whilst paper was rationed there was no opportunity to print supplements or substitute genuine news for promotional material.

In addition, if the Commission were to accept that a major advertiser could have a detrimental influence on the content of a paper, then, in 1947, it would have to censure the government. 'If any advertiser could, through sheer weight of expenditure, hope to influence the editorial policy of the newspapers,' the Advertising Association wrote, 'that advertiser must now be the Government itself'.[29] Government advertising, the Association pointed out, was running at around £3 million per year. This was significantly higher than any commercial body. The largest proportion of this expenditure went on the press. Furthermore, the government could secure more space in the newspapers than any other body, thanks to an agreement it had made during the war which Morrison had been able to prolong.[30]

New allegations: the influence of the government on the press

It was not in the original terms of reference of the Commission to examine the role of government influence on the press. But, to the surprise of the Commission many of the respondents, in interview and in writing, complained vigorously about the actual or possible threat of the Government Information Services.[31] This was despite the fact that, as the Guild of Newspaper Editors crossly reminded the Commission, they had 'omitted to ask us what are the responsibilities of public authorities to the press'.[32]

The criticism fell into three main areas: obstruction, inherent bias, and monopolisation of information. In other words, each of the accusations which had been levelled at the press were now being levelled at the government.

In addition to the central government obstruction already described, there were further obstacles at a local level. According to the Local Authorities Act of 1908 all local councils were required to let the press into their meetings.[33] There was, however, a loophole. If the council said they were meeting 'in committee' they could legitimately exclude journalists. By 1947, by the calculations of the Guild of Newspaper Editors, 867 local authorities were not allowing reporters into their meetings as against 130 which were.[34] Even when journalists were given minutes of the meetings, they were sometimes threatened that 'If you publish anything which we say should not be published in relation to particular minutes, then no minutes will be sent to you again'.[35]

Bias in departmental public relations departments was, many newspapers claimed, 'inherent within the situation itself'.[36] It was inevitable, the Institute of Journalists said, that 'the natural ambition of official bodies, national and local, [was] to have their virtues and accomplishments publicised'.[37] Stephen Tallents, the original Public Relations Officer (PRO) and now President of the Institute of Public Relations, acknowledged that as a PRO 'you are concerned, of course, to put over the point of view of your department; that is what you are there for'.[38] In practise, A.L. Cranfield, editor of *The Star*, told the Commission that this meant he received a couple of calls a week from PROs informing him that something in his newspaper was wrong, although, as he protested, it is only 'not right from their point of view'.[39]

The most serious of the accusations was the third, that the government had a monopoly of information and could retain or release this as it saw fit. Though many newspapers believed that the government did its best to pass on information, they were aware that it could misuse its power. Geoffrey Crowther, editor of the *Economist*, gave a good example of this. Prior to making sterling convertible on 15 July 1947 the Treasury told all the papers that this would not be costly for the country and provided figures to back up this claim. Many newspapers took the government at its word and used its analysis. As a result, when convertibility sparked off a massive run on the pound, the press was seen to have been 'unanimously ill-informed or unanimously wrong in its judgment'.[40] The danger was even more acute in areas like foreign affairs when the press regularly relied on the government as its sole source of information. *Tribune* called this 'Gleichschaltung' (establishment of absolute conformity) and thought its effect all the more damaging since, because the papers were not allowed to quote their source, they had to rewrite the stories in their own words.[41] This made them the equivalent of government sponsored news.

An offshoot of this monopolisation was the government's use of hand-outs. A hangover from the war, a hand-out would normally be either a transcript of a ministerial speech or a summary of an official document. Newspapers could use them but not refer to them. 'The sources of these hand-outs must not be quoted,' the Northcliffe Newspapers group told the Commission, 'in other words it must not appear to be official or semi-official'.[42] Editors could be forgiven for seeing a parallel between hand-outs and proprietorial directives. Moreover, the hand-outs could sometimes be wrong or misleading. Emmanuel Shinwell was due to give a speech at a rally in Edinburgh on 5 May 1947 to mark the introduction of the miners' five-day week. A text of the speech was distributed to the press an hour before it was given. Unfortunately, it did not match the actual speech made.[43] On another occasion in October 1947 the Board of Trade released the newly signed General Tariff Agreement late in the day. Since the document weighed over 8 lbs there was not time to read it before going to print. As a result all the papers relied on the 4-page summary written by the PRO.[44]

The press was partly defending itself from government attack by raising these concerns, but there was also genuine anxiety amongst many of them that they were being systematically blocked from finding information or were being given skewed information. This represented a significant threat for contemporary and future reporting; as the Institute of Journalists wrote in its evidence, 'If the road to the public relations section is the only one left to enquiring journalists, and the newspapers have to take their news solely from hand-outs, a condition approximating to official censorship of official news will have been established'.[45]

The Commission considers extending its terms of reference

Before Christmas 1947 the Royal Commission members reflected on their position and discussed whether they should issue an interim report. In general they were disappointed with the quality of evidence against the press ('astonishingly confused, thin and ill-supported' said Sir Geoffrey Vickers) and had trouble sustaining the claims about monopolistic tendencies.[46] They were not keen on the sensationalism of the popular press but this, members like Ensor thought, was a case of 'giving the people what they want' rather than through any conscious attempt to distort facts.[47] It was difficult, G.M. Young argued, to find a direct link between the nature of newspaper ownership or commercial control and restrictions on accuracy of information or freedom of opinion.[48]

However, they had been affected by the significant criticism of the government's information services and some of the members of the Commission voiced their concerns about other damaging influences of the government. Actions such as Hugh Dalton's November tax on advertisers, would do 'more harm than good' they thought.[49] And more important still, the government's strict rationing of newsprint created such unnatural conditions that it made it impossible for the Commission to judge the situation fairly and recommend serious changes. G.M. Young compared the Commission's job with 'trying to prescribe a healthy regimen for the inmates of a concentration camp, not knowing when, or by what stages, they will be discharged'.[50]

The members thought they could not recommend significant government intervention given their findings to date and their concerns about government behaviour. These concerns also, they thought, reflected the prevailing mood in which 'feelings against any kind of Government control over, or interference with, the Press is so strong that Parliament, I am sure, would not entertain a measure for the better regulation of the Press unless the need was demonstrated beyond all doubt'.[51]

They considered extending their inquiry to include other influences on the press, particularly that of the government itself. But this would force them to veer outside the original terms of reference. The Commission had been asked to inquire into 'the presentation of news' with the object of furthering 'the free expression of opinion' as affected by the current 'control, management and ownership' of the press. It was not expected to investigate the government as well. Despite discussion, by March 1948 the members were split on what they should do.[52]

As chair, Sir David Ross decided. We 'should limit the inquiries to matters plainly directed' by the questions within the terms of reference, he said. 'Matters external to the press such as the influence of PROs would be considered only insofar as they were put forward by the press as alternative explanations of shortcomings which seemed to arise from causes inside the press'.[53] In other words, they would ask the government to be interviewed in respect of the original terms of reference, but not with a view to extending the inquiry to a wholesale review of the influence of the government.

The Government is called to the Royal Commission

The secretary of the Commission, J.J. Nunn, wrote to the Treasury on 16 March 1948 and requested that the government come for interview.[54] The letter was deferential and apologetic and made it clear that the Commission had little choice. Attached to the letter was a summary of the criticisms, obligingly laid out so the government could respond.

The letter generated a minor panic within Whitehall. The Treasury tried to push the issue onto the COI.[55] But Robert Fraser felt it was not his responsibility because the departments dealt directly with the press and the Commission referred explicitly to the public relations officers who were based in each department.[56] So he suggested Philip Jordan take charge and work directly with top PROs to handle it. Though Philip Jordan was willing to take it on, the suggested PROs were not. Thomas Fife Clarke and Matthew Crosse, from the Ministries of Health and of Fuel and Power, refused to go in front of the Commission. It is likely they feared that the ignominy heaped on the information services and on PROs by the press, would fall on whichever poor soul chose to take the brunt of the criticism. Scrabbling around for other names the government eventually chose James Crombie (Treasury), Michael Balfour (Board of Trade), J.E. Holroyd (Board of Trade), and W.M. Ballantine (Scottish Office) to accompany Jordan.

These officials were still keen to make sure they were not sacrificial lambs. They insisted that, if they were to stand in front of a Royal Commission, they would only act as spokesmen for a government statement, prepared and submitted before their interview.[57] Philip

Jordan was made head of a sub-committee to draft this document and to prepare for the interview. All this would, however, take time, and so the government told the Commission they would not be ready for the proposed interview date on 1 April. They eventually met on 26 May.

In the meantime Jordan met with Morrison and quickly prepared a draft which was scrutinised by the official information services committee, the ministerial information services committee, the Lord President's office, and the Prime Minister.[58] At the same time Boon and Gore from the Lord President's office started collecting evidence of the activities of the PROs from each department (press conferences held, hand-outs distributed, facilities visits, and press inquiries handled).

The Ministers and civil servants went over the Jordan document very carefully, editing it, making sure there were no lines that could be used against the government. The idea was to make the statement as positive as possible and convince the Commission that the 'information sections were of equal importance as, for example, the accounts department and the typing pool, in the functioning of the Departmental machine'.[59]

Many of them had changes and adaptations to make. For example in paragraph 7, which read:

> The Information Division of a department has no view separate from that of the department as a whole. It is merely a section of the department discharging, as do all other sections, a specialist function for its minister. The facts it gives are provided by the department; and in presenting and explaining them, it is expressing its department's well-considered view of their significance.

Patrick Gordon Walker did not like this at all, 'it might well be taken out of context and quoted against us as showing that facts are twisted and presented in a way that we like'.[60] He therefore removed provocative words like 'present' and 'explain' and 'significance'. It ended up as, 'The information division of a department has no view separate from that of the department as a whole. It is merely a section of the department discharging, as do all other sections, a specialist function'. The irony that Gordon Walker and others were presenting a statement in the way that they liked was not commented on.

The eventual document which emerged had many fewer contentious words than Jordan's – no use of the word specialists, or indication that people were sifting the significant from the insignificant. Only that they were making the dissemination of information more efficient and less chaotic. It was sent, together with appendix giving examples of how the PROs worked (answers to phone queries, a diary of press conferences) to the Commission at the end of April.[61] Between then and 26 May when the interview took place, Jordan and the other representatives continued to receive instructions as to how they should react to the questions and what they should say.[62]

They should not have been so worried. Considering the range of criticisms levelled against the government their interview with the Commission was very brief and certainly not testing. Altogether the Commissioners asked 130 questions. This compared to the 598 they asked Lord Kemsley and his deputy chairman the following day.[63] The Commission voiced the main complaints of some of the papers but little more. At one point Sir David Ross even apologised that the questioning was so negative, 'We seem to be making nothing but complaints, although, of course, you will understand we are not making them ourselves, we are investigating them'.[64]

The official spokesmen accepted that there had been developments in government communication but disputed the press's interpretation of their effects. There had been a growth in staff numbers which was fully documented.[65] There were more formal mechanisms for dealing with the press which meant that most inquiries were directed to a central source, contact was channelled through this same source, and access to others within that government department had to be arranged through that source. But, though the press saw these sources and the mechanisms surrounding them as barriers to information and as prisms through which information could be shaped, the government saw them simply as more effective means of accumulating and distributing information in a timely manner. Holroyd replied at length to Sir George Waters, for example, about how, over time, each press office could add to its store of information available to the media and then make it easily accessible whenever it was required.

Waters tried to pursue this line of questioning by referring to specific complaints raised by newspapers. He talked, for example, about the papers of South Wales who told the Commission they found it 'much more difficult to get information with regard to mines than it was before'.[66] Crombie's response was to shift the blame, 'Of course the Coal Board are not Government departments, as you realise sir'. But this was Water's point. The growth of government, whether through nationalisation or bureaucratisation, had seriously reduced the accessibility of information. 'More channels are opened than are being closed' Crombie countered.[67]

The spokesmen had been well briefed and were well prepared. They stuck to a positive message about the information services. They did not answer questions which might have political repercussions or that required them to offer judgment. There were not many of these but Reverend Aubrey asked one towards the end of the interview. 'Do you feel' he asked, 'from your experience of this work, that the public is so much more fully informed and the press is so much helped that the expenditure is entirely justified?'. 'This is very difficult for me to answer' Crombie replied, 'I really think it is for Ministers to give an answer to that question'.[68]

The Commission remained true to the instructions of Sir David Ross. At no point in the interview did it seek to critique the government for its behaviour or search for specific ways to regulate it.[69]

International developments cast a shadow over government scope for action

The government's autocratic behaviour towards the press over the course of 1947 might have appeared less ominous to the newspapers had it not been for the very real constraints being placed on press freedom elsewhere in the world. During the period when the Labour government was berating the papers, increasing its executive powers over them, and considering alternative means of organising the press, the governments within the emerging Soviet bloc and many elsewhere in the world were all increasing their control of the media.[70]

In Hungary, for example, the acting Minister of Information, Mihalyfi, announced in June 1947 that all journalists would, from that point on, be liable for punishment, including the death sentence, for publishing 'reports which would harm the reputation at home or abroad of the Hungarian Republic'.[71] In October, following a secret conference of the Soviet Union and its East European neighbours in Warsaw, a communist information office was to be opened in Belgrade, the centre of a newly established Cominform. And even in pre-communist China, the government extended its control of the press at the end of January 1948, to the extent that *The Times* wrote, 'a censorship under that name may not exist, but Chinese newspapers which do not conform with Kuomintang views or directives are either deprived of newsprint or suppressed'.[72]

But it was the developing situation in Czechoslovakia in early 1948 which had the most damaging impact on perceptions of the role of government on the organisation of the press. Czechoslovakia had been seen by many in Britain as a successful marriage of socialism and freedom. In particular its organisation of the press was held up by many witnesses of the Royal Commission as a model which should be emulated. 'We have heard a great deal about Czechoslovakia and its press', one of the Commissioners, G.M. Young, said.[73] Kingsley Martin espoused the system of licensing, outlined above, in his interview and his book *The Press the Public Wants*. The NUJ lauded the single national union which contained all Czech journalists and by whose rules they were all held responsible.

Then, on 25 February 1947, the Czech president, Edouard Benes, appointed a new communist-dominated government. Immediately afterwards action groups started expelling journalists from the national journalists' association. Once expelled they were not allowed to write for any newspapers. Since all journalists were members and the government held the licenses of all the news groups it was quite straightforward to exclude dissident voices. Shortly afterwards it went further and threw all foreign journalists out of the country as well.

This came as a profound shock in Britain. Many immediately made direct comparisons with Western left-wing governments and saw developments in Czechoslovakia as a warning. 'What is a Czechoslovak internal crisis has its implications and its lessons for all western countries' said a *Times* editorial.[74] In a similar vein the *Sunday Times* wrote, 'Here too the grim example of Czechoslovakia has lessons for us which we disregard at our peril'. Lord Kemsley's paper went further and said that Socialism was 'a bridge of appeasement, over which the invading forces pass, openly or in disguise, to compel the capitulation of democracy'.[75]

Though most other commentators were not as pejorative as the *Sunday Times*, they did believe that Labour now had a choice. They could choose Socialism first and democracy second or democracy first and Socialism second. 'On one side lies the territory where power is held in trust for the people, who are free to criticise the Government and to change it. On the other lies the territory where the power is held by a party which allows no rivals and tolerates no criticism of its infallible creed'.[76] Labour recognised that it had to define its position and distinguish itself from East European Socialism. On 3 March the National Executive Committee released a statement to do just this: 'The issues before us' it said, 'no longer permit of any prevarication. Socialism is meaningless without democracy. Democracy cannot live without freedom of speech, press, and organisation'.[77]

This statement expressed a serious shift in the perceptions of Labour in Britain. 'A great change has come over the party since the Communist coup in Czechoslovakia' the *Observer* said.[78] Opinion had hardened against the Soviet Union and communists, and there was a heightened awareness of the values of freedom of speech and freedom of the press. As a direct result of the coup, some of the alternative models of press organisation had been thoroughly discredited. The Czech method of licensing specific 'responsible' groups to run newspapers, for example, was no longer tenable. Neither was the idea of enforcing a journalistic closed shop.

These suggestions became even more unfeasible since, from 9 February 1948, the transcripts of the Commission interviews were released. 'The impact of events leading to Communist domination of Czechoslovakia has particular interest for the British press' *Newspaper World* commented, 'as the Czech press organisation has been quoted in Left-wing circles in this country as a possible model for ensuring press freedom'.[79]

The coup also had a pronounced effect on some of the members of the Royal Commission. Sir George Waters, the most experienced member of the group, made a speech in Scotland in June 1948 in which he said he was worried about many left-wingers' praise of the Czech press system and warned his audience that the freedom of the British press from government was not necessarily assured.[80] R.C.K. Ensor, the only member of the Commission who still worked for a newspaper, wrote that 'the one good thing about the affair is the extent to which it has opened men's eyes'. 'Journalists [in Czechoslovakia]', he wrote, 'are particularly easy for totalitarians to deal with, owing to the post-war Czech law which made journalism a closed profession'.[81]

At the same time that the Czech government was imposing severe controls on its press a five-week international conference on Freedom of Information and the Press opened in Geneva. One of the primary concerns of the conference was how to protect the freedom of the press against the growth of government control. Discussion quickly polarised into two camps – East and West. The Soviet delegate, Bogolomov, accused the 'reactionary' press of Britain and America of fomenting an atmosphere of hostility and mistrust. The 'purer press' of the Soviet Union had shifted from being '"mere disseminators of news" into instruments for the education and enlightenment of the people'.[82] A role not dissimilar to the one to which some people believed certain members of the British government aspired.

Hector McNeil, the British delegate, roundly condemned the 'dictated thinking' of the USSR and its satellite states. He held the British press up as an archetype of democracy and independence. 'A supine press is a bad press' he said, and claimed that, 'There is within the British press endless opportunity for the expression of different views'.[83] He also submitted a resolution on behalf of the British government on freedom of the press which included a clause stating that each national press should have the 'freedom to impart and receive information and opinions without Governmental interference'.

With statements like these the discrepancy between Labour's rhetoric abroad and its behaviour at home became very apparent. 'Was this really a speech by a member of the British Government?' *World's Press News* asked after McNeil's address, 'because if so there must be two Government voices, one for abroad which tells the world what a fine democratic and independent press we have in Britain, and the other for home consumption'.[84] It was not true, for example, that there was endless opportunity for different views when they all had to be fit within four pages. Neither was it true that the British government had refrained from interfering with the press throughout 1947. 'Such resolutions' therefore, 'are mere lip service unless accompanied by practical evidence of concern for a properly functioning press' as *The Times* pointed out on 24 May.

It was becoming much harder for the government to ignore the parallels between its actions towards the press and those of socialist or communist governments abroad. It was no longer plausible for them to argue that they were promoting a free press at the same time that they were curtailing supplies of newsprint, limiting circulations, increasing costs, and penalising advertisers. The Americans were so concerned at the threat to democracy this represented that, at the beginning of May 1948, they offered to allocate $22 million in the first years' Marshall Aid in order to buy additional newsprint.[85] When the government rejected the offer the reaction of even the most neutral newspapers showed that the contradictions between Labour's assurances and their policies were becoming politically unsustainable. 'Newsprint cannot be treated on this side of the iron curtain as just another material commodity' *The Times* wrote.[86] 'We are finding it increasingly difficult' *World's Press News* said, 'to draw a real distinction between the objectives of the Communists of Czechoslovakia and the British Government of today in relation to the Press'.[87]

Direct government communication too expensive

In addition to the international developments that were making increased government control of the press politically unacceptable, there were domestic pressures that were making the alternative – mass government communication – politically and economically impractical, and pushing Labour towards some sort of modus vivendi with the newspapers.

Politically, there had been mounting criticism of the Government Information Services, particularly at the end of 1947 and beginning of 1948 (described in Chapter Four). Economically, expenditure on government communication was only slightly below its wartime peak and, in March and April, MPs were expressing serious unease. 'Disquiet over the Government's information service is not confined to Conservative circles' the *Observer* wrote, 'Many of the Government's own supporters realise that there is something very seriously wrong'.[88] This unease was vented in the Supply debate in May, after which both Cripps and Morrison insisted that cuts be made. Budget cuts in information services were symptomatic of a broader range of spending cuts across government departments and indicated that the government simply could not afford to produce all its own information via films, publications and advertising. It would have to rely on the existing channels, primarily the press.

The centralisation of the authoritarian state in Eastern Europe also coincided with increasing political uncertainty amongst some ministers as to further growth in the role of the state in private industry. Morrison led this uncertainty and, at the Labour Party conference in Scarborough in May, suggested it was time to slow the pace of nationalisation and focus on securing the gains reached so far. 'Whilst in the next programme it will be right' he told delegates, 'to give proper consideration to further propositions for public ownership, do not ignore the need, not merely for considering further public ownership but for allowing Ministers adequate time to consolidate, to develop, to make efficient or more efficient the industries which have been socialised in the present Parliament'.[89]

Morrison felt Labour needed to draw a distinction between socialisation in Britain and the restriction of freedom by state intervention within other socialist republics. The transparent reduction of the freedom of the press in the Soviet bloc and elsewhere gave a sinister hue to paper rationing and other government controls. Moreover, the practical need for budget cuts made it unfeasible for the government to keep spending on the production of its own information. Combined, these two developments made it politically and economically untenable for the government to justify a reorganisation of the press to fit within a socialist state or to push government intervention in newspapers any further.

The Royal Commission's own shift in focus, from the effects of monopoly ownership and commercialisation which it was asked to investigate, to the dangers of government control and intervention was, therefore, illustrative of a comparable political shift within Britain. Their interview with the government witnesses in May 1948 was demonstrative of wider anxieties as to the intentions of the government towards the press and of the ever-expanding role of the State in general.

Morrison's recognition of the limitations of the role of the State at the Scarborough conference coincided with his disillusionment in the Royal Commission. Once it became clear that the Commission would neither come up with alternative means of organising the press nor justify further government newspaper management he gave up on it as a vehicle for radical change. 'We are credibly informed' *World's Press News* reported on 27 May, 'that only a few days ago Herbert Morrison roundly and angrily turned upon a group of left-wing journalists to condemn them severely for having induced the Government up the garden path in the appointment of that Commission'.

The government and the press agree to disagree

Neither Morrison nor many within the government were yet reconciled to working closely with the press. Ministers continued to denigrate it when given the opportunity. Before the 1948 Labour conference Nye Bevan famously called it 'the most prostituted press in the world'. But they began to recognise that it would be impossible to bypass the newspapers entirely and that they were not going to be given the license to institute significant reforms. They therefore began to look for acceptable means of engagement. Generally this meant seeking to influence the press by informal persuasion and direction rather than formal controls.

In 1948 Labour ministers therefore began to tone down their comments and even to defend the British press. In May the Solicitor-General, Sir Frank Soskice, defended the newspapers' role as the public's watchdog, and its willingness to criticise the government to prevent any abuse of power.[90] In June Morgan Phillips, chairman of the Labour party, told the International Journalists' Club that Labour did not want State control of the press.[91]

Even Bevan was forced to subdue his language. He sat virtually silent in the House while, during an adjournment debate at the end of July 1948, the Opposition tried to push him to appear before the Commission and justify his accusations against the 'prostituted' newspapers.

The Home Secretary defended Bevan and said the Prime Minister had stopped the Minister of Health appearing on constitutional grounds.[92] In the words of *The Economist*, 'Having attacked a body whose case is at present sub judice, he [Bevan] was so hopelessly in the wrong that, for once, he had to rely upon others to conduct his defense'.[93]

Labour's anger at the press was also mollified by the results of the US election of 1948 which suggested that newspapers had little genuine political influence. Harry Truman had beaten his Republican opponent Thomas Dewey despite the overwhelming support Dewey received from the American papers. Morrison was particularly heartened by this. Speaking in Fife in November he said that 'the US has had an even more dramatic indication that the prognostications of the press of the Right are unreliable, and that newspaper circulations are no guarantee that their readers agree with them or vote in the way they urge'.[94]

The shift towards working informally from within was perfectly characterized by Morrison in a speech he made in London on 16 November 1948. 'I am a friend and protector of the press as a great institution' he told his audience, 'If I am a critic of the press it is because I feel I am part of the family'.[95] This mixture of protector and critic began to characterise the new relationship. Hartley Shawcross told an American audience in July 1949 that 'we have in Britain an active and vigorous Press, which cannot be bullied or bought, and is vigilant in protecting the rights and liberties of the subject', while in November Cripps accused the press of setting out deliberately 'to mislead and confuse the people of this country'.[96]

The press were similarly conscious of the shift away from institutional reform, but equally aware that the two estates had simply agreed to maintain a mutual distrust. A.J. Cummings, the author of the influential 'Spotlight' column in the *News Chronicle* told the Manchester Reform Club in October 1949 that 'it had been a tough fight to keep the British press free, and the fight was by no means over. Perhaps it never would be over'. Though the 'Shinwells and the Bevans were "maintaining a pulsating silence"' Cummings said, 'it was a pause in a battle that was never won'.[97]

The report of the Commission and its implications

When the Commission finally released its report, in June 1949, the debate had reached stasis. The report tried to fulfil Morrison's criteria by criticising the popular press for its sensationalism and overly emotive political bias. But by balancing this with statements like 'the

British press is inferior to none in the world' it ensured that the latter rather than the former made the headlines. Its dismissal of any intervention by government was understandably seen as a victory for the press and celebrated as such. 'The Press is Vindicated' the headline on the front page of the *Daily Express* read.[98]

Conversely, Morrison highlighted the report's criticisms of specific press coverage and quoted the report's warning that some of the journalism in the popular papers was leading to a 'further weakening of the foundations of intelligent judgment in public affairs'.[99] The Lord President's expectation that the report would shine a spotlight on the seamier side of newspaper production was dashed because the newspapers had no intention of advertising their own faults. But the government also escaped substantial criticism as the Commission did not think 'that up to now any harmful influence is being exerted on the press through the medium of the Government information services'.[100] If anyone had hoped the Commission would suggest preventative measures to protect the freedom of the press from the combined influences of owners, government or commercial pressures in the future, they would have been disappointed. The main recommendation, for a General Council of the Press, was accepted by the government but delayed and diluted by the press, eventually being set up in 1953.

The original promoters of the Commission argued that just by its appointment it had served its purpose. Ernest Jay of the NUJ said that the 'existence of Royal Commission has already had a salutary effect'.[101] It was true that Lord Kemsley had introduced a training plan for journalists, the Institute of Journalists had tried to create a 'code of honour' for the press, and John Gordon, the new President of the Institute and editor of the *Sunday Express*, called on his sub-editors to raise standards of accuracy.[102] But these were relatively minor developments given the initial hopes of the government and the NUJ.

Conclusion

Between 1946 and 1949 the government's efforts to change the structure of democratic communication, and its attempts to make the press do the same, had a number of important consequences for relations between the government and the press in Britain. The first was the confirmation of a perpetual distrust between the two estates that exists to this day. Neither the government nor the press was satisfied with the conclusion of their confrontation and as a result, they pursued their own ends without any clear resolution of the issues.

The press interpreted the government's new information services and its clumsy use of its executive powers (paper control, licensing, etc.) as methods of managing, censoring, and 'spinning' news. Many editors and journalists made this clear in their responses to the questionnaire of the Royal Commission. In these they said they believed the government now had significantly more control over information than before the war. Few of them cited instances in which this control had been misused, but almost all of them emphasised that it had the potential to be. Therefore they sought to preserve their independence from government influence, a goal not necessarily incompatible with, but certainly not complementary to, the government's attempts to encourage responsibility.

Indeed, this seems to have had a further detrimental effect. From the inception of the Government Information Services many members of the press became suspicious of the nature of government news sources and the way in which news was released. As a result they began to focus disproportionately on the process by which information was communicated rather than on the information itself – another factor which came to characterise modern spin. Journalists became increasingly suspicious of the motivations of politicians and of the information they received from their departments. The failure of the Commission to question the government fully or to recommend regulation of the new services helped ensure that this suspicion persisted.

The press' triumphalism, born out of the its perceived 'acquittal' by the Royal Commission, was also unhelpful. It fostered the impression that the press had escaped regulation by the government which would necessarily have restricted its freedom. And yet the newspapers had consciously and successfully framed the debate about their role according to liberal ideas of nineteenth century press freedom. This obscured the original purpose of the inquiry, to check the growth of monopolistic tendencies in the control of the press and constrain the influence of proprietors and rampant commercialisation, and prevented any realistic consideration of an extension to the definition of 'freedom of the press'.

The government had to accept that it could not force the press to be 'responsible' (its interpretation of responsible, of course), nor could it define the limits of commercial or proprietorial influence. However, it still believed that the political education of the public was critical to the health of a democracy. Therefore, it not only had to adopt some of the responsibility for that education itself, but felt it was justified in influencing the press with the means at its disposal. J.I.C. Crombie argued as much to the Royal Commission in 1948; 'If you have set up the [information] Division' he said, 'it is natural that the contacts with the outside press should be canalised through that Division'.[103]

Politicians have always tried to influence the press. But now the situation was materially different. The formal and informal mechanisms by which the government related with the press had been established: the Central Office of Information, the news distribution unit, official civil service grades for public relations officers within each department, written lobby rules, enhanced connections with the BBC, and a growing understanding of the process of communication. The government had much more ability to control information, package it, time its release, 'canalise it' to the media, observe its representation, follow up if necessary, and measure its effect.

In addition to its vastly increased apparatus of communication the government had also developed an entirely new conceptual understanding of State communication. As explained in Part I, it now consciously separated presentation from policy such that rather than being simply a corollary of policy, information was now a means to an end. Therefore when the government was unsuccessful in its attempt to remould the press into a shape more conducive to channelling government information, it was both able and willing to shift to other means, overt and covert, of manipulating the newspapers to ensure that it got its message across.

Part III

Government Communication in Practice: Broadcasting

8
A Model Communicator? The BBC Objects to Being a Mouthpiece of the State

The BBC came of age during the Second World War. Prior to 1939, despite aspirations towards greater political freedom, it remained in many respects diffident and restrained. This was as much due to the constraints the organisation imposed on itself, as those which were imposed upon it.

Formed as a private company in 1922 the BBC grew extraordinarily quickly in its first few years. During this time its character and direction were forcefully dictated by its first managing director (and subsequent Director General), John (later Lord) Reith. Reith stamped his immense Presbyterian will on the infant organisation and impressed upon it the public service values that helped it secure its first Royal Charter in 1927.

Reith's ability to gain not only a Royal Charter but a broadcasting monopoly was a remarkable achievement. But it came at a price. Politically Reith had been chastened by his experience during the General Strike of 1926. The BBC only just escaped being taken over by the government during the crisis (partly due to Reith's friendship with the Prime Minister, Baldwin). As a result, when the BBC received its first charter the following year it agreed to remain apolitical, impartial and, initially, entirely uncontroversial. Reith fought against this last stricture and in 1928 managed to have it removed. It was removed, however, only as long as the BBC behaved itself. If the government found any of its output objectionable, it could rescind this allowance. This de jure control by the State was formalised in the charter and license agreement.

Throughout the following decade the BBC continued to exercise considerable political restraint. In coordination with the government it carefully rationed access to the microphone, limiting almost all political appearances to speakers nominated by the government (leading to the exclusion of dissident MPs like Winston Churchill). Labour politicians complained that the BBC was far too supportive of the State but little changed in the years leading up to the war.

Before the war the BBC was equally conservative in its news output. It did not have its own news-gathering operation and relied entirely on feeds from the four press news agencies. It was not allowed to broadcast news bulletins before 6pm and many stories were embargoed until they had appeared in the morning newspapers (an early attempt by the press to monopolise scoops). The Corporation's news output was, in the main, earnest, uncontroversial, and unexciting. Listeners heard news they had probably already read, toned down to remove any contentious elements, without any BBC angle or reflection. When Chamberlain signed the Munich agreement, for example, BBC listeners would only have heard that it was an unparalleled success.

All this changed during the Second World War. The BBC began its programming earlier and ended it later. It started broadcasting news bulletins throughout the day. It developed its own news-gathering service and cultivated its own newsreaders and correspondents, some of whom became famous in their own right (the BBC had previously promoted anonymity). It launched a new national radio channel for the armed forces, the Forces Programme, which soon became more popular than the Home Service. Internationally, the BBC expanded its overseas services such that by the end of the war it was broadcasting news and information in 38 foreign languages. In the process its size and scope were transformed. In 1948 the Corporation had 11,349 employees, against 4,300 in 1939.[1] Its spending rose from £2.7m in 1938 to £6.7m in 1945.[2]

At the same time its audience at home and abroad grew and grew. On any given night during the war half the British adult population, 16 million people, could be found gathered around the radio listening to the nine o'clock news. Even more listened to Churchill's broadcasts. By the beginning of 1946 more than ten million homes in Britain were paying a radio License Fee. This equated to four out of every five households.

The BBC's national and international reputation grew even faster than its audience. By 1944 this was such that George Orwell could comment that 'I heard it on the BBC' had a new meaning – 'I know it must be true'. The BBC had consciously nurtured this reputation by emphasising its commitment to impartiality and its pursuit of the truth. Even though it was often simply passing on information given to it by the British government, it managed to give the public the impression of scrupulous propriety.

In addition to its effect on the listeners, this enhanced reputation had a profound impact on the BBC. It raised the organisation's self-consciousness and self-confidence, and made it much more aware of the principles for which it stood. The MP Herbert Butcher told the Commons in 1946, over the previous six years the BBC 'secured a consciousness of its strength and of the part which it played in the winning of the war'.[3]

In 1944 a new director general joined the Corporation, William Haley, who typified its new sense of confidence and self-belief. The BBC was, for Haley, a beacon of moral rectitude and objectivity. It can, he said in 1947, 'conceive that its highest duty is to the disinterested search for Truth. This is a stern concept. Absolute impartiality in all matters of controversy must be its golden rule'.[4] In this regard, Haley thought, it absolutely distinguished itself from the press.

Labour shared the BBC's belief that it was possible to inform the public truthfully, and in a balanced, impartial way. A broadcaster could, they both believed, report objectively and independently without favour to the government, to the Opposition, to pressure groups or to commercial interests. These shared principles encouraged the government to believe the BBC was a model communicator – in stark contrast to the 'instruments of political warfare', the newspapers.[5] Some even recommended the press be restructured such that it be made up of 'lots of BBCs'.[6]

And yet, within another six years, the BBC's independence had been so undermined that ending its monopoly was to become a key policy of the incoming Conservative government. Over the same period Haley had become so frustrated by the behaviour of the government towards his organisation that, in 1952, he quit to become editor of *The Times*. 'The more I reflect on broadcasting' Haley wrote in his diary, 'the more I am convinced that the greatest obstacle to its progress is the fact that people, especially the politicians, will not leave it alone'.[7]

The experience of the Attlee government illustrates some of the problems inherent in a system where the State has extensive connections with, and potential control over, major channels of mass communication. It shows how difficult, perhaps impossible, it is for a democratic government to resist using a monopoly public broadcaster to its advantage, whatever its avowed intentions. The State, claiming the 'national interest', will always be able to justify its interventions and to rationalise its attempts at control.

The government's blundering attempts at control were no longer acceptable in the post-war environment. A newly confident BBC was no longer willing to act as the mouthpiece of the government, and both the Opposition and the press believed broadcasting was now too important not to be made more transparent. As a result, the government was forced, over this period, to relinquish many of its means of direct control over broadcasting (although not without a fight of course).

Yet the State could not allow such an essential means of communication to slip from its grip entirely. Therefore, as its direct control diminished, so it built up its means of indirect control. Some of these were incorporated into the framework of broadcasting – first within the BBC's charter and later within the licences of commercial broadcasters (no such constraints existed for newspaper owners). Other techniques were developed at this time and have persisted ever since. These included: collaborating on the production of key programmes, stage managing the appearance of Ministers on air, blocking the appearance of alternative views, funnelling information through narrow government sources, 'explaining' bad news to reduce its potency, providing favours to encourage compliance, packing the BBC's board with a sympathetic Chairman and governors, and, when necessary, putting extensive political pressure on senior executives to conform to government policy. Cumulatively these equate to the techniques that characterise information management and modern spin.

Though earlier British governments had used some of these techniques, none of them had the communications personnel or machinery to administer or coordinate such control on a constant and extensive basis. Moreover, there had been less need since the BBC had previously been a more submissive partner.

By the time the BBC lost its monopoly in 1954, the government's new relationship with broadcasting had been established. The introduction of competition then further accentuated the need for informal means of State control, and accelerated their use.

Government – BBC consensus at the war's end

At the end of the war all the signs were that the new Labour government and the BBC would get along very well. Not only had the BBC worked closely with the government and Labour Ministers in the Coalition government during the conflict but its output had come to reflect the left-leaning consensus which characterised Whitehall and the nation at that time. As the war progressed the BBC started to broadcast an increasing number of programmes about post-war national reconstruction, about planning, education and full employment, such as 1943's 'The World We Want', and 1944's 'Jobs for All'.[8] These were not intended to be controversial but to capture the popular urge for regeneration and change: an urge which Churchill and the Conservatives consciously avoided (adamant that the war must be won before they discussed the peace).

But the new Labour government and the post-war BBC had more in common than a few specific programmes. The BBC shared much of Labour's heady idealism. It too wanted to promote egalitarianism and opportunity, for example by providing the cultural element of Labour's universal welfare state. To this end Haley added the Light Programme to the Home Service in July 1945 and had plans to add a Third Programme the following year. The aspiration, as a July editorial in *The Listener* explained, was that, 'If the horrid but convenient terms can be permitted, high brows, low brows and middle brows will each have a programme to themselves – thereby, one hopes, decreasing mutual jealousies and increasing the general stock of human happiness'.[9]

Such idealism extended to education. Like the new government Haley wanted the BBC to provide greater access to learning. He believed it was the responsibility of the broadcaster to bring education 'to much greater numbers of people than have ever been served before'.[10] For this reason he continued Forces Educational Broadcasting, and extended the BBC's Schools Broadcasting department.

Haley was conscious that as a child he would have been a beneficiary of such services. Having left school at 15 he found a job as a copy-taker with *The Times* in Brussels. He worked hard and by the time he was 30 was Managing Editor of the *Manchester Evening News*. Just over ten years later he joined the BBC as Editor-in-Chief and, within a year, was offered the post of Director General (DG). Throughout his adult life Haley was self-conscious about his lack of formal education, reading voraciously to make up for it, and even penning book reviews in his spare time while he was DG of the BBC.

Haley was a man of strong principles and considerable integrity as well as ambition. He fully endorsed, enhanced even, the Reithian principles which underlay the BBC. Perhaps the most important of these was to keep people politically informed. The BBC's duty, as he saw it, was 'to ensure that the idea of the British nation as an informed democracy shall not merely be an ideal but a reality'.[11]

But it was also the BBC's job, according to Haley, to act as a channel for political broadcasting, not to have a voice of its own. As the DG put it in 1947, 'the BBC has principles rather than policies, and... while we should supply all the ingredients for the informing – and thereby the forming – of public opinion, the actual catalyst should always be outside ourselves. Our task in relation to public opinion is to transmit, not to transmute'.[12] This meant avoiding controversy not courting it. It is difficult to imagine any newspaper adopting a comparable approach.

It was this unexamined commitment to impartiality that made the post-war BBC, like the post-war Labour government, determined to deal in 'facts'. The BBC even started a programme on the Home Service in 1945 called 'Facts First'. Each week this 15 (then 10) minute show was supposed to give a 'Picture Post level audience' a brief sketch of the background on current, topical issues.[13] At its heart should be dry facts, without too much illustration or description. As the BBC's Vincent Alford said, 'The 'pictorial' or the 'topographical' should only be introduced when it is relevant to the elucidation of the subject of the talk, and then sparingly'.[14]

The commitment also turned the BBC into a sort of political accountant. It began to count the appearances of every politician at the microphone and record their political allegiance and the time they spent there.[15] That way it could not only try to maintain an exact political balance but could also prove to its detractors that it was maintaining that balance.

Commercialism in broadcasting, Labour and the BBC both agreed, would soil political communication and sully the benefits of public service broadcasting. Herbert Morrison had an instinctive dislike for commercial programming. His often quoted comment in the House in July 1946 gives a good flavour of this: 'Personally, I find it repugnant to hear, as I have heard [in the US] a programme of beautifully sung children's hymns punctuated by an oily voice urging me to buy somebody's pills'.[16] The BBC shared Morrison's dislike and his belief in 'Gresham's Law' that in commercial broadcasting 'The good, in the long run, will inescapably be driven out by the bad'.

Neither did either of them think there was any demand for competition. When Patrick Gordon Walker asked Morrison why he would not allow an additional commercial station to broadcast, even under the control of the BBC, Morrison replied that he doubted whether there 'is really a very strong demand in Britain for this sort of programme'.[17]

So, when Labour came to office it found a national broadcaster whose ambitions were similarly idealistic, whose programmes reflected the national consensus for reconstruction, and whose aspirations to political objectivity were irreproachable. Moreover, and perhaps most significantly, the Corporation's very structure seemed to provide evidence of the success of nationalisation. The BBC was a national monopoly intended for universal benefit, paid for by a direct tax on radio owners, with an independent Chairman and Board of Governors overseeing the executive. As Herbert Morrison said in 1946 it was 'an outstanding achievement in socialisation' and, more remarkably, 'a socialised institution for which the nation has to thank successive Conservative Governments'.[18]

Consensual appearance disguises fundamental tensions

The apparent congruence of attitude and purpose between the BBC and the government disguised fundamental differences in each of their perceptions of the role of the national broadcaster. The BBC wanted to build on the reputation that it had earned during the war, assert its autonomy, and distance itself from government. The government (and this would have been equally true had the Conservatives won power) wanted a compliant organisation with which it could continue to work closely and through which it could communicate its policies – 'unmediated' – to the people.

The war had demonstrated that the BBC need not simply be a common carrier like the national grid but could be much more politically constructive. Rather than simply transmit, it could actively promote the objectives of the state. As well as passing on information, it could raise morale, encourage a sense of shared citizenship, direct people towards specific goals, and provide rationales for government action. It was not a passive participant in the war but played an active role in winning it.

Not only were the government and the Corporation conscious of this new role, neither of them wanted it to end. Both now believed that the BBC had a critical part to play in actively sustaining democracy. The microphone could properly be used, Haley said, 'to inculcate citizenship, to [motivate people to] pay proper attention to public affairs, to encourage tolerant discussion'.[19] Far from being simply a channel, the BBC should now help to ensure 'that an informed Democracy shall function'.[20] The government signalled its approval of this role by agreeing that the BBC should now broadcast the edited highlights of Parliamentary debates each evening.

In 1945 neither the government nor the BBC recognised that there were two concepts of the BBC's role, nor that those two concepts were incompatible. There was the active, independent BBC which acted as the government's watchdog and promoted democratic debate. And there was the passive, quiescent BBC which collaborated closely with the government and provided tacit support for its policies. The inherent, as yet unrealised, tension between these two roles was bound to generate friction.

Government keen to maintain the broadcasting status quo

At the war's end, however, the shared attitudes and values of the BBC and the government were much more apparent than their differences. Combined with the exalted reputation of the broadcaster it is not at all surprising that in 1945 Morrison believed the BBC charter should be renewed. Indeed he had so few doubts about this that he pressed for it to be renewed without an inquiry, unlike on the previous two occasions.[21] He had made this decision based on the deliberations of his own Broadcasting committee and its predecessor, the Coalition Committee on Broadcasting.

Shortly after Labour took office Morrison chaired a Labour Broadcasting Committee to discuss the future of broadcasting policy. It met three times in total, in August, September and October 1945.[22] It was building on the work done by the Coalition Committee on Broadcasting which had met eight times between May 1944 and April 1945.[23]

The Coalition Committee on broadcasting had considered the issue of an inquiry and been unable to reach a consensus. Brendan Bracken was the source of disagreement, as the one member of the Committee who believed there should be an inquiry into the BBC, along the lines of the Ullswater Committee of 1935–36, before the Charter was renewed.[24] Therefore though the Coalition Committee wrote a report before the Caretaker government took over in May, it remained unsigned.

Morrison's Committee had much less trouble coming to an agreement. He, and the other three Ministers, agreed that broadcasting was now too 'closely bound up with politics', that an inquiry would cover the same ground as had been covered before, and that the technicalities had been already been sanctioned by an acknowledged expert.[25] Their report, in its essentials, was the unsigned Coalition Committee's report with some minor amendments. It went before Cabinet on Monday 17 December 1945.

The paper sailed through Cabinet with almost no debate. The Lord President and his colleagues, the minutes note, 'were satisfied that there need not be any inquiry by an independent committee, on the lines of the Ullswater committee, before the charter of the BBC was renewed and that the BBC should continue to be the sole authority licensed to broadcast in the UK for the further period of 10 years from 1 January 1947, covered by the new charter'.[26]

At the end of the same week Sir Eric Bamford, acting Director General of the Ministry of Information and present at the meeting, called William Haley to tell him the Broadcasting Report had made it through Cabinet. The Licence Fee would be doubled, from 10s to £1, just as the BBC wanted, the Third Programme could go ahead as planned, and BBC broadcasting to Europe would continue. Also, there would be no inquiry into the BBC.[27] The government and the BBC were both happy with the situation as it stood. So happy indeed that Haley was given a knighthood in the New Years Honours list for 1946.

This cosy mutual appreciation would not last. Indeed since the end of the war the BBC had been conscious that it needed to detach itself from the government and assert its independence.

The BBC seeks to establish some distance from government

At the end of the war the Director General was eager to establish some distance between the BBC and the government. They had grown very close over the previous six years and Haley believed it was important to assert the BBC's independence. He therefore sought greater financial, editorial and political autonomy.

The BBC's financial independence had been suspended for the war. Rather than being funded predominantly by the Licence Fee as it had been since its inception, during the war the BBC's money came directly from the Treasury under grants-in-aid. Not only did removal of the Licence Fee ceiling mean that expenditure increased significantly, it also meant that the BBC grew quite used to having the Treasury as its paymaster. According to Maurice Gorham, editor of the *Radio Times* during the war and head of the Light Programme immediately after it, 'during the war broadcasting was a national service and it was not difficult to go to the Treasury and get more money for staff, studios and equipment... People had got used to the feeling that if new things were needed the money could always be found'.[28] As a result the Corporation's expenditure rose by 150 per cent in seven years.

Haley was determined to return to the BBC's financial independence. But, given the increase in the Corporation's size, and the investment required in developing the new services and television, this meant a major increase in the Licence Fee. Haley suggested doubling it, and the

Labour government agreed. Since the number of Licence holders surpassed ten million early in 1946 the BBC would now receive yet another increase in income to add to that which it had enjoyed over the course of the war. The rise took effect from June 1946 but it was not until 1947 that the BBC gained full control of its finances once again.[29]

The BBC's enhanced reputation after the war was mainly the result of the perceived accuracy and impartiality of its news. Its authority was such that by 1945 '"I haven't heard it on the BBC" was sufficient justification for popular disbelief'.[30] This reputation was nurtured and protected during the war by separating the BBC's news services from other departments. After the war Haley decided to perpetuate this separation. Looking back on it he described how he 'isolated the News Division from the rest of the Corporation, and made the news itself immune from the Programme Heads. Fixed slots, the lengths and timings of which were decided by the Director-General, were imposed on each programme. They could not be varied. What went into them was the News Division's responsibility alone. No programme head was allowed to concern himself with the news audience's figures, or their effect on his programme'.[31] Haley hoped in this way he could sustain both the perceived and the actual impartiality of the BBC.

Haley also wanted to clarify the BBC's position on post-war Party political broadcasting and make it more transparent. Political broadcasting had always been an issue at the BBC. After granting its first Licence in 1927 the government stipulated that the BBC could not engage in any controversy nor could it express any political opinions of its own.[32] In 1928 this stipulation was relaxed so that the BBC could broadcast controversy, as long as it remained balanced and impartial.[33] However, throughout the 1930s the Corporation was unable to find agreement amongst political parties as to the nature of these broadcasts and remained politically very restrained as a result.[34] Party political broadcasting was suspended during the war.

In the weeks after Labour took office Sir Allan Powell (then Chairman of the BBC) and Haley began talks with the government to restart Party political broadcasting within clearly articulated parameters. Haley soon became aware that this would not be straightforward. Labour did not want to give up their current advantageous position. 'We are now talking to Arthur Greenwood [Lord Privy Seal] about political broadcasting' Haley wrote in his diary in November, 'The Labour Govt. have authoritarian leanings in this'.[35] Haley tried to overcome these leanings by capturing the BBC's proposals within an Aide-Memoire. This was discussed at length in the penultimate Cabinet before Christmas. But the Cabinet were concerned that written rules would diminish the government's current advantageous position and instead felt 'these matters should continue to be governed by understandings as to the normal practice'.[36] Greenwood explained to Haley on 23 January that such rules could as easily be written down as could 'conduct befitting an officer and a gentleman'.[37] The issue therefore remained temporarily unresolved and the other political parties without ready access to the microphone.

Haley was more successful at rebutting clumsy efforts by the government to interfere with specific BBC programming. After a World Affairs talk by the historian A.J.P. Taylor in September 1945 which Ernest Bevin found objectionable it was suggested that the BBC submit all scripts dealing with overseas matters to the Foreign Office.[38] Haley refused. In October, after the dockworkers went on an unofficial strike, George Isaacs, Minister for Labour and National Service, wanted the union leader, Donovan, to broadcast a 'factual statement' on the BBC. Haley blocked Isaacs, telling him that if Donovan broadcast they would have to let the strikers broadcast as well. Attlee then called Haley directly to question this 'extraordinary argument'.[39] But the DG held firm and was backed by the Chairman and Governors.[40]

Therefore Haley was trying, after July 1945, to assert the BBC's independence from government; in its news output, in its financing, and in its political broadcasting. However, the extent of this assertiveness should not be exaggerated. The BBC did not challenge the government openly, neither did it introduce a raft of new political discussion programmes. In fact, it seemed to play down domestic politics in the period after the war. Asa Briggs has argued that this was 'through fear of broadcasting being used for propaganda purposes' although it seems odd that an organisation trying to assert its independence from government should do so by avoiding politics.[41] The newspapers, for example, took the opposite approach and celebrated their peacetime freedom with much greater discussion and criticism. Moreover, there were many aspects of the BBC where the wartime closeness persisted, and this closeness compromised the Corporation's aspirations to independence.

The BBC remains 'enmeshed in government'[42]

Given the depth and length of the wartime relationship between the government and the BBC the legacy was bound to extend into peacetime.

There were too many official, unofficial, attitudinal, and habitual connections to shed quickly. However, whilst the BBC was conscious of many of these connections and keen to let them go, the government was both less conscious and much less keen. This was true of both the formal and the informal connections.

The government had always held de jure powers over the BBC via its constitution but rarely used them. During the war it increased its influence significantly. At the end of the war, instead of letting this influence go, it perpetuated, and in some cases even formalised it.

Given the power of radio at this time this is not surprising. The BBC's monopoly of broadcasting combined with the popularity of the wireless gave the broadcaster a direct channel into 80 per cent of households in the country.[43] It was a very valuable and influential channel, as the wartime Coalition had found. It could be used for announcements, for appeals, for campaigns and for Ministerial broadcasts. During the war there was rarely a day when a listener would not be treated to an abundance of government information.

Government announcements continued after the war but slowly wound down. In November 1945 there were still many public service broadcasts for the home listener. Martin Flett's research identified '77 informative talks given in the course of one month chosen at random' including 'The Small Farm – Labour Problems', resettlement information and citizens advice.[44] The official announcements period on Mondays, Fridays and Saturdays disappeared, first to be replaced by a more flexible arrangement each weekday, and then to be reduced to a single slot on a Tuesday from December 1945.[45]

Ministerial broadcasting was, however, too useful for the government to let go. During the war the procedure was that any minister could approach the Ministry of Information and request time to broadcast on air. He or she would then be given a slot of up to 15 minutes to broadcast live to the nation, in monologue not dialogue. Once in office Labour did not ask the BBC if it could maintain this privilege; it notified the Corporation that the practice of wartime Ministerial access would continue. 'Dear Haley', Sir Eric Bamford wrote to the Director General in mid August 1945, 'You may wish to know that Mr. Attlee has reaffirmed the procedure with regard to Ministerial broadcasting which was laid down by the Coalition Government'.[46]

Morrison was well aware of the importance of Ministerial access. When, at the end of September, Martin Flett wrote a memorandum to Morrison about home broadcasting which suggested there was general agreement that government control should revert to the pre-war position, Morrison wrote in the margin, 'Yes, but it may include require-ments as to Ministerial or official broadcasts'.[47] This led to a follow up note in which Flett made certain that the BBC were still bound to 'send out any matter which any government department may require to be broadcast'. 'I think that these terms are sufficiently wide enough to enable the Government to arrange for any Ministerial or official broad-casts it wishes', Flett wrote.[48]

The government also maintained a formal connection with a large part of the BBC after the war, the BBC Overseas Services. These had expanded enormously after 1939.[49] During the course of 1944 there were many discussions as to whether they should be maintained and if they were, whether they should become independent after the war or remain within government. In 1945 Attlee decided they should be kept. They could not, however, be given back entirely to the BBC. The government believed they were too important a political instrument for that. Instead, they would sit in an uncomfortable middle ground, ostensibly free to determine their own programming, but always in 'close consultation' with the Foreign Office and always in pursuit of the national interest.[50]

In addition to these formal connections many of the unofficial links between the government and the BBC still existed. Over the course of the war departmental officials had become very familiar with pro-gramme heads and programme makers at the BBC, sometimes going as far as 'writing or re-writing their scripts and rehearsing them'.[51] Some BBC personnel had also worked directly for the government during the war. Mary Adams, post-war head of BBC television talks, was Director of Home Intelligence at the Ministry of Information from 1939–41. A.P. Ryan, Editor of BBC News after the war, was seconded to the MOI to be 'Adviser to the BBC on Home Affairs'. His task, according to his *Times* obituary, 'was to put the government's point of view to the BBC on domestic matters'.[52] Or, put less diplomatically, to keep a careful watch on the broadcaster.

The closeness of personal and departmental relationships extended to information sharing. From late 1945 through 1946 the government and the BBC cooperated closely on the preparations and packaging of the broadcasting White Paper and subsequent BBC Charter. As noted above, for example, Bamford was happy to contact Haley shortly after he knew the outcome of the Cabinet meeting on the BBC White Paper in December 1945 – even though Parliament would not know of the government's intentions until late January 1946 and after.[53] The BBC then worked collaboratively (and secretly) with the government to prepare the White Paper on broadcasting throughout the first half of 1946.[54] When, prior to the Broadcasting debate in July, pressure began to build for an inquiry into the BBC, Morrison even asked Haley for information about the BBC's reorganisation that he could use to argue against an inquiry. At this stage Haley 'pointed out to Abbott [at the Post Office] the BBC would have to be circumspect in such a matter. It cannot be put in the position of seeming not to want an inquiry'.[55]

As important as the formal and informal connections with government was the profound psychological legacy of the war years on the BBC. As a result of its self-censorship and its increased stature the BBC felt an overwhelming sense of responsibility which encouraged its conservatism. For example, Maurice Gorham, head of the Light Programme, asked in a Coordinating Committee meeting in August 1945 whether there were any limitations on the use of MPs in entertainment programmes. He was told that they 'should not be allowed to broadcast in a context which might be derogatory to their dignity' and that this was 'Of the greatest importance, MPs <u>must</u> be protected agst [sic] themselves. They are not always good judges in such matters'.[56]

Associated with this conservatism was a lack of initiative which characterised BBC news output at the end of the war. The government had led so many campaigns and required so much help from the Corporation in communicating information during the war that the BBC became used to receiving news rather than gathering it. This was highlighted by a BBC memorandum reviewing liaison with government departments in mid-1946: 'Before 1939 contact with government departments was made on the initiative of the Corporation when it required guidance. During the war numerous regulations, eg. rationing of food, brought about a complete change in relations'.[57]

The persistent formal and informal closeness between the government and the BBC enhanced the inhibiting sense of responsibility and passivity within the Corporation. It made it difficult to shake the feeling that the BBC and the government were working together, sharing information and coordinating programme making. Equally, it gave the government a continuing sense of control and assumption of BBC acquiescence. It saw the BBC as its natural ally, and encouraged it to treat the Corporation as a subordinate. For example when R.A. Rendall, controller of talks, spoke to John Strachey's office about the nature of the Minister of Food's proposed broadcast in July 1946 the office 'suggested it was not for us to cross question the Minister, and although I [Rendall] pointed out that the Corporation had a great responsibility in these matters, it was clear that he did not think it was our job to do anything but say yes, or his to do anything but get us to say it as quickly as possible'.[58]

This relationship inherently tended to favour the government; it was invariably given the benefit of the doubt, was normally used as the first source for information and questions, and was consulted regarding scripts which might offend. This was important because, as time went on the closeness not only encouraged a sense of partiality, it compromised the BBC's independence. This is shown by a *News Chronicle* poll conducted in June 1946 that asked, '*Which do you think the BBC most resembles, an independent concern like a newspaper, or a Government controlled body like the Ministry of Information?*' 37 per cent answered that it resembled an independent concern, 52 per cent answered that it was like a government controlled body.[59]

Free access to microphone leads to monopolisation and partiality

The advantages to the government of the connections with the BBC became apparent as 1945 wore on. Ministers used their right of access to the microphone liberally. From 14 August to end of December, there were 15 Ministerial broadcasts (this does not include ministerial appearances on the news or on other BBC programming – just direct broadcasts to the nation). They included informational talks by George Isaacs about demobilisation, appeals from Sir Stafford Cripps for the Workers Educational Association, and Aneurin Bevan explaining government policy on nurses.[60]

Though some of the broadcasts may have seemed innocuous, there were a number of difficulties with them. First, the government did not seem to recognise that the country was no longer striving together towards a single, shared goal. In November, for example, the government asked the BBC for the right 'on certain occasions' to broadcast on foreign affairs without prompting any right of reply. The Director General was concerned that this would be unrepresentative. 'They [the government] plead there will be some isolated emergencies when it will be necessary to speak as a united people, so that other countries, such as Russia, may be impressed', Haley wrote in his diary, 'But what if we are not a united people?'.[61]

Second, it was very hard for Ministers not to sound partisan in their broadcasts. It was only natural that, in making an appeal, a Minister should seek to justify his or her policy and outline its goals. Therefore Nye Bevan, when speaking about the need for nurses in November

1945, explained that the new government nursing charters 'are intended to establish the nursing profession on a much more satisfactory basis and to provide for conditions of work, and for salaries which will meet the highest status of the profession. The government intends that nurses shall have a square deal'.[62]

Ministers could not help, when broadcasting bad news, but try to explain what happened and put it in context. This context would naturally emphasise the good intentions behind government policy and highlight the influence of factors outside of the government's control which undermined those intentions. John Strachey, broadcasting about bread rationing in June 1946, told listeners that 'It is the destruction, and even more the disorganisation that is the inevitable aftermath of the war' which forced the policy on the government.[63] As explained in previous chapters, this was not true, it was done to stress the seriousness of the situation to the US.

Third, in trying to make their broadcasts as effective as possible, some Ministers wanted to stage manage the way in which they were made and how they were scheduled. This might mean setting the date and time of broadcast, or using contrived techniques to bring their point across. In March 1946, for example, P.H. 'Puck' Boon from Herbert Morrison's office contacted the BBC with a request that the Lord President broadcast a progress report on the production campaign. This would not have elicited much comment except that Morrison had special requirements. Boon asked the BBC if it could arrange to have 'a working man and his wife in the studio to put questions to him, answers to which could not be given in a straight speech. He suggested that the man should be a good trade unionist, preferably a manual worker, and that his accent did not matter. He must be a genuine character and be <u>willing to put the questions selected by the Lord President</u>' [Boon's underlining].[64]

The BBC were uncomfortable with this, as Boon later reported to Morrison. 'I tried to avoid an argument' Boon wrote, '(mainly because I didn't want anyone to steal the idea) but the idea of a common man and his common wife on the air at the same time as a Cabinet Minister has shaken the BBC'.[65] The issue was referred to the DG who suggested that if such a broadcast was to go ahead, Morrison must find his own worker and wife.

By February 1946 the Director General was becoming frustrated by the number of Ministers who wanted to broadcast. 'Ministers who wish to broadcast are becoming a nuisance' he wrote in his diary on 9 February.[66] Since the beginning of the year Pethick-Lawrence, Ben

Smith and Emmanuel Shinwell had already spoken on air.[67] There would be a further 18 Labour broadcasts before the end of June, almost the equivalent of one a week. By May the BBC Programme Policy committee noted the 'Recent unsatisfactory handling of ministerial broadcasts on the government side'.[68] It did not help that there were virtually no broadcasts by the Opposition (since 'political broadcasting' had not been re-established). In its first year of office the government broadcast 38 times compared to the Opposition twice (both Opposition broadcasts were by the shadow Chancellor, John Anderson, about the budget).[69] This monopoly of the airwaves could not help but have a naturally positive effect on listeners' perceptions of government policies.

BBC self-censorship and the impression of consensus

This positive impression was further enhanced after 1945 by the prohibition of any debate about issues under discussion in the House of Commons. For this prohibition the BBC had itself to blame. Shortly before the White Paper on Education was to be debated in July 1943 'Rab' Butler, then president of the Board of Education, asked the BBC if he could make a broadcast about education. Anxious that this type of broadcast might constitute competition with Parliamentary debate, the BBC drafted a resolution the following year which precluded discussion of a topic on radio that was the subject of legislation in the House, the so called '14 day rule'.[70] This draconian ruling, if taken literally, would have meant the BBC could broadcast about almost no current ongoing political issues. Though they did not adhere to it to the letter, the BBC did abide by the ruling's broad intention. Coupled with its reluctance to broadcast controversy this meant programming on the post-war BBC inevitably played down argument and encouraged an impression of consensus.[71]

The BBC's treatment of food and bread rationing provides a good example of this. As outlined in the previous chapters, bread rationing became a highly political issue in the first half of 1946. From February to July there was rarely a week without some coverage of bread in the newspapers. And yet there was not one BBC discussion programme on the topic during this time.[72] Specific items were covered in news broadcasts but not in discussion programmes. At the same time there were six long statements on food and bread made by government Ministers – Ben Smith, Edith Summerskill, Tom Williams (three broadcasts) and John Strachey.[73] There were also other talks (as opposed to discussions) on the world food shortage – by Arthur Salter and D.G. Bridson.[74] The last, on the UNRRA, 'The Battle Against Starvation and Want in Europe' was broadcast at 9.30 pm on Sunday 30 June, immediately after Herbert Morrison's production talk.

A listener would therefore come away from the BBC with the impression that there was a terrible shortage of bread worldwide, that the government was doing all it could to alleviate the world food crisis, and that people within Britain would have to work harder and eat less as a consequence. They would not have heard any Ministers being challenged on the statements they were making about food and bread, nor would they have heard a spokesperson broadcasting from the opposite perspective, against the rationale for rationing.

The BBC was not in a strong position to object. It was avoiding debate on issues that were under discussion in the House and it was allowing Ministers to make 'non-controversial' broadcasts as it was obliged to do under Clause 4(2) of the BBC Licence. Though the BBC ostensibly had the right to turn down a broadcast, it rarely did. It did eventually draw the line, however, at a request by John Strachey to broadcast on Sunday 21 July 1946, the evening before bread rationing began. Though the government claimed the broadcast would deal only with administrative details, the BBC responded that '(a) it is impossible for a Minister to speak on bread rationing without being deemed controversial (b) that if purely administrative explanation is aimed at an administrator could do just as well'.[75] On this occasion the government agreed to the BBC's request not to broadcast.

One reason for this is that Labour's free use of the microphone had, by this time, attracted the attention of the Opposition. The specific catalyst was a broadcast by Herbert Morrison on Sunday 30 June 1946 when the Lord President spoke for 15 minutes under the title 'Britain Gets Going Again'. Winston Churchill sent a letter to the BBC arguing that this talk could not be considered non-controversial and merited a response from the Opposition. It is hard not to have sympathy for Churchill's view. Morrison's broadcast was packed full of examples of the government's successes since the end of the war; 'Since June last year we have cut down the number of people working for the forces and their supplies [sic] by about six millions – that is by about half a million every month... ninety-seven out of every hundred now ready for work are employed... the building industry is being doubled in size over eighteen months... How are our exports looking? They are reviving wonderfully'.[76] He even made an ambitious political claim that if Labour's attempt 'to combine order with liberty' was successful, 'we will have invented something as revolutionary as some of the previous social inventions which we have given the world, such as our parliamentary system'.[77] Morrison, however, did not believe he had been partial and would not agree to an Opposition reply.[78] As a consequence the Conservatives insisted that the two Parties enter discussions about political broadcasting.[79]

The government was therefore using the BBC to its advantage and the BBC was favouring the government by its own self-censorship. The Opposition and the press could not fail to notice and to react.

The growing pressure for an inquiry into the BBC

From the end of 1945 until the Broadcasting debate on 16 July there was growing pressure on the government to hold an inquiry into the BBC. Barnett Janner MP asked the first question to the Labour government on 13 December and was told by the Prime Minister that the administration were undecided on whether there would be an inquiry before the Licence was renewed.[80] On 24 January 1946 the *Daily Mirror* said it felt it was 'quid pro quo' that if the licence fee payer was to be required to double the amount he or she paid, the BBC should be required to explain why.[81] Janner asked again about an inquiry on 29 January and on 19 February.[82] It was not until this third occasion that Attlee told him there would not be an inquiry. This rejection sparked further debate in the press. In April *The Times* in a leader column and a serving BBC Governor, Arthur Mann, in a letter to *The Times*, both called for an inquiry.[83]

The pressure coalesced in a motion put forward by Winston Churchill in June. Brendan Bracken was almost certainly the driving force behind this motion. Bracken had, as noted above, been the only proponent of an inquiry whilst on the Coalition Broadcasting Committee. He was one of the main signatories of a note sent to Churchill by James Stuart on 5 June 1946 asking the leader of the Opposition to lead the charge for an investigation: 'A Motion has been drafted by Messrs Bracken, Crookshank and WS Morrison' Stuart wrote, 'which has been approved by the Committee of Chairman and which reads as follows: – "To move that the question of the renewal, with or without amendment, of the Charter of the BBC be referred to a Joint Select Committee of both Houses"'.[84] Churchill agreed to head the list and tabled the motion on 20 June.

By this time there was virtual unanimity amongst the Opposition, the press and interested outsiders, of the need for an inquiry. The extent of support can be seen in the debate about the issue in the Lords on 26 June when Lord Listowel, the Post Master General, had to defend the government's decision not to have an inquiry almost single handed.[85] And, to an even greater degree, it can be seen in the editorials of the press and periodicals. 'It is almost impossible to find a single person who, on due consideration of the question, fails to see the need for a full and public discussion of the working of British broadcasting' *The Spectator* wrote.[86] Whilst *The Times* said 'the public is unquestionably entitled, before the Charter is renewed, to the benefit of a thorough survey and adjudication'.[87]

There were a variety of different motivations driving interested parties to call for an inquiry. Some, like *The Daily Mirror*, were triggered by the rise in the Licence Fee. Others, like Arthur Mann, were motivated by political and personal reasons.[88] Most, however, were motivated by the desire to investigate the enormous changes that the BBC had undergone over the course of the war, in size, in structure and in purpose. As well as an increase in spending of 150 per cent, the BBC had 7,049 new employees, more than two and a half times more than in 1939.[89] It had two national channels, soon to be three, and was broadcasting an overseas propaganda service to over twenty countries. There had also been rumours of internal crises left unreported during the war (such as that surrounding the departure of Sir Frederick Ogilvie, Reith's successor as Director General until 1942).[90]

Some of those calling for an inquiry were also concerned that the 'heavy hand of Whitehall' which had controlled the BBC during the war 'was never quite removed'.[91] A *Times* editorial on 22 June suggested that, over the last six years, 'The BBC has entered into fundamentally new relations with the Government' which deserved to be examined.[92] On 29 June *The News Chronicle* wondered 'What should be the relationships between broadcasting and Government?' and suggested that it was up to an inquiry to find out. Some Conservatives were equally anxious to illuminate the tangled relationship of the BBC and the government and protect it from Cabinet Ministers. Brendan Bracken told Sir Ian Fraser, an ex-Governor of the BBC, on 24 June that he had tabled the motion, 'To strengthen the BBC' and 'to ensure its independence against Herbert Morrison'.[93]

When the government presented its reasons for not having an inquiry in the Broadcasting Policy White Paper issued on 2 July it increased rather than removed the speculation.[94] The three reasons it gave for not having an inquiry were: that the BBC had only been operating in normal (peacetime) conditions for less than a year which was not enough time to evaluate its position; that technology was moving forward too quickly right now to make a proper assessment; and that international agreements on wavelengths had yet to be revised.

The Spectator called the White Paper 'completely unacceptable... in almost every respect a thoroughly bad document'.[95] The three reasons all seemed surprisingly weak. It was the changes wrought by war that the public were interested in, said *Time and Tide*, not the twelve months of peace.[96] The argument that technology was moving too quickly could have been made at any time in the post-war period. And in the broadcasting debate Ian Orr–Ewing suggested that an inquiry should strengthen the government's position when negotiating future international agreements on wavelengths.[97] The naïveté of the government's arguments made some people even more suspicious of the relationship between the state and the national broadcaster; 'the White Paper is indeed very disquieting' *Time and Tide* wrote, 'It seems to view the monopoly as taking its place in the national propaganda machine'.[98]

There is no evidence to suggest that, despite the significant amount of pressure, Morrison ever reconsidered his original decision not to have an immediate inquiry. Rather the government papers indicate that he spent his time preparing for the broadcasting debate by collecting additional arguments not to have an inquiry. He asked his Assistant Secretary Martin Flett to look over the papers of the Coalition Broadcasting Committee to confirm that but for Bracken's contrariness they too would have voted against an inquiry.[99] He calculated the length of time it took the government to appoint the Ullswater Committee and react to its report.[100] And he contacted William Haley and asked for information showing how the BBC's reorganisation would make an inquiry very difficult.[101]

There are a few probable reasons why Morrison was not affected by the pressure for an immediate inquiry. He was conscious that the BBC was in the midst of launching new services and restructuring the organisation and that an inquiry would make this more difficult. He may well still have been worried about the implications of an investigation for the BBC's new overseas services. This had been one of the original reasons against an inquiry which Flett had raised immediately before the meeting of the August 1945 Broadcasting committee.[102] But most importantly, Morrison was very happy with the situation as it stood. This was particularly true because he could make a direct comparison between political communication on the BBC and political communication in the newspapers. From Morrison's perspective the

BBC was responsible and impartial, the newspapers were irresponsible and partisan. If there should be any inquiry, Morrison believed, it should be into the press, not into the BBC.[103]

Morrison did, however, have to make a concession. Calls for a BBC inquiry had spread to his own party and he faced a potentially difficult battle to force the Charter through without some sort of compromise. He therefore told the Parliamentary Labour Party that he would reduce the length of the Charter to five years and promised to hold an inquiry before the end of that date.[104]

The government's intransigence up to this point and its determination to preserve the status quo unquestioned caused people to raise fundamental questions about the nature of the BBC and about its relationship with government.[105] It increased awareness of this relationship going forward and ensured that the Conservatives would not give the government unchallenged access to the microphone again. It also led people to question Labour's commitment to openness in other socialised industries.[106] Morrison had always argued that socialised industries would maintain public trust via frequent open inquiries. His refusal to have one into the BBC made this claim seem much less credible.

Had the government recognised people's concerns and opened the BBC to public scrutiny in mid-1946 it might have allayed suspicion about the Corporation's independence and impartiality. That it did not meant these suspicions were encouraged and one of the key arguments in favour of the continuation of the monopoly was undermined.

Morrison's concession on the BBC inquiry did not represent a shift in Labour's attitude towards broadcasting. The government remained outwardly unconscious of the potential problems associated with its excessive closeness to and control of the BBC. It maintained and in some cases increased its formal and informal connections. The BBC's new Charter and Licence perpetuated the key elements of government influence. Ministers continued to use the broadcaster to make frequent statements to the nation. Departments remained convinced that the BBC should be their ally on government campaigns and receive most of its information from government sources. The Cabinet began talks with the Opposition regarding political broadcasting but did not question its assumption that the BBC was incapable of organising political broadcasting on its own. Over the course of the next three years each of these would be questioned, by the BBC itself, by the Conservative Opposition, and by the press, such that eventually, not only would the persistence of government control seem untenable, but so, to some, would the maintenance of the BBC monopoly.

9
'Necessity' Justifies New Techniques of Manipulation

The BBC Charter that was renewed in December 1946 was essentially unchanged by the heated discussions of the summer. It maintained the Postmaster General's power of veto. It perpetuated the right of any department to broadcast whatever it liked whenever it liked.[1] It made regular coverage of Parliament a written BBC obligation, and it allowed the Postmaster General to require the BBC to 'refrain from sending any broadcast matter (either particular or general)'.[2] Even more remarkably, this requirement could also 'specify whether or not the Corporation may at its discretion announce that the note has been given'.[3] In other words, the government could use the microphone whenever it wanted. It could censor anything to be broadcast on the BBC. And, it could ask the BBC not to tell anyone that the content had been censored. In television the government's powers were made even broader still.[4] Though these clauses were similar to those included in the 1936 licence, the reaction of the press and the BBC to their renewal illustrates both how far broadcasting had changed over the previous decade and highlights contemporary fears about the BBC-government relationship.

Some of the press were appalled at the breadth of powers taken by the government. The Charter contains 'the foundations for an almost limitless censorship' *Time and Tide* wrote.[5] 'There is too much at the present time of the Government taking powers "which will naturally never be used"', the magazine continued, 'The fact is that under the monopoly's charter the Government has taken powers so unspecified and therefore so wide as to enable it to control completely, if it wants, what the listener can hear'.[6] *The Spectator* was of the same opinion, writing that 'To give that authority, without qualification or reservation, to every Government department in Whitehall or its purlieus is altogether excessive'.[7]

The BBC had been brought in, very late in the process, to make final alterations to the draft.[8] Haley was able to remove some of the more stringent aspects of government control but was still unhappy with the outcome, especially clauses 4(3) and 4(4). He and the Governors were particularly bothered by 4(4) which specified that the government could stop the Corporation broadcasting something and prevent the Corporation telling anyone it had been stopped. They felt the government should only be allowed that power of veto on issues of national security.[9]

The Governors were anxious enough about it to take legal advice the following February. They asked Sir Cyril Radcliffe, the highly respected barrister and later Lord of Appeal, whether they could challenge the clause. Radcliffe confirmed their fears. He advised them that they had to interpret the word 'announce' in the final sentence of Clause 4(4) extending 'to any communication of the facts addressed to the public or intended to reach the public' whether on the radio or by any other method of communication.[10] To challenge this the BBC would have to wait until the renewal of the Charter in five years time. Until then government power over the BBC would remain very much intact.

Morrison was unable to see the problem. As far as he was concerned it was only right that the government should hold such powers. They were not meant for everyday use, only in the case of an emergency. 'Nominally, the Government's powers of dictation over the Corporation are... absolute', Morrison told the House in 1946, 'In practice, there is a clear understanding that the Government will not use their powers as long as the Corporation does not misconduct itself'.[11]

But it was this 'clear understanding' which was now under scrutiny. The nature of government, and of the government-BBC relationship had changed and it was no longer acceptable for the state to assume BBC collaboration and compliance. The government was increasingly being made aware of this change, by the BBC itself, which was no longer willing to be the mouthpiece of the State, by the press, and by Parliament and the Opposition. As a consequence the government had to begin to release some of its formal control of broadcasting. As this formal control weakened, so the government started to develop new techniques with which to maintain less formal control.

Technique 1: Appoint a sympathetic chairman and governors

A critical aspect of continued control was ensuring the government had a close relationship with those at the top. Or, as any good newspaper proprietor knows, making sure those in senior positions had views sympathetic to one's own. The manner of the appointment of the BBC Chairman and Governors in 1946 and 1947 therefore gives an insight into the degree to which the government genuinely sought independent and impartial appointees or respectable yet acquiescent supporters. The BBC Governors were the guardians of the BBC's freedom from political and commercial influence. To quote Morrison in the 1946 broadcasting debate, 'The Governors are the BBC'.[12] Their integrity was also important as a validation of Labour's other nationalisation plans. The BBC board was the model which Labour said it would use when structuring other nationalised industries.

In 1946 and 1947 there was plenty of opportunity to demonstrate the proper manner in which to appoint BBC Chairmen and Governors. In April 1946 all five wartime Governors of the BBC were set to complete their five-year terms and needed replacing. And towards the end of 1946 Morrison decided to ask Sir Allan Powell, the BBC wartime Chairman, if he would step down to make way for a new candidate.

Morrison had been considering who should succeed the BBC Governors since February 1946. He and John Pimlott put together an initial list of 22 names which they then discussed with Patrick Gordon Walker and Maurice Webb before passing on to the Cabinet Secretary Sir Edward Bridges. This then increased to over 45 potential candidates from whom Morrison picked five (with a couple of alternatives) to recommend to the Prime Minister.[13] He also forwarded the list to the PostMaster General, Lord Listowel. The five first choices were Ernest Whitfield (unsuccessful Labour candidate in 1931 & 1935), I.J. Hayward (prominent trade unionist and Chairman of Education Committee of LCC), Barbara Ward (active member of the Labour Party), David Low (well known cartoonist with Labour sympathies), and G.M. Young (historian with Conservative sympathies).

Listowel was taken aback by the predominance of left-wingers on Morrison's list. 'I think it would be a serious mistake' he wrote to Morrison, 'if four of the new Governors were either members of the Labour Party or familiar to the public as exponents of Labour views'.[14] Morrison accepted the criticism and Hayward was replaced by the non-political Air Marshall Sir Richard Peck, David Low was dropped in favour of the Chair of the Women's Volunteer Service, Lady Reading and G.M. Young was exchanged for the more outwardly Conservative Geoffrey Lloyd. Had Lord Listowel not made such a vocal objection to Morrison's choices there is no reason to believe he would have changed them.

When it came to choosing a chairman later in 1946, Morrison was equally keen to find a left-winger. In October he wrote to Attlee, 'My own mind has been working on the lines of appointing a Chairman whose sympathies are towards the Left – though not necessarily violently so'.[15] He found his ideal candidate in Lord Inman, 'a sane and reasonably left figure, not too tarred with "party" but making no secret of his membership of the Labour Party'.[16] Unfortunately, only three months after Morrison appointed Lord Inman he was asked to become Lord Privy Seal and in April 1947 Morrison had to find another candidate. Once again Morrison looked for someone with clear Labour sympathies. He decided on another Labour peer, Lord Simon of Wythenshawe.

The appointment of Labour sympathisers as Chairman and Governors of the BBC was not, in itself, surprising or necessarily detrimental to the integrity of the BBC. However, it does demonstrate the determination of Morrison to maintain the closeness of the government to the BBC and increase Labour's influence over broadcasting policy. This was not lost on outsiders. Lord Reith, who had been hoping to be invited to be chairman, told Haley that the reason he was not was that, 'He was not a member of the Labour party [and] He was not amenable to the Government'.[17]

Of course the Chairman and Governors could themselves only exert indirect influence over the day-to-day running of the BBC. If Morrison wanted greater executive control he would need to target the Director General, William Haley. And indeed the Lord President did target Haley, frequently. In May 1947 Haley noted in his diary that 'Morrison had complained I was reserved towards the Govt. He had apparently no complaints to make agst my impartiality but he thought I could be a bit more forthcoming. This is about the fourth time in the last 18 months Morrison has aired this complaint'.[18] Between 1945 and 1951 Haley repeatedly blocked government attempts to encroach upon the independence of the BBC, by Morrison and others. He refused to be influenced even when directly criticised by the Prime Minister and he spoke frequently about the need for the BBC to stay aloof from government. In the late 1940s it was not the Board which was the most determined defender of the BBC's integrity but the Director General.

When Haley remained non-compliant Morrison sought to dilute the power of the Director General in favour of the Chairman and Governors. Immediately before Lord Simon's appointment Morrison talked to him about the structure of public corporations and the relationship between the Board and the Executive. He told Lord Simon that the DG of the BBC was too powerful.[19] Morrison would later tell Lord Beveridge about the same thing and Beveridge would eventually make this dilution of power one of the recommendations of his 1951 broadcasting report.[20]

Technique 2: Dominate the broadcast agenda

Despite the fracas surrounding Morrison's talk of June 1946 and Strachey's attempt to broadcast in July, Ministers continued to use the BBC microphone freely. Tom Williams, James Griffiths, Stafford Cripps and ten other Ministers made radio statements before the end of the year.[21] On top of this many Labour MPs and Ministers were appearing on BBC discussion programmes. Ministers now seemed to assume it was their right to talk to the people directly without being challenged, edited or interrupted.

By late 1946 the Conservatives became convinced that Labour voices were being significantly over-represented on radio. To prove it Lord Woolton hired a media research firm called 'Watching Briefs' to monitor the amount of airtime each party received on the BBC.[22] Basing its analysis on the month of December 1946, Watching Briefs counted 32 talks on political subjects by 22 different speakers. 15 of these speakers were, according to the research, socialists, six were Liberal and 11 were independents. None were given by Conservatives.[23]

Though publicly the BBC disputed the figures recorded by the Conservatives, privately it had already recognised there was a problem.[24] Prompted by a comment in the House by Woodrow Wyatt in November Haley had written to Morrison's Private Secretary, John Pimlott, to make him aware of the disparity between government and Opposition broadcasting. In the note he quoted the 1935 Ullswater report to the effect that these Ministerial statements 'tend naturally to stress the beneficence of Government activities'.[25] Pimlott drafted a follow-on note to Morrison in December.[26] As a consequence, Morrison spoke to Attlee about reducing the number of Ministerial broadcasts, and John Pimlott set about the unenviable task of trying to define impartiality.[27]

This experience did not, however, lead Morrison to question the government's dominance of broadcasting. Instead, he was anxious that the imbalance between government and Opposition broadcasting was becoming too noticeable, and that the Ministerial broadcast had been over-used as compared to other methods of communication.[28] His office made sure that Rowan's draft of the Prime Minister's Cabinet

Paper spelled this out. Excessive numbers of Ministerial broadcasts, it said, 'debase their value and reduce their effectiveness'.[29] By reducing the number of broadcasts and seeking alternatives they could make the remainder more powerful. Attlee issued a note to Ministers on 3 January to this effect.[30] As a result, the number of Ministerial broadcasts dropped to nine in the first half of 1947 (two of them by Attlee).

However, after the economic crisis in July Morrison sought to increase the number again. On 31 July he told the Home Information Services committee that 'there might with advantage be somewhat more such broadcasts'.[31] Though this was followed by three in the next four weeks (four including Morrison's Party Political Broadcast), the number then dropped again so that in November the Lord President talked to Attlee about having a regular, monthly broadcast about the economic situation. Attlee thought that these might be given by Stafford Cripps but Morrison, concerned in case other Ministers might think this disproportionately raised Cripps' stature, suggested they be given by a range of Ministers.[32]

Morrison was particularly concerned that these broadcasts be perceived to be absolutely impartial. This was less to protect the listener from possible party political influence than to make sure that they would not provoke a response from the Opposition. Morrison was very explicit about this. 'The scope and tone of these broadcasts would have to be national' he told Attlee, 'and it would be essential that they should not give rise to opposition replies. If this could not be secured then I think the idea should be dropped'.[33] Morrison and other Ministers remained convinced that a 15-minute monologue given by a Minister could be impartial.

Haley found it hard to agree. Reviewing the status of Ministerial Broadcasting for the BBC's Board of Governors at the beginning of 1948 he said that while 'It is true that they were considerably reduced last year... the basic difficulty remains'.[34] How could the listener tell the difference between factual information communicated by a government Minister from straightforward party political propaganda? Regarding Hugh Gaitskell's recent broadcast on petrol rationing, for example, Haley said it was questionable whether it 'was necessary in the interests of carrying on the King's Government or whether it put the Government in a more favourable light'.[35] Similarly, how could a review of the economic progress made by the government in 1947, due to be made by Sir Stafford Cripps in January 1948, fail to be politically partisan?[36] On February 17 Haley brought up his concerns at a meeting between the BBC and the government. 'Ministerial broadcasts on controversial subjects caused difficulties for the BBC', the Director General said.[37] It was hard to distinguish between controversial and non-controversial subjects, 'especially when the 'facts' of the situation were the subject of dispute between parties'. Despite Haley's concerns, Morrison would not agree to stop or even reduce Ministerial broadcasts but said he understood the issue and would 'keep a close watch'.[38]

For Labour Ministers the BBC had been a channel through which they could speak directly to the people. Unlike the newspapers the BBC was not, they thought, a filter but simply a means of access to the homes of their electorate. When they were denied access Ministers tended to become quite angry (as with John Strachey in July 1946). Equally, when Ministers gave the BBC statements, they expected them to be read out verbatim. When they were not, they attacked the BBC for irresponsibility and misrepresentation. In May 1947 George Isaacs accused the BBC of prolonging the dockers' strike by not reading out his three paragraph statement on the news, in full. A.P. Ryan, Editor of News, responded that the BBC had read out two of the paragraphs and had only briefly mentioned the first paragraph because it 'summarised past history'.[39] Unmollified, Isaacs told the BBC that in future he would make it clear when an important announcement should, for policy reasons, be read out in full.[40]

As well as being a platform from which to make their case Ministers also saw broadcasting as a means by which to counter adverse coverage elsewhere. In January 1949, for example, Philip Noel-Baker wrote to the Prime Minister requesting time to broadcast on the Commonwealth because 'there has been a good deal of irresponsible comment in the press and elsewhere implying that the Labour Government is giving the Commonwealth away, or at least letting it break up'.[41] Though he assured Attlee that the talk would be non-controversial it was clear that the Minister was using the BBC as a means to counter unfavourable comment in other media. Attlee approved the broadcast.

During this period, however, it became clear that circumstances had changed. Ministerial broadcasts were now too blatant a means of government propaganda. Each one was eliciting a complaint from the Opposition or comments in the media. In addition to which, the Opposition were scrutinising all Labour's appearances at the microphone and the BBC was no longer comfortable reading out pre-prepared government scripts verbatim. Ministers and their departments would, therefore, have to find more subtle ways of using broadcasting which attracted less attention and less criticism. Though Ministerial broadcasts continued after 1947 the number declined slowly.[42] In their absence the government sought alternative means of dominating the broadcast agenda.

Technique 3: Conceal government involvement in independent programming

The shift towards an alternative, more collaborative approach to the management of broadcasting is seen nowhere more clearly than during the economic campaigns of 1947. This year was the country's 'economic Dunkirk' and the government expected the BBC, in contrast to the press, to support it as it had in the difficult days of 1940. The BBC did its best but was increasingly uncomfortable with the government's interference and direction.

After receiving considerable criticism from the press and from its own supporters the government decided it should put much more effort into its communication. The BBC, it determined, should play a central role in this effort. The BBC was already looking to help the country cope with the developing national crisis, by temporarily stopping television broadcasting and the Third Programme to save fuel, and by organising a whole series of talks and discussions on the crisis. But the government wanted a much closer arrangement. It wanted the BBC to be part of its broader communications strategy.

Francis Williams, in his role as head of the Prosperity Committee, invited the BBC Controller of Talks, the head of the Home Service, the editor and deputy editor of news, the head of features and the head of television to No. 10 Downing Street. He told them that the government was keen that the BBC help explain the White Paper to the country and make the crisis and its implications comprehensible to the listener. Williams wanted to know 'what plans the BBC has for further explanation of the economic state of the nation to its listeners in the way of discussions, feature programmes and so on'.[43] The government's intention was to create a 'successful chain of persuasion' across various media to increase national productivity over the course of 1947.[44]

The BBC was doing what it could but was constrained by limited information. It lacked 'a central point where they could obtain information, ventilate their own ideas, or find out where information was to be got; and the lack of a news gathering organisation which would supply them with hot news-stories on the production front, in specific factories'.[45] The Lord President's office thought it could be this source and made Puck Boon the principal conduit of information between the BBC and the government on the production drive. Boon began collecting stories from departments to give to the BBC and became the central point of contact for senior BBC staff. The relationship was evidently fruitful, as Rendall wrote to the Ministry of Food in April that 'the arrangement with the Lord President's office... is proving very useful to some of our programme departments, particularly the Features department'.[46]

The government was equally keen to ensure the BBC used this information to explain the crisis in a way which supported the government's position. They therefore worked closely with the Corporation on the production of certain landmark programmes. One of these was a major series called 'Britain's Crisis'; eight talks at 9.15pm each Wednesday on the Home Service, presented by Graham Hutton, an independent economics expert.

Harman Grisewood, the Assistant Controller of Talks, had spoken to Boon about the series. Grisewood even went so far as to ask 'the [Prosperity Campaign] committee to assist him by suggesting names of people to take part in the debate, and by giving guidance on the emphasis to be given in the programme'.[47] The Committee were sent synopses of the talks and, at their meeting on 8 May, discussed them with the BBC producer, G. Steedman. They questioned him in some detail. For example John Pimlott asked Steedman 'if full justice was done to the treatment of planning in a democracy. The discussion in [programme] No. 8 dealt with the administrative details of planning and not with the place that planning occupied in a democracy. Mr. Steedman explained that Mr Hutton was very much alive to that point, and that it would run all the way through the series'.[48]

Despite this close involvement the BBC was keen to maintain the impression of independence. An editorial in *The Listener* introducing the new series on 8 May 1947 went out of its way to stress the lack of government–BBC collaboration. 'The government has published a White Paper and launched a propaganda campaign: 'We work or want' with graphs illustrating the production and export targets that have been set. Parallel but entirely independent of this – and here we may stress the non-party nature of the programmes – a new series of broadcasts began yesterday under the general title of 'Britain's Crisis'.'[49] As already demonstrated, this was not actually true. Presumably the BBC was self-conscious about its connections and felt the series might be compromised if the government's involvement was revealed.

In addition to 'Britain's Crisis' the BBC broadcast an impressive range of programmes to explain Britain's economic circumstances in 1947. The Corporation counted 62 broadcasts on the economic situation for the three months between 1 June and 31 August. This

included the Home, Light, Third and Regional Programmes and everything from Graham Hutton's talks with the follow-up discussions, to
educational broadcasts, pieces on Woman's Hour, feature programmes,
and Ministerial broadcasts (this list does not include mentions of the
crisis on the news).[50]

Technique 4: Emphasise broadcaster's 'responsibilities'

When the economic situation was made much worse by the July currency crisis even this was not enough. The government put even greater
pressure on the Corporation to soothe national anxieties and encourage
greater economic effort. The Chairman and Governors of the BBC were
'frightfully anxious to live up to their responsibilities'.[51] Lady Reading,
Governor and Deputy Chairman of the BBC, wanted the BBC to explain
the crisis to ordinary people and tell them 'what they personally could
do in the way of food preservation, salvage, and national savings'. Her
fellow Governor Barbara Ward 'suggested encouragement and enlightenment were needed, particularly on the world food situation, inflation,
coal and incentives'.[52]

   William Haley, though conscious of the BBC's 'responsibilities', was
concerned that it might be moving too closely into line with the government. He felt the Board of Governors 'do not face up to the fact it is
predominantly a political crisis' and the BBC must not immediately
assume the position of the government.[53] He therefore drew up a long
memorandum which he gave to the Board and to senior BBC staff outlining how he thought the BBC should behave. It split the BBC's
responsibilities into the moral, the economic and the political. The
BBC should try to help morally and economically by discouraging the
black market and explaining the economic situation to people as best it
could. 'On the political side', however, Haley said that 'it was important that the BBC should not try to make out that there was political
unity when in fact the country was divided'. 'It is <u>not</u> the BBC's duty'
he wrote, 'to win any political battles'.[54]

   The three way split of the BBC's responsibilities was difficult to
maintain in practice. Economic issues dominated the political agenda
throughout this period and the BBC was showing rather a lot of the
'Dunkirk spirit'. Shortly after distributing his memorandum, therefore,
Haley found himself telling programme makers to be careful about
how they used the economic information the government was giving
the BBC (prepared by the recently formed Economic Information
Unit). The *Bulletin* which was distributed by the EIU, 'should be used as

background information and in no sense as a guide as to what Corporation should put out' Haley wrote.[55]

The Director General also found himself having to police any further encroachment of the BBC's impartiality by the government. In November 1947, at a meeting of the Information Services Committee, Morrison 'drew attention to recent announcements which had been made over the BBC regarding the cut in sugar and the rationing of potatoes'. Morrison was concerned because 'Both these announcements had been couched in extremely bald terms'. Though the Lord President 'recognised that Departments had in all probability provided the BBC with explanatory notes' it seemed they had not been used. Morrison therefore 'thought it would be helpful if Departments which had unpalatable announcements to make should, where possible, agree with the BBC the terms of a short explanation which would accompany the official announcement'. Morrison 'also drew attention to the importance of proper timing, bearing in mind the political repercussions which such announcements might cause'.[56] The Lord President was advocating the use of news management techniques across other departments.

Haley was not prepared to sanction such an infringement of BBC news' autonomy. All government announcements should be treated on their news merit, he told the Programme Policy meeting on 18 November. 'The wording of news items in the BBC news bulletins is a Corporation responsibility' not a government one.[57]

However, the fact that Haley had to become so involved in protecting the integrity of the BBC demonstrates the extent to which, even by 1947, the government was trying to use the BBC to its advantage. The BBC did not make it any easier to define the parameters of the relationship by cooperating with the government and using the government as its main source of information. The editorial in *The Listener* and Haley's autumn memorandum show how concerned the BBC was about its proximity to the government. The government showed no such signs of concern. Morrison in particular was determined to maintain the closeness and was not worried about the risk of partiality.

The ways in which the government sought to influence the BBC during 1947 also shows how, in addition to the formal and overt use of broadcasting for Ministerial monologues and official announcements, it was beginning to use the machinery at its disposal to institute less formal, more constant communication. Moreover, following the economic crises, it was shaping the presentation of news and of talks in its favour, without telling the listener it had done so.

Technique 5: Exclude unwanted political voices

Under increasing constraints in the extent to which it could use the microphone, the government not only found alternative ways in which to promote its agenda but also set out, unofficially, to censor its detractors. By making private agreements with the BBC, by undermining the financial viability of overseas commercial broadcasters, and by exerting intense but covert political pressure, the government was able to exclude non-mainstream political voices, commercial voices, and communists from the airwaves. Their exclusion enhanced the impression of post-war consensus and ensured that political debate was restricted to the leading figures from the two main parties.

After Morrison's broadcast of 30 June 1946 Churchill insisted that Labour begin discussions about political broadcasting. The two Parties then met on July 30 1946, without the BBC, and then on 5 November, with a further discussion after the completion of the Aide Memoire on 28 February (the BBC was invited to the latter occasions).[58] At the first meeting, in the BBC's absence, Labour and the Conservatives decided that Party political broadcasting should be resumed. Each Party should be allocated a number of political slots on the radio each year according to the number of votes it received at the last election. The Parties could choose to use these slots as they wished (including which politicians should be allowed to broadcast). In addition, the government should be allowed to make national broadcasts as long as they were absolutely impartial. They gave these proposals to the BBC to be discussed at the second meeting on political broadcasting on 5 November 1946.

The Chairman at that time, Sir Allan Powell, and William Haley were unhappy with the proposals. They suggested that they represented a return to the practice of the 1930s when the Party Whips would decide who did and did not broadcast. This had meant that dissident voices (most notably those of Winston Churchill and David Lloyd George) were blocked from appearing on the radio. The initial draft of the 1946 Aide Memoire on political broadcasting would have effectively formalised this procedure rather than changed it. The BBC Chairman believed this would compromise the Corporation's freedom to safeguard broadcasting in the national interest. The BBC must, he argued, be allowed to invite persons of public eminence to the microphone if the circumstances required it.

But neither Morrison nor Churchill was keen to change the draft.[59] Churchill said there were 'no such eminent men' outside the mainstream today so it did not matter'.[60] If there was such a person, Morrison said, the BBC could always consult the Parties and gain their agreement. This, Haley replied, rather defeated the object. After further discussions they eventually agreed that the BBC could invite people of 'outstanding national eminence' to the microphone. This definition was specifically exalted enough that it would prevent all but very rare invitations, and even on those occasions the Parties would have room to object, should they choose to.[61] This was included in the Aide Memoire on political broadcasting which was eventually agreed and signed off on 6 February 1947.

Throughout the November meeting and those subsequent to it Haley was conscious that the politicians did not think the BBC was competent to organise political broadcasting on its own. On 5 November 'There was a great deal of talk of the responsibility of the political leaders to guide political controversy and the difficulty of the BBC treading in this field on its own'.[62] This attitude was equally apparent during an argument over political broadcasting a few months later, in August 1947. Clement Attlee had just made a national broadcast regarding the currency crisis. The Conservative Chief Whip then contacted the BBC to tell them Winston Churchill was keen to reply. Told that Churchill would have to use a coupon (one of the Conservative's five political slots) since Attlee's broadcast was 'national' and not political the Chief Whip complained. An argument ensued between the Lord President's office and the Opposition. 'At no stage has any reference been made to the BBC' Haley noted in his diary. 'It is strange how even in a row the politicians keep this affair a close c...[illegible]. They would do almost anything rather than let the BBC decide the issue – as it legally can under the Aide Memoire'.[63]

Though outsiders were unaware of the internecine arguments behind the scenes at the BBC, they were clearly aware of the end result. Only a small number of politicians ever made Party political broadcasts. Those that made broadcasts did so on their own terms not those of the BBC. Once again the BBC was seen to be abdicating its position in favour of the leaders of the political Parties. Not only were other politicians blocked from appearing on air, but so were other non-Party political voices. Haley lamented that 'all the politicians regard their world as a closed world. So long as a reply is forthcoming from an official opposition they really feel all duty of impartiality has been meet [sic]. It does not occur to them there are other forces in the community, such as the Church, which may have a right to a say in some matters'.[64]

A comparison can be made between this 'closed world' of the politicians on air and the blacklists of the newspaper owners that caused such a stir during the Royal Commission on the Press. Both the owners and the politicians made sure their media outlets were exclusive and that those who they did not want to gain publicity were prevented from gaining it. An important difference, however, was that since Britain had a competitive press there was normally an alternative newspaper through which someone could make sure they were heard. No such alternative existed in broadcasting.

Technique 6: Exclude unwanted commercial voices

It had been a consistent policy of the British government since the early 1930s to try to prevent commercial broadcasting to the UK from abroad in order to uphold the monopoly at home. The Labour government continued this policy after 1945 but with even greater urgency.

The most prominent target of Labour policy was Radio Luxembourg. Radio Luxembourg had been broadcasting to Britain since 1933 and had gained quite a following before the war. As a commercial station broadcasting music and entertainment its programming was quite different from the rather staid BBC (especially on Sundays when Lord Reith insisted the BBC desist from all forms of entertainment).

During the war Radio Luxembourg was twice taken over. First by the Germans in 1940 (who used it for propaganda), and then, in 1945, by the American Army (who did the same). At the end of the war the commercial station was very keen to start broadcasting again. The British government, however, was determined to stop it. Initially, the Foreign Office thought it might be able to take control of the station's transmitters itself and use them to broadcast the BBC overseas service to the continent.[65]

When it became clear this would not be possible and that Radio Luxembourg might be able to get back on air the F.O. and the Lord President's office began desperately searching for ways to prevent it. They had already encouraged the BBC to counteract the potential revival of Radio Luxembourg by supporting the launch of the Light Programme. This was supposed to give listeners an alternative to overseas commercial radio and undermine its competitive advantage.[66] But the Lord President wanted to go further and stop Radio Luxembourg broadcasting entirely. In May and June 1946 Morrison tried to alter the defence regulations to prevent the channel selling advertising time on air to British companies.[67] When this did not work he had Flett ask the

Treasury if they could do the same thing via the Finance Bill. When even this was unsuccessful he asked the Board of Trade to introduce exchange controls which would stop Luxembourg buying British records.[68]

Labour justified its concerted campaign against Radio Luxembourg by saying that it was committed, like other British governments before it, to sustaining the broadcasting monopoly. It also defended its actions by arguing that it was maintaining standards which, it suggested, would inevitably be reduced by a commercial broadcaster. But there was another reason why it found Radio Luxembourg objectionable. One which was outlined in a memorandum from Morrison's office: 'it might be said that an additional reason for disliking programmes like those of Radio Luxembourg is that we have no control over their content'.[69]

This control over content was important not only for maintaining standards but also for preventing specific people or organisations from gaining airtime. Puck Boon, from the Lord President's office, discovered in February 1946 that if Radio Luxembourg began broadcasting again, 'There is a probability that two of their clients will be THE CONSERVATIVE PARTY and the ROAD HAULAGE ASSOCIATION' [his capitals].[70] Three months later Boon confirmed that this was the case and that 'there was talk to the effect that the Iron and Steel Federation are being approached to work a program on similar lines'.[71] Morrison's office redoubled its efforts to keep the station off the air. In May and June it worked directly with the Treasury to try to stop British companies being able to pay Radio Luxembourg to advertise.[72]

The government was not successful and Radio Luxembourg did eventually begin broadcasting again on 1 December 1946. Morrison's efforts had, however, scared off a number of potential advertisers and Morrison himself continued to try to bring down the commercial station throughout 1947.[73]

Labour's treatment of Radio Luxembourg is interesting for three reasons. It suggests that the government was not aware of the contradictions inherent in its actions. Morrison told Patrick Gordon Walker in June 1946 that he doubted 'there is really a very strong demand in Britain for this sort of programme' and yet he exerted an awful lot of effort trying to block it.[74] It also seems to reveal a remarkable lack of self-consciousness. Labour was desperately attempting to prevent all foreign broadcasts to the UK while, at the same time, broadcasting the BBC Overseas Services to over twenty countries around the globe. And, Labour's treatment of Radio Luxembourg demonstrates the government's

204 The Origins of Modern Spin

determination to retain absolute control of broadcasting to the UK. Its reasons for this were not only to maintain standards but also to control who gained access to the microphone and for what purpose.

Technique 7: Exclude unwanted communist voices

If the government was able to exclude non-mainstream voice by its Aide Memoire with the BBC, and exclude commercial voices by threatening their economic viability, when it came to objectionable political voices the government shifted to bullying and intimidation. It did this when it suspected the BBC had been infiltrated by communists.

On 17 February 1948, Churchill wrote to Morrison about the 'undue prominence being given by the BBC to Communist and near-communist speakers, the featuring of Mr. Horner etc.'.[75] The following week he brought it up at the political broadcasting meeting with the BBC.[76] The leader of the Opposition said he thought the BBC had within it a nest of 'Communist vipers' who were using their influence to give communism a disproportionate amount of coverage on air. Lord Woolton presented analysis to back up these claims.[77]

Given the fear aroused by the Czech coup at the end of February, the issue was raised in Cabinet on 5 March. At this meeting 'the suggestion was made, in the course of the discussion, that Communist influences might be at work in the BBC' which the Lord President undertook to look into.[78] Due to its sensitivity, the Cabinet secretary intentionally did not record this in the Cabinet minutes.[79] A small Ministerial committee was set up to examine the infiltration of communists westward. Morrison was given responsibility for reporting on communism in the BBC.

The Lord President's office began listening out for signs that communism was being treated too favourably in BBC broadcasts. After a speech by Harry Pollitt received coverage on the BBC news on 21 March Morrison sent Stephens, from his private office, to the BBC to find out who was responsible. Haley refused to say, telling Stephens he would not submit to what he called 'witch hunting of the worst type'.[80] Astonishingly, he also told Stephens that he was well aware of the danger of BBC infiltration and that the BBC had been vetting people according to their political affiliations with the help of MI5 for ten years.[81] Undeterred, the Lord President then contacted Lord Simon and told him to sack whoever had produced the broadcasts.[82] Though Lord Simon did not go this far he insisted to Haley that from now on the

BBC keep a careful record of all references to communism and any airing of communists on the BBC.[83]

The BBC Governors discussed the issue of communism on 4 and 18 March and 1 April.[84] Acting on Haley's advice they confirmed that the Corporation did not employ people with overt communist sympathies. If, however, there was a communist already on the staff, they did not think it right to remove them unless their political affiliations were affecting their work. They emphasised the need for 'vigilance' as well as the need to 'preserve a proper perspective' about communism.[85]

Morrison, however, continued to harry them. In early April he had dinner with Lord Simon and Haley and asked them about an invitation which BBC Manchester had made to a fascist speaker. Haley explained how it was 'some minor blunder' but Simon was appalled that such a thing could have happened without him knowing about it. After the meal he said to Haley that in future he should 'be told of every communication written or verbal, from any government department that has occupied, or may occupy, the attention of a Minister'.[86]

Only a few days later the Lord President was in contact with Lord Simon again. He now wanted the BBC to appoint someone to watch over BBC staff and act as a contact between the broadcaster and the government. He had a specific candidate in mind.[87] He asked Lord Simon if the BBC would take him on as an advisor. This time the Chairman agreed and rang the DG to ask him to appoint Morrison's candidate. Haley objected, saying he was unable to see how this person would fit in. Though Lord Simon pushed the issue he dropped it after Lady Reading also raised serious objections.[88] Morrison continued to badger the BBC during the summer, at one point going as far as asking for attendance records of the Board meetings, before temporarily abating.[89]

The government's behaviour towards the BBC in the spring of 1948 once again emphasised the difficulties inherent in a single national broadcaster maintaining its independence. As soon as the communist scare arose after the Czech coup the government and Opposition began attacking the BBC. The government treated the staff of the Corporation like members of the civil service, calling for them to be vetted, policed and even fired if the government required it. Though the experience says quite a bit about Lord Simon's 'appalling susceptibility' [Haley's words] it also emphasises the willingness of the government to transgress the boundaries that were designed to separate the BBC from the government.[90] Had Haley not been so firm in his own defence of the Corporation's staff it is likely that there would have been many more concessions to the government's demands.

The communist issue came up again in 1950 immediately prior to and during the Korean War.[91] For a second time the government and the Conservative Opposition pressured the BBC and its staff and sought to influence its programming.[92] Through its actions the government showed that not only was it prepared to limit access to the microphone to itself (with occasional broadcasts by leaders of the Opposition), but that it was also willing to use its powers to prevent other voices from being heard.

The Beveridge inquiry

As the government had promised in 1946, it eventually set up an inquiry into the BBC. Sir William Beveridge took the chair in May 1949 and set to work with characteristic earnestness. Over 19 months he collected copious evidence, from the BBC and its detractors (640,000 words from the BBC alone) and conducted exhaustive research (including sending some of his committee on a field trip to America). By Christmas 1950 he had prepared a report of 327 pages, with 100 recommendations, complete with 583 pages of evidence.

Unfortunately its length and its complexity counted against it. Once it was clear that Beveridge was not going to recommend an end to the BBC monopoly, people assumed his whole report was an endorsement of the status quo. The press certainly chose to emphasise the conservatism of his recommendations, the *Spectator's* headline reading 'BBC for Ever', and the New *Statesman and Nation* leading with 'No Revolution at the BBC'.[93]

Much of the report was indeed conservative. Beveridge believed that the monopoly was the best way in which to preserve 'a public service for a social purpose'.[94] He opposed using popularity as a means of determining programming; 'We reject as a guiding principle in broadcasting competition for numbers of listeners'.[95] Neither should a broadcaster always aim to make programming people liked. 'Broadcasting should not' recommendation 57 read 'be governed automatically by regard to what will please the listeners'.

When it came to relations with the government the Committee's report suggested virtually no change. It recommended keeping Clause 5 from the 1946 Charter, giving the government sweeping powers over television.[96] It proposed that the 'friendly arrangement' by which the BBC arranged government broadcasts should be maintained.[97] It even said the Governors should fulfil a 'Ministerial function' and compared the BBC to a department.[98]

But Beveridge was also highly conscious of the dangers of monopoly and spent a great deal of time thinking of ways in which to guard against them. Over time, he believed, the BBC should be required 'to make steady progress towards greater decentralisation, devolution and diversity'.[99] To ensure that the monopoly did not become complacent or unresponsive he suggested strengthening the role of the Governors. They 'must be the watchdogs against dangers of monopolies' and, in an unfortunate turn of phrase, be 'agents of democratic control'.[100] Internally, the 'Charter should place them in unfettered control of the staff and all its activities'.[101] Externally, they should make sure that the BBC remained responsive to public opinion.

But this, and other safeguards, were too intangible for people anticipating Beveridge would recommend major structural changes. Certainly the government seemed to welcome the report as an affirmation of its current policy and chose to ignore all its warnings and challenges. Ministers failed to respond to the report and the government did not even issue its broadcasting White Paper until July.

Part of the reason for this was the turmoil in Cabinet at the start of 1951. This was the highpoint of the Korean War, Ministers were split due to the impact of the rearmament budget on welfare spending, and a number of members of Cabinet were seriously ill. In March, Morrison took over from Ernest Bevin as Foreign Secretary and handed over his responsibility for information policy. A very ill Bevin briefly oversaw BBC matters until his death in April after which time Patrick Gordon Walker took charge.

Beveridge himself was understandably dissatisfied with the government's treatment of his report and the White Paper they wrote in response to it. He did not believe Labour had engaged with the problems of broadcasting and did not comprehend the dangers inherent in the relationship between the government and the BBC. 'My Committee' he said to the House of Lords in July 1951, 'were profoundly impressed by the dangers and disadvantages of monopoly in so vital a service as broadcasting. The Government, to judge by their White Paper, are not conscious of any dangers at all.'[102]

Selwyn Lloyd's Minority Report, at only ten pages, was much easier to read and its message was more succinct. Lloyd was unable to agree with the other members of the Committee and wrote a separate short report recommending an end to the BBC's broadcasting monopoly. His report was taken up by a Conservative Broadcasting Policy Committee formed in February 1951. This ten member committee 'summoned witnesses, including Haley, and looked at alternative models of future broadcasting'.[103] Though not able to come to a unanimous conclusion (Brendan Bracken was one member of the committee), they were all agreed that there had to be more competition and diversity. The findings of the group were to form the basis of the Conservative government's broadcasting policies after they won the election later that year.

After Churchill returned to office in October the Conservatives extended the current BBC Charter for six months. This was enough time to reconsider the position of the BBC and draft a White Paper which stated that 'in the expanding field of television provision should be made to permit some element of competition'.[104] This provision was introduced two years later and was enough to inaugurate the advent of commercial television and, subsequently, commercial radio.

Conclusion

The BBC, and broadcasting more generally, had changed radically over the course of the war. It had increased immeasurably in importance, multiplied its range of services, and significantly widened its scope. The development of television after 1946 increased this still further. Though the post-war government appeared to be conscious of this change and outwardly applauded the BBC's coming of age, it also wanted to perpetuate the cosy, collaborative arrangement the State had enjoyed with broadcasting in the 1930s. There were distinct benefits to the government of a helpful, deferential, and essentially submissive monopoly national broadcaster.

Yet such a relationship was no longer sustainable. The BBC was too large, had too many listeners and too great a reputation. Its new Director General, William Haley, typified the organisation's new sense of self-confidence and aspiration to independence. 'We may have to wage a great battle' he anticipated in July 1945 'for the British way of Broadcasting'.[105] At the same time the press (particularly the political journals) and Parliament also recognised broadcasting's altered status and called for a shake up in the State's relationship with it.

Initially the government tried to ignore these calls and maintain its privileged position. It refused to launch an inquiry in 1946 and, only after pressure had spread within the Labour Party, agreed to have one within another five years. Ministers continued to expect to use the microphone at will, assumed the BBC would be complicit and compliant, and took it for granted that they could rely on the BBC to censor anything politically uncomfortable or controversial.

This prolonged attempt to preserve the status quo had three important repercussions. First, it convinced some Conservatives of the need to end the BBC's monopoly and introduce competition to broadcasting. In May 1947, while the BBC was supporting the government's economic education and productivity campaign, Lord Woolton, the Chairman of the Conservative Party, spoke about these concerns to John Coatman on his way back from dinner in Pembroke College. The following day Coatman told the BBC Director General how Woolton had confided that 'it was touch and go whether the Conservative Party would make the destruction of the BBC's monopoly a plank in the new Tory programme'.[106]

Second, it undermined the validity of the broadcasting model. The idea that other industries could be reorganised to reflect the structure of broadcasting was no longer supportable. This was particularly important for the press. The 'Czech press model', which had many similarities to broadcasting in the UK, was strongly advocated by a number of left-wingers to the Royal Commission on the Press. In this model, the Czechoslovakian government granted licences to responsible groups, not individuals, to publish newspapers. The licences had to be renewed on a regular basis and could be revoked or suspended if the newspaper group did not conform to set rules.

To Selwyn Lloyd, whose Minority Report eventually had such influence, it was this very model that was, by 1949, highly objectionable. It epitomised the idea of the Labour socialised industry which Lloyd viewed as paternalistic, centralist, and uncompetitive. He strongly objected to the principles expressed in the BBC's evidence to the Beveridge Committee which he summarised as: 'it is the BBC's duty to decide what is good for people to hear or to see, and that the BBC must elevate the public taste and constantly be ahead of public opinion and public wishes in their programmes'.[107]

He, like a number of other Conservatives, took issue with Morrison's defence of the BBC as an integral part of the Corporate State. As Selwyn Lloyd's biographer has put it, 'For the younger Conservatives this sharpened the thrust of the argument: it became free enterprise versus centralism; the market economy or the planned economy'.[108] Lloyd even used the idea of this model transferred to the press as a criticism of the structure of British Broadcasting: 'It is just as though a British Press Corporation were to be set up with a monopoly of publishing newspapers, and were to decide what choice of newspapers people were to have and what it was good for them to read in them'.[109] Therefore Labour's appreciation and praise of the BBC helped to poison the Conservatives against it.

The provocation of a wider challenge to the government's control of broadcasting was the third, and most important, repercussion of Labour's approach towards the BBC. As a result of this wider challenge the government was forced to relinquish some of its control. Given the significant and increasing power of broadcasting, however, it did not want to relinquish this control without developing corresponding alternatives. It found two such alternatives. It made sure that the regulatory structure of broadcasting was much more rigorous than that of the press, and it developed informal techniques that would allow it to preserve (and in some cases enhance) its influence without appearing to constrain freedom.

These informal media management techniques included everything from the careful control of information at source (in terms of content, timing and choice of media outlet), the establishment of reciprocal channels of information (as with the Lord President's Office in 1947), the provision of pre-packaged news summaries and statistics (as with the Economic Bulletin), the contextualisation of bad news to dilute its impact, the targeting of specific audiences with tailored messages, the assiduous management of Ministerial appearances, the deliberate exclusion of dissenting voices (either through prior agreement or through intense political pressure), and the appointment of malleable board members. Necessity, in other words, led to the introduction of new techniques of manipulation.

These techniques would be further amplified and justified by the country's descent into Cold War and the introduction of commercial competition to broadcasting. Competition in particular would have a profound impact as it loosened the direct ties between the State and broadcasting still further. But though they continued to mature and multiply, this was the period in which these techniques, within which modern spin was an integral part, emerged.

Conclusion: Communication Moves Centre Stage

If they could see Britain in the 21st century, Herbert Morrison and his colleagues would be astonished by the extent to which communication and presentation have come to dominate modern government. Though the Lord President was far ahead of his time, government communication was still in its infancy by the time he left office. Where, in 1945, the government was spending a total of less than £5 million on information services, in 2003 it spent £230 million on paid publicity alone (mainly advertising and direct marketing). It spent another £90 million on the salaries of the 2,600 communications specialists employed by the government. And these figures represent only the most easily quantifiable expression of the growth in the importance of communications.

What Herbert Morrison and his colleagues might find even more remarkable is the way communication has moved from a supporting role to being a major player in the political drama – yet it was their actions that laid the foundations for what followed. This book has attempted to show what their government did and why, and it is for future studies to trace how subsequent governments used and developed the ideas and techniques Attlee's government pioneered. This conclusion, however, will simply highlight four of the most significant features of contemporary democratic government that have their roots in events this book has described.

The first is the constant effort by governments to direct and control the agenda and approach of the independent news media. For the most part this is for understandable and democratically justifiable reasons – for example, to make sure the public is made aware of actions which are being taken which have a direct bearing on them. The government tries to do this through a range of different methods. Central to these is the daily lobby briefing. At this a Number 10 spokesman briefs the lobby journalists about the government's plans for the day, gives them its take on current issues in the news, and responds to specific questions. Throughout the day the government then uses ministerial speeches, interviews and other public appearances to communicate its actions and try to establish its political agenda and news values. For more specific information the departmental press offices will send out press releases or contact specific media outlets.

Each of these finds its origins in the period immediately following the Second World War. It was in 1945 that Francis Williams began regular daily lobby briefings from Number 10 for the first time. The Economic Information Unit identified the importance of ministerial speeches and public appearances for establishing 'news values'. All departments only gained a press office by the end of the war, and information officers were not established within the civil service until 1949. The COI news run, distributing departmental news to all the key media outlets, was initiated by Robert Fraser in 1946. Of course the degree of communication was vastly different but the methods remained much the same.

However, none of these methods can guarantee control over the media's multiple agendas and approaches, so the government also uses a variety of other means which are less open and often less democratically palatable. Less open but defensible are the government's attempts to integrate entertainment values to its communication to increase the likelihood of media take-up and public consumption. At its simplest this might mean a staged photo opportunity such as a Minister kicking a football to introduce a new sports initiative. At its more complex it might involve the production of promotional material – films, magazines, websites. But as the communication increases in complexity and becomes more staged, so it shifts further from its original essence and becomes less democratically justifiable. Presentation is consciously separated from policy and communication becomes less about informing and explaining and more about persuading and directing – more, indeed, like modern spin. As Clem Leslie of the EIU said in 1947, in each case 'the task is to project, and win acceptance for, news information and ideas about a complex and changing situation'.[1] Less defensible still is the production of pre-packaged material to be passed on to the media disguised as independent news.

Again, it was during the Attlee administrations that these methods were first developed in earnest and these problems encountered. It was during the great film-making experiment that Films Division realised how hard it was for the government to produce, and to justify producing, drama and entertainment to promote its policies. So the EIU commissioned material designed to be given to the newsreels and passed off as their own. The Information Research Department infiltrated the news and editorial columns of the press.

If these methods to dominate the news agenda fail the government can always resort to the age old practices of personal intervention – appealing directly to heads of media organisations (as Morrison did to Sir William Haley and Lord Simon), denial of access – to individual journalists or whole organisations (as local authorities did after the war) or by the illegitimate use of regulation (for example when Cripps withheld paper from the fascist periodical, or when Morrison searched desperately for regulatory tools which could be used to prevent commercial broadcasting to the UK).

A second important feature, characterising communications in the modern democratic State, is its ongoing attempts to coordinate communication across government. This is done to prevent important policy announcements and initiatives clashing, to avoid information being released inopportunely, and to try to project a single, simple message from government which will not be overly distorted by the media and which people will take notice of and understand.

By the 21st century the government had developed a particularly sophisticated way in which to try and do this, called the 'Grid'. Each week would be mapped out on a grid, held centrally at Number 10. The grid would detail when every government announcement was due to be made, which ministers were due to give interviews, when important statistics were to be released and so on. At the same time it would also detail non-government events which were liable to be covered heavily in the media; international news, cultural festivals, even football matches. In this way the government hoped to schedule its communication to ensure there were no clashes, to reduce unpredictability, and to increase the likelihood of good media coverage.

Though this is a degree of attention and application previously unparalleled in British government, efforts at coordination for the sake of media coverage emerged under the Attlee government. Herbert Morrison first saw the need for such coordination and repeatedly emphasised this to ministerial colleagues and officials. Ministers, he said in 1948, when seeking authority for a particular course of action 'should, as a regular practice, give some indication of how the publicity would be handled... bear in mind the publicity value and, where appropriate, to consult with their publicity experts'.[2] Moreover, the position of Number 10 Press Secretary, which was invented for just this purpose, was set up in 1945. Francis Williams, the first to hold this position, sought to do just this in 1947 by creating a 'successful chain of persuasion' across all contemporary media to explain why Britain was in such dire economic straits and to convince people to work harder.[3] But the most compelling precedent for centralisation and coordination of information was the EIU. The EIU acted as the central conduit for all economic information during Labour's 'economic Dunkirk' of 1947 and after. It not only collected information from across government and shaped it for the media, but put together briefings for Ministers so they would communicate a consistent message, provided more detailed information for the media to back this up, and commissioned surveys of public opinion to ensure that communication was targeted at the right people with the right message. The EIU was the precursor to numerous subsequent attempts at centralised command and control.

As with the government's efforts to direct and dominate the independent news agenda, its attempts at coordination also have a less salutary side. A single, straightforward message repeated consistently across government gives only one, frequently over-simplified, perspective (the government's 'spin'). This represses the healthy discussion of an issue and militates against independent mindedness within government (and against the collegiate style of government which so wonderfully typified the Attlee administration!). Such an over-simplification can limit people's understanding and give the impression the State is hiding something. In addition, the government can choose to release uncomfortable or damaging information at a time when it knows it will be least noticed, burying it beneath other, more newsworthy news.

This raises a third significant feature which emerged from this period and which has since come to characterise modern democratic government: the reliance of the State on the measurement and assessment of public opinion to help it govern. This reliance represents a fundamental shift in the nature of government, in which the government relinquishes the moral obligations of political leadership. In 1948 George Gallup wrote that public opinion polling 'speeded up democracy' by providing a constant measure of the public's levels of approval and disapproval. By the same token it undermines the legitimacy bestowed by the five year electoral mandate and can turn government into a perpetual popularity contest. It also, as Francis Williams pointed out in *Press, Parliament and People*, diminishes the role of Parliament as the representative 'voice of the people' and replaces it with the media and focus groups. Moreover, in practice opinion research is as often used to identify resistance to policy rather than to develop or adapt policy, so that in the communication and application of that policy the resistance can be overcome.

If Nye Bevan could have seen how dependent government was to become on polling and public opinion research he would have been appalled. But it was while Bevan was in office that the government first began consistently to use public opinion surveys to inform policy and presentation. Morrison steered approval of the wartime Social Survey through Cabinet after the war and the departments, though slow to start, soon began to use them habitually. Bevan himself became a convert to public opinion surveys after being persuaded by his officials.[4] Williams, Leslie and Fraser found them particularly useful for learning how to tailor communication for specific groups of people and how to choose which media to use to reach them. They also learnt that using rational, functional language had a limited effect and that 'Emotional appeals are more effective than rational'.[5] Therefore, if the government wanted to elicit a particular reaction, communication had to be simple and emotive. This helped limit the explanatory ambitions of later government communication and encouraged the adoption of marketing techniques.

Using public opinion as a guide to success has also increasingly determined the type of people appointed to senior positions within the parties. It is not possible to imagine a figure like Clement Attlee, for example, being considered 'media friendly' enough for a prominent position in government by the 21st century. He would be neither telegenic enough, nor able to speak in sufficiently emotive soundbites. Likewise, it effected the type of people advising Ministers. Those with experience and expertise at dealing with the media became more prominent and gained in status, to the detriment of those without.

Many aspects of these three features of modern government would not have emerged had the government trusted the independent media to communicate its actions as it wanted. But it did not. The media was, and still is, similarly cynical of government communication. The public, the eventual target of both the government and the media, has become unsurprisingly disillusioned with both. This distrust, cynicism and disillusion is the fourth notable feature of modern democratic communication whose roots can be traced to this period.

The Attlee government tried to create an environment in which it could trust the media to translate its actions faithfully. It was for this reason that it undertook the first exhaustive review of the role of the press within society. Yet the Royal Commission rejected all radical measures for reform and Herbert Morrison had to settle for its recommendation of self-regulation. This led, in 1953, to the formation of the General Council of the Press. From the government's perspective this was a palpably inadequate means of ensuring accurate communication and lacked any real strength to take effective action against newspapers. Though it was reformed in the 1960s and then replaced by the Press Complaints Commission in 1991 it remains inadequate. In broadcasting the government had to accept that it could not collaborate too closely with a monopoly broadcaster without undermining that broadcaster's independence. Once, by 1951, it had undermined that independence the subsequent Conservative administration conceded much of the government's power over broadcasting by introducing competition. Though this was much more heavily regulated than the press and overseen by the ITA, the government had to accept that it would never have the degree of influence over broadcasting it had once enjoyed. Unable to trust the independent media the government therefore felt justified using its own methods, both palatable and less palatable, to make sure it got its message across.

Media distrust of the government meanwhile, though already well-established, was extended and enhanced in this period. This was because, though the government transformed the means by which it communicated with the people it did not institute adequate controls over those means of communication. There were no guidelines set up for how the State should, and should not, communicate. There were no constraints put on the way in which the government produced communication or worked with the independent media (over and above the insufficient civil service code of neutrality). There was no way to ensure the government was giving the news media sufficient or equal access, and no way to ensure any consistent representation of information. The government entirely failed, in other words, to make its communication accountable. Given that any such controls would have limited its freedom of action when dealing with the media, this is not entirely surprising. However, the government missed a critical opportunity to make its communication transparent. As a result the media became suspicious of the process of government communication from the outset and have since regularly portrayed it, whatever its intention, as sinister and Machiavellian.

This portrayal has led to disillusionment amongst the people about both the government and the media. People are understandably loath to trust the government given the impression of its veracity provided by the news media. Equally, they find it difficult to believe what they see in the media given its limited and inadequate self control. Until the government scrutinises its own communication much more rigorously, and until the news media regulates itself effectively, there is no reason to think that trust will revive.

Each of these four features of modern democratic government communication can be traced back to the period examined in this book. Hindsight puts into sharp relief the origins of these aspects of the contemporary scene, but there were people then who recognised the importance of what was happening. Many of the most senior officials involved – Robert Fraser, Clem Leslie, Francis Williams, John Grierson, John Pimlott, Thomas Fife Clark – all wrote and commented about government communication and the importance of the government's relationship with the mass media. All of them concluded that not only was mass communication a new and necessary feature of modern democratic government, but that it needed organisation, direction and management. Each started with high minded ideals about the obligation of government within a democracy to communicate and then had to compromise those ideals as they reacted pragmatically to events.

When the Conservatives came to office in October 1951 they were determined to reverse Labour's commitment to communication. For them it was far too closely associated with socialist propaganda. Within weeks of coming to power Churchill appointed Lord Salisbury, the Lord Privy Seal, to head a Ministerial committee tasked with finding extensive cost savings in the information services. Salisbury considered all the options, even the abolition of the COI. To this end, in December 1951 he asked the Treasury to assess whether doing this made economic sense.[6] Though the Treasury told him it did not, his Committee still recommended swingeing cuts.[7] As a result the government shut down the Crown Film Unit, ended the theatrical distribution of films, stopped the mobile screenings, cancelled the government lecture service, halved the budget for exhibitions, and cut back the Social Survey's spending and personnel. Between October 1951 and April 1952 the new administration reduced the number of COI employees by 31 per cent.[8] Winston Churchill even decided he could do without a press secretary and could revert to the situation that existed prior to the Second World War.

It quickly became apparent, however, that such a reversal was not possible. Modern government communication, once started, could not be stopped. For one thing, the mass media would not allow their main source of news to disappear. The newsreels, for example, would not accept Churchill's decision not to be photographed or interviewed by them. They protested at how unfair this was given their previous relationship with the Conservative party. They even went so far as to offer the Prime Minister the same level of control as the Royal Family. This meant only one camera following him and 'absolute censorship over what is actually shown in the cinemas'. 'Nobody has ever complained' the Chairman of the Newsreel Association wrote, 'that the Royal Family has at any time been depicted in an unfavourable light'.[9]

Churchill capitulated and within a year of taking office Lord Swinton, Chancellor of the Duchy of Lancaster, quietly organised for Fife Clark to act as the Number 10 public relations advisor (in all but name). This was the last time that a Prime Minister tried to do without a press secretary. The position was subsequently amplified, particularly by Joe Haines under Harold Wilson and by Bernard Ingham under Margaret Thatcher, reaching its apogee (to date) when Alastair Campbell held the post under Tony Blair.

Churchill's government also had second thoughts about its decision to reduce the government communications machinery. In 1952 the Foreign Secretary, Sir Anthony Eden, asked Lord Drogheda to examine the government's current policy and assess what role the State should play in communication. Although specifically tasked to look at overseas communication Drogheda's findings had important repercussions at home as well. By the time he released a summary report, in April 1954, expenditure on the information services had sunk to its postwar nadir. In 1954–55 the government spent less than a third of the amount on government information as Labour had in 1947–48. The Drogheda report stated that this was grossly insufficient. In the context of the Cold War and the shift from Empire to Commonwealth it was critical, Drogheda said, that Britain explained itself to the world. 'It would be better' the report read, 'not to do the work at all than to skimp it'.[10] The following year spending on information began to increase again. By 1959–60 it had more than doubled.[11] By 1970 it was almost five times higher again.

But for the Conservatives in the 1950s, as for Labour in the 1940s, it took a national calamity to force home the new attitude to communication. The Suez debacle of 1956 convinced Ministers that they had not put enough effort into presentation. MacMillan therefore brought in Lord Hill, the famous 'radio doctor' of the Second World War, to coordinate it. This was the first time that a Cabinet Minister's primary responsibility was to oversee information and presentation. Hill's approach and his language illustrate how far attitudes had already changed and how central information and news management had become to the process of government. Hill told Ministers, for example, that when dealing with the mass media it was important to establish a strong narrative. 'Every story' he said, 'needs a peg, whether it be a speech, party statement, White Paper or other'. Similarly, long before the arrival of 24-hour television news, Hill said that the government should always have a response ready for the media, and should never allow a gap to open up, 'Never leave a vacuum in the output of news'.[12]

This increased attention towards the mass media had become much more urgent due to the arrival of television. In 1950 less than 350,000 households had television licenses. By 1960 over ten million did.[13] This accelerated the patterns established in the 1940s, particularly the focus on the independent media as the primary means of government communication. It also encouraged an emphasis on style over substance. '[T]he viewers will not remember many of the words he [the Minister] used' Hill said about the television interview, 'It is the general impression he made as a man that matters, not the pungent phrases he thinks he has used'.[14]

The government's approach to communication since 1951 was not predetermined in 1945. It was the result of the circumstances encountered by the Labour government and their reaction to those circumstances. The approach would have been different, for example, had communication initially been considered essential to Labour policy. It would have been different had the administration not experienced the crises of 1947, after which it felt justified in centralising and coordinating its economic information. And it would have been different had not the Cold War, and in particular the Czech coup of 1948, not limited the government's freedom to contemplate alternative structures of press control.

Moreover, the approach was significantly affected by the personalities involved. Morrison's attitude towards communication clearly had a major impact on its direction. But it was certainly not the case that all members of the administration were convinced of the necessity of communication or converted to it by 1951. Four different attitudes can be identified. First, there were those who were evangelical about the importance of communication to the modern State. Patrick Gordon Walker was one of these. He argued that communication was fundamental to the process of government and he had no qualms about using information to persuade as well as inform, as he made clear in his 1951 book, *Restatement of Liberty*, quoted already in Chapter 4. 'Persuasion' he wrote, 'is particularly necessary to help achieve the sorts of natural behaviour that the new State is almost wholly debarred from bringing about by the use of its direct powers'.[15]

The second attitude was characterised by Sir Stafford Cripps. Cripps believed that communication was necessary but had reservations about its use and extent. Third, there were those who resisted on principle, such as Aneurin Bevan. And finally, there were those who paid almost no attention to communication, like Clement Attlee. In today's world, there are no longer any politicians of the fourth type.

Notes

Introduction: What is Modern Spin?

1 Margaret Scammell, *Designer Politics* (1995); Pippa Norris et al., *On Message: Communicating the Campaign* (1999); Bob Franklin, *Packaging Politics* (2004); Dominic Wring, *The Politics of Marketing the Labour Party* (2005), Martin Rosenbaum, *From Soapbox to Soundbite: Party Political Campaigning in Britain since 1945* (1997); Dennis Kavanagh, *Election Campaigning: The New Marketing of Politics* (1995), Nicholas Jones, *The Control Freaks* (2001); Michael Cockerell, Peter Hennessy and David Walker, *Sources Close to the Prime Minister: Inside the Hidden World of the News Manipulators* (1985); Bernard Ingham, *The Wages of Spin* (2003).

2 Pippa Norris et al., op. cit.

3 Edward Bernays, *Propaganda* (1928), 2005 edition, p. 119.

4 Electorate 1910: 7,694,741. Electorate 1931: 29,960,071, Butler & Sloman, *British Political Facts* (Fifth Edition, 1980), p. 208.

5 Ibid. By far the largest increase was in 1918 itself.

6 Thanks to the introduction of radio broadcasting in the 1920s and cinema sound in 1930 the inter-war period was 'the point in British politics at which the medium and the message became inescapably intertwined', John Ramsden, *Appetite for Power* (1999), p. 256.

7 Richard Crossman, 'The Lessons of 1945', in Perry Anderson et al., *Towards Socialism* (1965), p. 155.

8 Cabinet Paper, CP(47)150, 'The Number and Cost of the Civil Service', 15 May 1947, CAB 129/18.

9 Murdock and Golding, 'The Structure, Ownership and Control of the Press' in Boyce, Curran and Wingate, *Newspaper History from the Seventeenth Century to the Present Day* (1978) p. 130. Hulton Readership Survey (1947).

10 Perilli, 'Statistical Survey of the British Cinema Industry' in Curran and Porter, *British Cinema History*, (1983), p. 372, Table 1.

11 The number of households paying a BBC Radio Licence Fee passed 10 million in January 1946. See Programme Policy Meeting minutes, 29 January 1946, R34/615/4, BBC-WAC.

12 Walter Lippman, *Public Opinion* (1922), 1997 Edition, p. 165

13 PEP Broadsheet, No. 230, 'Government Information Services', 2 February 1945.

14 Peter Hennessy, *Never Again – Britain 1945–51* (1992), p. 118.

15 Marquand, 'Our Production Plan', essay based on lecture given in the autumn of 1945, re-printed in *Forward From Victory! Labour's Plan* (1946), p. 52.

16 Ian McLaine, *Ministry of Morale: Home Front Morale and the Ministry of Information in World War II* (1979), p. 281.

17 William Crofts, *Coercion or Persuasion? Propaganda in Britain after 1945* (1989), p. 250.

18 Cook and Stevenson, *The Slump* (1977), p. 29.
19 'Government Public Relations', PEP Broadsheet, No. 14, 21 November 1933.
20 Mariel Grant, *Propaganda and the Role of the State in Inter-War Britain* (1994), p. 45.
21 Colin Seymour-Ure, *Prime Ministers and the Media* (2003), p. 128.
22 Grant, op. cit. (1994), p. 5.
23 For more detail on the effectiveness of propaganda in the First World War, and on attitudes towards propaganda in inter-war Britain see Niall Ferguson, *The Pity of War*, Ch. 8, and Grant (op. cit.), chapter 2.
24 See Philip M. Taylor, 'If War Should Come: Preparing the Fifth Arm for Total War 1935–39', in *Journal of Contemporary History*, Vol. 16:1 (1981), pp. 27–53, Temple Willcox, 'Projection or Publicity? Rival Concepts in the Pre-War Planning of the Ministry of Information', *Journal of Contemporary History*, Vol. 18:1 (1983), pp. 97–117, Temple Willcox, 'Towards a Ministry of Information', History, 69 (1984), and Mariel Grant, *Propaganda and the Role of the State in Inter-War Britain* (1994), Chapter 7, 'Centralization Rebuffed 1935–46'.
25 Chamberlain response to Greenwood that, at home at least, the MOI was 'a war time measure only', Parliamentary Debates, Vol. 348, col. 1501–02, 15 June 1939.
26 Interview with Anthony Eden, 25 September 1968, Morrison Biographical Papers, Section 6–2, Donoughue and Jones, BLPES.
27 Donoughue and Jones, *Herbert Morrison* (2001 edition), p. 349.
28 Dictionary of National Biography (DNB), Sir Robert Fraser 1904–1985, Anthony Pragnell.
29 Francis Williams, *Nothing So Strange* (1970), p. 207–8.
30 S.C. Leslie, Obituary, *The Times*, 11 January 1980, p. 16.

1   Idealistic Intentions: Striving to Speak to the People

1 David Low, 'On the Higher Level', *Evening Standard*, 26 June 1945.
2 Aneurin Bevan, *Tribune*, quoted in Michael Foot, *Aneurin Bevan* (1997), p. 238.
3 Jonathan Rose, *The Intellectual life of the British Working Classes*, (2002), p. 292. 'The Labour victory of 1945 moved AE Zimmern to proclaim, "It is an England largely moulded by the WEA that has been swept into power"'.
4 Such as the meetings of the Public Opinion Action Association in Birmingham whose first debate, on 'What is Democracy' was attended by hundreds, see William Harrington and Peter Young, *The 1945 Revolution* (1978), Ch. 9.
5 Harold Nicolson, Diary, 5 June 1941, quoted in Ian McLaine, *Ministry of Morale* (1979), p. 250.
6 Stephen Taylor, INF 1/292, 1 October 1941, quoted in McLaine, op. cit., p. 251.
7 Douglas Jay, quoted in Austin Mitchell, *Election '45: Reflections on the Revolution in Britain* (1995), p. 118.
8 GEN 85/1, Memorandum, 'Post-War Organisation of Government Publicity', Minister of Information, 4 September 1945, CAB 78/37.

9 GEN 85/2, Memorandum by Lord President, 14 September 1945, CAB 78/37.

10 GEN 85/2nd, Minutes, Post-war Organisation of Government Publicity, 3 October 1945, CAB 78/37.

11 Mariel Grant, 'Towards a Central Office of Information: Continuity and Change in British Government Information Policy 1939–51' in *Journal of Contemporary History*, 1999, Vol. 34, No. 1, p. 60.

12 It would include provision for poster advertising, exhibitions, photographs, publications and films, and a central channel for the distribution of government news.

13 Lord President's Report, later to become CP(45)316, CAB 124/987.

14 Chamberlain, Parliamentary Debates, Vol. 348, col. 1501–02, 15 June 1939.

15 Dictionary of National Biography, Robert Armstrong.

16 Radcliffe to Bracken, 1 November 1943, INF 1/941.

17 Brendan Bracken, Parliamentary Debates, Vol. 465, 23 May 1949, col. 966.

18 MG(O)47, Report by Official Committee on Machinery of Government, 24 April 1944, CAB 87/74.

19 'Your views have influenced us a good deal' Barlow to Radcliffe, 25 March 1944, T 222/68.

20 IS(48)6, Cost of Government Information Services, 12 April 1948, figures for 1944–45, CAB 134/458.

21 Ibid. Figure for those working abroad on overseas information services at this time is not given.

22 Letter from Civil Servant (who chose to conceal identity) to Treasury, undated – by implication January–February 1945, T 213/404.

23 Treasury Study Group 1944 – original memorandum date unknown, re-circulated to Home Information Services Committee in July 1947, IH(O)(47)35, 1 July 1947, CAB 134/356.

24 Barlow to Radcliffe, 28 March 1944, INF 1/941.

25 MG(44)12, Memorandum, Home Secretary, 'The Future of the Ministry of Information and Government Publicity', 2 June 1944, CAB 87/74.

26 Donoughue and Jones, *Morrison*, p. 209.

27 Correspondence to JIC Crombie at the Treasury 1939–41 from range of Ministries requesting sanction for employment of Chief Information Officers and Press Officers, T 213/404.

28 'Government Public Relations', PEP Broadsheet, No. 14, op. cit., 21 November 1933.

29 PEP Broadsheet, 'Government Information Services', No. 230, 2 February 1945.

30 P.H. 'Puck' Boon, Morrison's Public Relations Officer, refers to the report in the Lord President's files

31 GEN 85/2, Memorandum, Morrison, 14 September 1945, CAB 78/37.

32 Donoughue and Jones, *Morrison*, p. 350.

33 PEP's July 1947 report, 'The Plan and the Public', was also important and will be discussed later. See also 'Men, Management and Machines' No. 260, 3 January 1947, in CAB 124/908.

34 MG(44)13, Memorandum, Postmaster General, 'The Future of the Ministry of Information and Government Publicity', 6 June 1944, CAB 87/74.

35 *Evening Standard*, 18 September 1945, 'Who wants the MOI?', 'Leader of the survivalist group is Mr. Herbert Morrison'. Clipping in LP's files, CAB 124/985.

36 *Daily Express*, 'Keep the MOI – Socialist Demand', 17 September 1945, p. 1.

37 Bracken, response of Minister of Information to PM's Directive WP(43)476, 'With regard to the Ministry of Information itself the Minister proposes that it should be dissolved at the conclusion of the war with Germany... In the Minister's opinion it is inevitable that, as a general rule, Government departments should resume responsibility for the conduct of their individual activities in the field of publicity', BCS, 11 November 1943, INF 1/941. Churchill to E.E. Bridges, INF 1/942.

38 See letter from Ministry of Health (signature illegible) to WS Murrie regarding Bevan's views, Cabinet Offices, 10 September 1945, CAB 21/2011.

39 'Unfortunate start' from Barlow Report, MGO(44), April 1944, CAB 87/74. 'Relapsed into...', Michael Balfour, quoted in Ian McLaine, *Ministry of Morale*, p. 250.

40 MGO(44)41st, Minutes, Official Committee on the Machinery of Government, 8 February 1944, T222/68.

41 Barlow Report, MGO(44), April 1944, CAB 87/74.

42 GEN 85/2, Memorandum, Lord President, 14 September 1945, CAB 78/37.

43 Ibid.

44 The Ministerial Committee on Home Information Services (IH) met only twice in 1946 and three times in 1947, CAB 134/354.

45 Attlee, Parliamentary Debates, 7 March 1946, Vol. 420, Col. 522.

46 Leslie to Barlow, 'A Note on the Future of Departmental Public Relations', 15 May 1944, T222/68.

47 Leslie to Barlow, follow-up letter, 18 May 1944, T222/68.

48 BD Fraser to Barlow, regarding Leslie's letter, 22 May 1944, T222/68.

49 Ibid.

50 Morrison to Ted Williams, 23 November 1945, CAB 124/988.

51 E.M. Nicholson to Morrison, 20 November 1945, CAB 124/988.

52 Stephen Taylor, 'The Future of Government Information Services', *Fabian Quarterly*, No. 48, December 1945, filed in CAB 124/988. Also in LP's correspondence for November 1945, CAB 124/988.

53 Ibid.

54 His biographers called him the ''The maestro of cunning', Donoughue and Jones, *Morrison*, p. 150

55 Francis Williams, *The Triple Challenge* (1948) pp. 87–88.

56 Personal Note on 'Government Publicity', Morrison to Attlee; 'My dear Clem, I have been trying my hand at helping you in connection with the Government information problem. Result is enclosed which is not for the Committee but for your own information' 2 October 1945, CAB 124/985.

57 Preparation of PM's statement, JAR Pimlott to Bamford, Rowan et al, 5 March 1946, CAB 124/990.

58 Grubb to Williams, 10 September 1945, INF 1/942.

59 Comparison of draft plans for organisation of post-war government publicity, October 1945, CAB 124/987.

60 Clement Attlee, Labour Conference, Scarborough, 19 May 1948.

61 Stephen Taylor, letter to *The Times*, 5 October 1945, p. 5.

62 Morrison speech,' The Labour Party and the Next Ten Years', Autumn 1945 to Fabian Society, *Forward from Victory! Labour's Plan* (1946) p. 16.

63 Interview with Christopher Mayhew, 3 July 1968, Morrison Biographical Papers, Section 6–3, Donoughue and Jones, BLPES.

64 Dominic Wring, Media Messiahs, *Tribune*, 5 April 1996.

65 Donoughue and Jones, *Morrison*, p. 359.

66 'Government Publicity Services', Morrison draft, 14 November 1945, CAB 124/987.

67 Ibid.

68 CP(45)316, 'Government Publicity Services', Annex 1 by Lord President, 23 November 1945, CAB 129/5.

69 OI & IH(46), Overseas and Home Information Services Joint Meeting, Minutes, 8 April 1946, CAB 124/990.

70 Cabinet Papers, CP(45)316, CAB 129/5; discussed at CM(45)60, 6 December 1945, CAB 128/2.

71 Cabinet Conclusions, CM(45)60, 6 December 1945, CAB 128/2.

72 Attlee reply to Maurice Webb, Parliamentary Debates, Vol. 417, Col. 916–917, 17 December 1945.

73 First meeting of Official Committee on Government Information Services, GIS(O)(45)1, 19 December 1945, T219/38. Report of the Official Committee on Government Information Services, CP(46)54, CAB 129/7.

74 W. Douglas, DoH, 6 February 1946. Ministry of Labour, 'Semi-detached Departments always land the Government in trouble', 8 February 1946, INF 1/958. Approval by Cabinet (46)16, 18 February 1946, CAB 128/5.

75 Morrison speech to *News Chronicle* Centenary dinner, 21 January 1946, Labour Party Archives, Manchester.

76 There were still 5 million men in the Services – most to be demobilized. 500,000 homes had been destroyed, and a further 250,000 severely damaged. Five million people were working in civil defence or munitions – from Peter Hennessy, *Never Again* (1993) p. 99.

77 Treasury Report 1944, exact date unknown – re-circulated at meeting of Home Information Services, IH(O)(47)35, 1 July 1949, CAB 134/356.

78 Fife Clark, 'Public Relations Policy', 20 August 1945, forwarded to Aneurin Bevan 27 August 1945, MH 151/62.

79 Fife Clark to Neville, 10 September 1945, MH 151/62.

80 Fife Clark, 'Public Relations Policy', 20 August 1945, op. cit., MH 151/62.

81 E.g. *The Times*, 20 November 1945, 'This Winter its Vital not to Waste Bread', p. 7.

82 E.g. *The Times*, 24 December 1945, Santa Claus, 'And thank you, Savings Workers; May your energies never flag, you shorten my road, you lighten my load, and put savings in the bag'.

83 E.g. *Manchester Guardian*, 18 December 1945.

84 Meara's summary of 'Points arising from correspondence between the Treasury and the Home Departments in connection with the constitution and functions of the COI', 1 March 1946, attached to letter from Bamford (acting DG) to Fraser, INF 1/958.

85 Ibid. Also following Barlow Report on Structure of Information Services sent to Ministerial Meeting of Home and Overseas Information Services, February 1946, INF 12/308.

86 IH(O)1st, Minutes, 11 April 1946, CAB 134/355.

87 IH(O)3rd, Minutes, 19 June 1946, CAB 134/355.

88 Ibid. Eric Bamford.

89 List of standing committees and working parties, IH(O)(47)29, CAB 134/356.

90   In 1943 a decision was taken under the Emergency Powers (Defence) Acts that explanatory material be issued along with subordinate legislation (and instructions issued in TC7/43). After these expired, 'the Legislation committee had decided that explanatory material should be issued with all subordinate legislation and that central machinery should be established to supervise their form and scope'. IH (O)(46)2, Minutes, 16 May 1946, CAB 134/355.

91   IH(O)(47)3, Memorandum, 'Pamphlets on new Acts of Public Importance', 4 February 1947, CAB 134/356.

92   IH(O)(47)6, Memorandum, Ministry of National Insurance, 20 February 1947, CAB 134/356.

93   PC(O)C(47)3rd, Minutes, Robert Fraser, 16 January 1947, CAB 124/908.

94   IH(O)(47)4th, Minutes, 2 April 1947, CAB 134/356.

95   Cabinet Papers, CP(46)32, 'Economic Survey for 1946', memorandum by Lord President, 30 January 1946, CAB 129/6.

96   Report of Douglas Jay, 28 May 1946, CAB 124/905.

97   Original meetings of PC Committee not minuted. Reference from IH(O)(46)2, Minutes, 16 May 1946, CAB 134/355.

98   PC(O)C meeting, 1 May 1946, CAB 124/904.

99   'Central Office of Information – National Production Drive Publicity', Note by DG, 16 July 1946, CAB 124/906.

100 Ibid.

101 A.G. Millikin to PC(O)C, 14 January 1947, CAB 124/908.

102 PC(O)C(46)25, Memorandum, 'Prosperity Campaign – Future Arrangements', 1 October 1946, CAB 124/906.

103 Ibid.

104 Ibid.

105 Paul Addison, 'Keynesianism... was so deeply embedded in Whitehall that it had to come and, whether they realized it or not, the party leaders were proto-Keynesians already', *The Road to 1945*, (1994), p. 289.

106 PC(O)C(46)30, 'Publicity for Production (Notes prepared by Mr. Leslie)', 11 October 1946, CAB 124/906

107 See, in particular, Survey of Knowledge and Opinion about Economic Situation, CAB 134/365–373.

108 During the war the newspapers agreed to allow the government paid for advertising space as part of a 'gentleman's agreement'. The Cinema Exhibitor's Association (CEA) agreed to screen government short films and trailers free of charge. The BBC gave the government airtime each week and Ministers access to broadcast. Factories agreed to put up posters and allow speakers, exhibitions and film screenings (see IH(O)(46)12, 16 July 1946, CAB 134/355).

109 E.g. 'Memorandum on Issue of Trailers', IH(O)(46)11, 12 July 1946, and 'Memorandum on Works Relations', IH(O)(46)12, 16 July 1946, CAB 134/355.

110 COI Meeting Minutes, 9 April 1946, INF 12/135.

111 Ibid.

112 Cockerell, Hennessy and Walker, *Sources Close to the Prime Minister* (1984), p. 59.

113 From 'The Report of the Committee on Cost of Home Information Services', Cmd. 7836, November 1949.

114 The Report of the Treasury Select Committee on Estimates 1938 calculated that the amount spent on staff wholly or partially employed on press, intelligence and/or public relations in 1931 was £18,650. T162/479/36055 cited in Mariel Grant (1994), p. 225.

115 Op. cit., Cmd. 7836, 1949.

116 Figure for 1947–48, according to Cmd. 7836; £4,537,883.

117 Annual Report of the COI, 1949–50 reports that that there were 1,601 staff at the COI in 1946 (p. 31). The figure of 800 departmental staff is from letter from Fraser to Wardley, 30 September 1946, INF 12/29. In 1931 there were 44 people employed wholly or partially on publicity work (Treasury report 1938 cited in Mariel Grant (1994) p. 45).

118 Donoughue and Jones, *Morrison*, p. 209.

119 Robert Fraser to DJ Wardley, 30 September 1946, INF 12/29.

120 Fraser to Morrison (via J.A.R. Pimlott), 28 September 1946, CAB 124/1017.

121 Cabinet Papers, CP(49)95, 'Questions of Procedure for Ministers', 29 April 1949 (collection of notes issued since 1945), CAB 129/34.

122 Quoted by Francis Williams in his autobiography, *Nothing So Strange* (1970), p. 215.

123 Francis Williams, *Press, Parliament and People* (1946), p. 100.

124 *World's Press News*, 29 August 1946, p. 9.

125 Winston Churchill, Parliamentary Debates, 17 October 1946, Vol. 427, Col. 1054 (Oral Answers).

126 J.B. Usher to Leonard (presumably Hornsby, CIO at Ministry of Labour), June 1946, CAB 124/1004.

2 Expedient Outcomes: Communication Proves Harder than Expected

1 Donoughue and Jones, *Herbert Morrison* (2001), p. 350.

2 John Pimlott, first draft to Nicholson and Boon, sent 28 November 1946, to become IH(47)2, 'Some Observations on Information Policy', CAB 124/1004.

3 Ibid.

4 Ibid.

5 Boon to Pimlott, 29 November 1946, CAB 124/1004.

6 Fraser's comments to Pimlott, Boon, Nicholson & Morrison, 2 January 1947, CAB 124/1004.

7 Reference to Morrison's Christmas reading in Donoughue and Jones, *Morrison*, p. 390.

8 Morrison to PC Committee, quoted in PC(OC)(47)1, 31 December 1946, CAB 124/908.

9 *The Observer*, Charles Davy, 29 December 1946. Copy in CAB 124/908.

10 Donoughue and Jones, *Morrison*, p. 391.

11 Ibid. p. 393.

12 Peter Hennessy, *Never Again*, p. 277.

13 *News Chronicle*, A.J. Cummings, 'Spotlight', 11 February 1947.

14 *Daily Mail*, Editorial, 'Why be Afraid of the British People', 11 February 1947.

15 *Daily Herald*, 10 February 1947.

16   IH(O)(47)2nd, Minutes, 28 February 1947, CAB 134/356.
17   *Daily Mirror*, 11 March 1947, p. 1.
18   FR 2462, 'The language of leadership', 20 March 1947, Mass-Observation Archive. Attlee responded to survey in the Commons, 24 March 1947, see March correspondence in T 273/299.
19   Memorandum from Ritchie Calder, 14 April 1947, T 245/2.
20   Interview with Kingsley Martin, 1 February 1968, Morrison Biographical Papers, Section 6–3, Donoughue and Jones, BLPES.
21   Entry for Ritchie Calder, 1982. Calder also wrote Francis Williams' entry in the DNB.
22   E. Castle, 46th Labour Annual Conference, 29 May 1947.
23   Maurice Webb, 46th Labour Annual Conference, 29 May 1947.
24   Ibid.
25   'The Plan and the Public', PEP Broadsheet, No. 269, 25 July 1947.
26   Home Production Conference Minutes, 8 August 1947, INF 12/66.
27   GEN 169/2nd, Minutes, Ministerial Economic Planning Committee, 7 March 1947, CAB 130/17.
28   Williams to Attlee, 25 March 1947, T 273/20.
29   E.E. Bridges, note regarding Cripps authorisation, 1 April 1947, T 273/20.
30   Leslie's salary would be £3,750 a year compared to £2,500 for Fraser. The Chancellor, Hugh Dalton, agreed the figure 'with great reluctance', Dalton to Morrison 15 May 1947, T 273/20.
31   IH(O)(E)(47)1st, Minutes, 12 June 1947, CAB 134/361.
32   EPC(47)14, Economic Policy Committee, Memorandum, 'Economic Information Unit, Functions Of', 10 November 1947, CAB 134/215.
33   S.C. Leslie to Morrison, 30 June 1947, T 245/2.
34   Ibid.
35   Ibid.
36   IH(47)1st, Minutes, 31 July 1947, CAB 134/354. Subsequently called the 'Survey of Knowledge and Opinion about the Economic Situation'.
37   IH(O)(E)(48)8th, Minutes, 7 May 1948, CAB 134/364.
38   IH(O)(E)(47)13th, Minutes, 31 October 1947, Economic Information Programme – included 'special material for women's organizations', CAB 134/361.
39   IH(O)(48)26, Memorandum, 20 April 1948, report on meeting with Group of Editors of Women's Magazines. Unlike the actual material produced by the government for women's organisations, these editors had actually initiated the meeting with the Home Information Services Committee, CAB 134/357.
40   'Report to the Women of Britain', No. 9, CAB 134/365.
41   IH(O)(49)18, Memorandum, 'On the Work of the EIU Briefing Section', SC Leslie, 1 March 1949, CAB 134/358.
42   'Crisis Publicity', Note by the EIU to EPB, October 1947, T245/2.
43   Ibid. 'It is for other information divisions to decide whether and how far its [the briefing section's] methods, and its relation to the operations of the Unit as a whole, contain any lessons for them'.
44   Ibid.
45   IH(O)(E)25, Memorandum, 6 August 1947, CAB 134/362.
46   IS(48)1, Memorandum, Morrison, 21 January 1948, CAB 134/354.

47 Leslie to Fraser, Memorandum, 'Economic Publicity Policy', 27 January 1949, T245/3.
48 Mr. Hoffman (American Government European Aid Administrator) to Morrison, 1949, quoted by Morrison in the Commons Supply Debate, 23 May 1949, Parliamentary Debates, Vol. 465, Col. 1009.
49 Empire Publicity Committee: 'The EPC was set up in October 1946 as a sub-committee of the Home and Overseas Information Services Committees and reports to both these' Back of file hand written note, 9947/181/950, EPC(48)7, 25 October 1948. Quote from EPC Memorandum, 'Schools Broadcasting on Empire Subjects', 3 February 1948, FO 953/132.
50 'Schools Broadcasting on Empire Subjects', op. cit.
51 Ibid.
52 John Dwight Jenks, 'Hot News/Cold War: The British State, Propaganda and the News Media 1948–53' (Ph.D. Thesis, University of California, Berkeley, 2000), p. 131.
53 In particular, Paul Lashmar and James Oliver, *Britain's Secret Propaganda War* (1998). For fuller list see bibliography.
54 Leslie to C.F.A. Warner, 8 January 1948, T245/2.
55 Leslie to Cripps, 7 January 1948, T245/2.
56 Norman Brook, 'Note for the Record', 4 June 1948, CAB 21/2219.
57 Fraser, Home Production Conference, 19 June 1947, INF 12/65.
58 After the first article was published on 4 December 1947, Morrison began a search of the Information Divisions to find out who leaked the information, CAB 124/992.
59 Frank England, *World's Press News*, 4 December 1947.
60 Ibid.
61 Ibid. There was even a photo of a suitably enigmatic-looking Leslie beside one of the articles, *World's Press News*, 1 January 1948.
62 *World's Press News*, 1 January 1948
63 *World's Press News*, 4 December 1947.
64 Morrison to Nicholson, 14 January 1948, CAB 124/992.
65 1st (joint) meeting of IH and OI, minutes, 21 January 1948, PREM 8/723.
66 Morrison to Attlee, 6 December 1947, PREM 8/723.
67 Minutes of information meeting, 12 January 1948; Lord President, Gordon Walker, Stephen Taylor, E.M. Nicholson, Philip Jordan, Robert Fraser, P.H. Boon, D. Stephens, INF 124/992.
68 Francis Williams, *Evening Standard*, 3 December 1947.
69 *World's Press News*, 23 October 1947, p. 1. *The Times*, obituary, 7 June 1951.

3   Slipping towards Spin: The Film-Making Experiment

1 Based on COI annual reports 1947–1951.
2 Answer to Parliamentary Question, Sir T Moore to FS Treasury, Hansard, Written Answers, 25 July 1949, Vol. 467, Col. 93. Not all of these were for home consumption. Some were aimed at overseas, particularly Colonial, audiences.
3 Robert Fraser Memorandum, 'The Film Programme 1949–50', attached to letter to Grierson, 17 May 1949, INF 12/130.

4 Perilli, 'Statistical Survey of the British Cinema Industry' in Curran and Porter, *British Cinema History*, (1983), p. 372, Table 1.

5 Street & Dickinson, *Cinema and State: The Film Industry and the Government 1927–84* (1985), p. 183.

6 1945–46; estimated non-theatrical audience 7,160,000. 1947–48; 5,312,000. 1949–50; 3,528,000. COI Annual Reports 1947 to 1951.

7 See Rachel Low, *The History of British Film 1914–18* (1950), pp. 36–37.

8 Some Ministries, such as Health, made sporadic use of some film publicity, for example in promoting hygiene, (Paul Swann, *The British Documentary Film Movement, 1926–1946* (1989), p. 52).

9 As John Grierson wrote later, 'In official records you would find the E.M.B. Film Unit tucked away in a long and imposing list of E.M.B. Departments and Sub-Departments, forty-five all told', in 'The E.M.B. Film Unit', in Forsyth Hardy (ed.), *Grierson on Documentary* (1946), p. 97.

10 Grierson Profile, *The Observer*, 31 August 1947, p. 6.

11 John Grierson, 'The Documentary Idea: 1942' Documentary News Letter 1942, in *Grierson on Documentary* (1946), p. 180.

12 Grierson wrote in 1937, 'the documentary group has learned freely from Russian film technique', John Grierson, 'The Course of Realism' (1937), reprinted in *Grierson on Documentary* (1946), p. 140.

13 The Arts Enquiry report states the documentary movement made over 300 films in the 1930s but many of these were non-government sponsored and of those that were, Swann points out that the figure is inflated by the many 'simple and cheap instructional films made by the Post Office' (op. cit. p. 68).

14 IH(O)(47)58, Memorandum, 'COI Films – Production and Distribution', 30 December 1947, CAB 134/356.

15 See Helen (Lady) Forman (née Helen de Mouilpied), 'The non-theatrical distribution of films by the Ministry of Information' in Pronay and Spring, *Propaganda, Politics and Film, 1918–45*, pp. 221–233.

16 'Shown by Request', Crown Film Unit (CFU), 1946, INF 6/382.

17 The government was also able to negotiate deals with the cinemas not represented by the CEA on a more ad hoc basis.

18 'This enables us to have twelve films a year shown in over 3,000 cinemas each [out of a total of about 4,700], which is far wider distribution than any normal commercial film could ever get' IH(O)(47)4, Memorandum, 'Film Distribution: theatrical', 7 February 1947, CAB 134/356.

19 6 in 1941, 7 in 1942, 12 in 1943 and 10 in 1944, according to IH(O)(47)58, 'COI Films – Production and Distribution', 30 December 1947, CAB 134/356.

20 Each reel equated to 1,000 feet of film which in turn equated to approximately 10 minutes.

21 'Documentary Today', Irmgarde Schemke, *Sequence*, Spring 1948, p. 12.

22 MOI, memorandum sent to departments, 'Post War Film Needs of Government Departments', 22 February 1945, INF 1/947.

23 COI Annual Report, 1947–48, Cmd. 7567, p. 22.

24 Robert Fraser to IH(O) meeting, 28 February 1947, CAB 134/356.

25 Grierson wrote in a typically pedagogical article in 1948 that 'the Government did not always want films. It was taught by the documentary people to want them because the documentary people saw the possibility of com-

bining their interest in the medium with the Government's interest in public service' 'Prospect for Documentary – What is wrong and Why', John Grierson, *Sight and Sound*, Vol. 17, No. 66, Summer 1948.

26 Morrison meeting with the MOI heads, 15 October 1945, CAB 124/988.

27 CP(45)316, 'Government Publicity Services', Annex 1, Lord President, 23 November 1945, CAB 129/5.

28 HG Welch to Sendall, 18 October 1945, Reference F.1183, INF 1/947.

29 'The Nature and Form of a Government Information Service', Grierson, 20 November 1945, CAB 124/988.

30 Cripps to Morrison, 3 December 1945, CAB 124/988.

31 Morrison to Attlee, 5 December 1945, CAB 124/988. In particular, Morrison thought that Parliament would sit on it – see hand written note to Pimlott on Nicholson letter, 4 December 1945.

32 In addition to the official government film unit, the '*Crown Film Unit*', the COI and departments were free to offer their commissions to the independent film companies.

33 For a good description of the process see Philip Mackie's article, 'Production History of a COI Film', in *Documentary News Letter*, November–December 1947, Vol. 6, No. 60, p. 157.

34 'Information Please', *Documentary News Letter*, April–May 1947, Vol. 6, No. 56.

35 Paul Rotha complained in 1947 that 'there seemed to be no justification for many of the cancellations made by the COI and the net result was certainly not to make films impact on the public more timely and therefore telling'. Interview No. 1, Marquand Inquiry, 25 September 1947, CAB 124/1028.

36 International Trade (One World), script written by Realist. Failure described in Philip Mackie memorandum on 'COI "Feature" Films', 10 May 1949, INF 12/542.

37 The documentary producers Sinclair Road and Mr Alexander (*Federation of Documentary Film Units*) thought the COI 'tackled programming in a haphazard way. There was no sense of urgency, no leadership or imagination'. Interview No. 15, Marquand Inquiry, CAB 124/1028.

38 'UK Documentary Film Problems 1947' Grierson, attached to accompanying letter by Grierson to Nicholson, 14 August 1947, CAB 124/1025.

39 '*Getting on with It*' (Merlin and Films of Fact compilation for COI 1946), viewed at BFI.

40 Tritton to Malherbe, 'Notes on Theatrical Distribution', 2 December 1947, INF 12/564.

41 Tritton to Sendall, 2 December 1947, INF 12/564. *The World is Rich*, Films of Fact, 1947.

42 See Marquand Inquiry, Interview No. 9, Helen de Mouilpied, CAB 124/1028.

43 IH(O)(E)(47)2nd, Minutes, 19 June 1947, 'Films on economic and production themes', CAB 134/361.

44 Robert Fraser to Sendall, 23 June 1947, INF 5/39.

45 IH(O)(E)(47)10th, Minutes, 'Film Programme – Factory Newsreel', 29 August 1947, CAB 134/361.

46 IH(O)(E)(47)11th, Minutes, 'Economic Information Programme – Films', 19 September 1947, CAB 134/361.

47 Ibid.

48 'Crisis Publicity – Note from the Economic Information Unit', E.P.B. 47, October 1947, T245/2.
49 IH(O)(E)(47)54, Memorandum, 'Directive on Factory Newsreel', 6 November 1947, CAB 134/363.
50 Ibid.
51 IH(O)(E)(47)13th, Minutes, 'Economic Information – Films Programme', 31 October 1947, CAB 134/361. See also 'Report by Films Sub Committee' – based on a meeting held on 23 October 1947, IH(O)(E)(47)50, CAB 134/363.
52 Memorandum by Ronald Tritton, 1 July 1947, to Bernard Sendall, Films Division, regarding films suggestion, INF 12/564.
53 Ibid.
54 Helen de Mouilpied, 'Draft Memorandum on Production Prospects', 16 July 1947, INF 12/564.
55 Ronald Tritton, op. cit., INF 12/564.
56 De Mouilpied, op. cit., INF 12/564.
57 IH(O)(47)42, Memorandum, 'COI Films', in the words of the Director of the Films Division, 3 September 1947, CAB 134/356.
58 See Marquand, 'Documentary Film Enquiry. Terms of Reference', 9 October 1947, CAB 124/1026.
59 Ibid. Regarding the COI, Marquand particularly blamed, as the documentary makers did, its lack of departmental status.
60 Ibid.
61 'UK Documentary Film Problems 1947' Grierson memorandum, attached to accompanying letter by Grierson to Nicholson, 14 August 1947, CAB 124/1025.
62 Note by Robert Fraser, response to Marquand report, 1 November 1947, CAB 124/1026.
63 JA Lidderdale, Lord President's Office, to EM Nicholson, 6 November 1947, CAB 124/1026.
64 Morrison response to Marquand, IH(47)12, 'Documentary Film Enquiry', 10 November 1947, CAB 134/354.
65 Malherbe to Leslie, 11 November 1947, CAB 124/1026.
66 IH(47)2nd, Minutes, 12 November 1947, CAB 134/354.
67 Ibid.
68 JA Lidderdale on behalf of Gordon Walker, 19 November 1947, CAB 124/1026.
69 SCL (Leslie) to Spicer (Treasury), 9 December 1947, CAB 124/1027.
70 Sendall to Lidderdale, 22 December 1947, INF 12/564. Though Sendall's letter suggests the concession was Fuller's idea it does seem highly coincidental that the General Secretary of the CEA should suggest it just at this moment, unprompted.
71 Sendall to A.G. White (BoT), 24 December 1947, INF 12/564.
72 A.G. White memorandum (BoT), 21 January 1948. Watson to Sendall, 16 January 1948, INF 12/565.
73 Tritton to Sendall, 2 February 1948, re the meeting with newsreel companies that morning, INF 12/565.
74 IH(O)(E)(48)2nd, Minutes, 6 February 1948, CAB 134/364.
75 Tritton to Sendall, 2 February 1948, INF 12/565.
76 IH(O)(E)(48)2nd, Minutes, 6 February 1948, CAB 134/364.
77 IH(O)(E)(48), Ministry of Supply, Report on Progress of Economic Information, 6 May 1948, CAB 134/366.

78 Harold Wilson to Morrison, 25 November 1947, INF 12/564.
79 Tritton to Sendall, 1 December 1947, INF 12/564.
80 Philip Mackie to Helen de Moulpied, 17 December 1947, INF 12/133.
81 Bernard Sendall, following dialogue with Woodburn and Campbell, 23 January 1948, INF 12/133.
82 IH(O)(E)(47)2nd, Minutes, 19 June 1947, CAB 134/361.
83 Ibid.
84 IH(O)(E)(47)8th, Minutes, 31 July 1947, CAB 134/361.
85 Helen de Moulpied was thinking of Meredith for the part as early as 17 June 1947, after her initial conversations with Leslie. Moulpied to Tritton & Sendall, 17 June 1947, INF 12/544.
86 De Moulpied to Meredith 2 July 47. Forman to Malherbe on 12 August 1947; Meredith 'would like to write the script', INF 12/544.
87 Denis Forman, brief for Meredith, 4 September 1947 – the idea was that the film would overcome domestic preconceptions of Britain, namely that 'Britain's Lazy, Britain's Old Fashioned, Britain's Short of Everything, Britain's Gloomy', INF 12/544.
88 Meredith telegram, 10 October 1947, INF 12/544.
89 De Moulpied to Watson, 21 November 1947. Fraser agreed to 2-reeler on 13 October, INF 12/544.
90 Philip Mackie memorandum to Robert Fraser, 'COI "Feature" Films', 10 May 1949, INF 12/542.
91 IH(O)(E)(48)56, Memorandum, 'Economic Information Programme – Feature Films', 18 March 1948, CAB 134/365.
92 IH(O)(48)14, COI Films programme 1948–9, Appendix D; 'Plans for the Production of Second Feature Films', 26 February 1948, CAB 134/357.
93 'Stafford Cripps, when he became Chancellor of the Exchequer, personally initiated the Charley Cartoon series', Halas and Manvell, *The Technique of Film Animation* (1976), p. 116.
94 The first was originally titled *Jeremiahs and Jonahs* and distributed as 'What a Life', monthly release, January 1949. Tritton to Grierson, 6 May 1948, INF 5/53.
95 IH(O)(48)7th, Minutes, John Grierson, 2 July 1948, MH 79/588.
96 IH(O), Film Programme Sub Committee, FP(49)1st, Minutes, note prepared by EIU for meeting, 25 January 1949, INF 12/57.
97 IH(O), Home Film Programme Committee, Monthly Releases, Note by the Chief Distribution Officer, Films Division, COI, (Reference FP(49) 11th Meeting, Agenda: Item 4), 29 December 1949, MH 79/597.
98 Though the EIC and COI had started to plan the films programme in the autumn of 1947 (via the film programme sub committee) they were given more latitude after 12 November and much greater impetus by the arrival of John Grierson. Morrison, see IH(47)12, CAB 134/354.
99 For example, Sendall to Fraser, 28 August 1947, 'Even under Socialism there is a wide field of human life in which the Public Service has little part to play... the problem is docs beliefs because of Grierson and his 'public process'. Grierson is a socialist and a propagandist; his main interest is in the social and political aspects of human life' INF 12/564.
100 Grierson saw, for example, radio and cinema as 'necessary instruments in both the practice of Government and the enjoyment of citizenship', *Grierson on Documentary*, p. 78.

101 John Grierson, 'Education and Total Effort', (1941), reprinted in *Grierson on Documentary* (1946), p. 209.

102 Grierson to Morrison & Cripps, 'Nature and Form of a Government Information Service', 20 November 1945, CAB 124/988.

103 IH(O)(48)7th, Minutes, Grierson, 2 July 1948, MH 79/588.

104 Ibid.

105 Grierson, 'To the Producer, Crown Film Unit', 31 August 1948, INF 5/32.

106 IH(O)(49)24, Memorandum, 'Information Services Film Programme', Paper 'C', 'COI Film Programme 1949–50 (Series)', 30 March 1949, MH 79/592. There was also a 'This is Britain' series, mainly for overseas distribution.

107 IH(O)(48)7th, Minutes, Robert Fraser, 2 July 1948, MH 79/588.

108 IH(O)(49)24, Memorandum, 'Information Services Film Programme', 30 March 1949, MH 79/592.

109 IH(O)(48)9th, Minutes, Robert Fraser, 24 September 1948, MH 79/588.

110 Terms of reference of Film Programme Sub Committee (FP(48)1, 23 November 1948), MH 79/596.

111 Wilson to Morrison, 25 November 1947, and subsequent Tritton-Sendall correspondence in December, INF 12/564.

112 Tritton to Malherbe, 2 December 1947, 'Notes on Theatrical Distribution' (from request by Leslie), INF 12/564. Sendall also wrote to JA Lidderdale to explain the issue, 5 December 1947, CAB 124/1027.

113 Lidderdale to Sendall on Gordon Walker's behalf, 16 December 1947, INF 12/564.

114 For a detailed assessment of the so-called 'Dalton Duty' and its effect on the government and the film industry see Street and Dickinson, *The Film Industry and the British Government 1927–84* (1985), Ch. 9.

115 In particular at the meeting on 'Production and Distribution of British Films for the "Supporting Programme"', 20 January 1948, with Morrison, Wilson, Gordan Walker et al. INF 12/565.

116 The Cinematograph Act, first passed in 1927 and then renewed in 1938, was the means by which the government sought to promote British film production and distribution. It set minimum quotas for the rental and exhibition of cinema films. For more details see Street and Dickinson, op. cit.

117 Lidderdale to R.C.G. Somervell, 3 January 1948, INF 12/565.

118 'Production and Distribution of British Films for the "Supporting Programme", Minutes, 20 January 1948, INF 12/565.

119 Cinematograph Act 1948, Bills, Public, 1947–8, Vol. 1, Numbers 26, 44, 63, pp. 571–651.

120 See coverage in Kinematograph Weekly, 24 June 1948. For example the reaction to the 25 per cent figure for the support programme; 'It is difficult in the extreme to see where on earth this footage is to be found', in 'Even Enough Films to Cover Quota Will Not Ease Product Headache', p. 6.

121 IH(O)(48)3rd, Minutes, 27 February 1948, Robert Fraser, regarding consideration of COI Film Production Programme 1948–49 memorandum, IH(O)(48)14. MH 79/588.

122 Ibid.

123 IH(O)(48)7th, Minutes, Robert Fraser, 2 July 1948, CAB 134/357. Number of films achieving commercial release 1947–48; 21, 1948–49; 26. COI Annual Reports.

124 IH(O)(46)4th, Minutes, Plumbley, 18 July 1946, CAB 124/1013.

125 Though a meeting was arranged between Morrison and the CEA (including Rank) for 20 November 1946, Sir Alexander King and Morrison were able to reach an agreement to extend the arrangement before the meeting (King to Ethel Donald, 16 November 1946), CAB 124/1013.

126 Morrison to Fraser, 'I have been trying to smooth things with CEA' because relations had become rather strained, 15 June 1948. Met with representatives 9 July 1948, CAB 124/1013.

127 IH(O)(48)7th, Minutes, Grierson, 2 July 1948, MH 79/588.

128 From preparation for COI Annual Report 1950–51 (compiled Nov 1950–Jan 1952), not published, INF 12/345.

129 The working party agreed that 'factory film shows offer the only certain means of reaching the men and women in the factories', IH(O), Factory Film Shows Working Party, Minutes, 7 June 1949, MH 79/604.

130 Ibid. The proposals were eventually unsuccessful due to government economies in information services.

131 Transcript taken from *Report on Coal*, CFU for Economic Information Committee, monthly release September 1947. Viewed at BFI.

132 *From the Ground Up*, CFU for Economic Information Committee, monthly release August 1950. Viewed at BFI.

133 Transcript taken from *From the Ground Up*.

134 See letter from Geo. W. Crowe to SC Leslie, 14 February 1948, re Coal Report: 'It may or may not interest you to know that I strongly object to having propaganda pushed down my throat at a place of public entertainment, and for which I have to pay', INF 12/565.

135 Audience reaction to 'A Yank Comes Back'– survey made in August 1948, by H.D. Willcock. NS-132, RG 23/533.

136 Ibid. Quotes from Survey.

137 Quoted within article in the *Daily Mirror*, 14 June 1948, contained within Fraser-Morrison correspondence on CEA deal, CAB 124/1013.

138 Boyd Carpenter, Parliamentary Debates, Adjournment Debate, 19 March 1948, Vol. 448, Col. 2538.

139 A. Marlowe, Parliamentary Debates, Supply Debate on Information Services, 13 May 1948, Vol. 450, Col. 2339.

140 J.A.R. Pimlott to Morrison, 9 January 1950, CAB 124/85.

141 'Note by the Economic Information Unit – Second Feature Films'. Tritton to Mouilpied, 22 March 1948. These suggestions included a film on cotton, on the black market, on women in the home and shipbuilding, INF 12/133.

142 De Mouilpied to Tritton, concerning second features, 7 April 1948, INF 12/133, her underlining.

143 J.A. Lidderdale to Bernard Sendall on Gordon Walker's behalf, 16 December 1947, INF 12/564.

144 *Life in Her Hands* (dir. Philip Leacock, CFU, 1951), viewed at BFI.

145 *Out of True*, CFU 382, Fife Clarke letter to Philip Mackie, 'Origination of project', 3 May 1947, INF 6/33.

146 *Four Men in Prison* (dir. Max Anderson, CFU), INF 6/410.
147 Fraser to Grierson re Philip Mackie memorandum of 10 May 1949, 'COI "Feature" Films', 2 June 1949, INF 12/542.
148 Ibid.
149 According to Woodburn, letter to Treasury, 3 November 1948. Total cost of the film estimated at £19,776, INF 12/545.
150 Mackie memorandum to Fraser, 'COI "Feature" Films', 10 May 1949, INF 12/542.
151 Cost of films based on reference to COI Films made for theatrical release in COI Films Programme, 28 February 1950 (FP(O)(50)2), FP(O)(50)3, MH 79/600.
152 Based on budgets for second features agreed in 1948, IH(O)(48)14, Memoranda, 'COI Films programme 1948–9', 26 February 1948, Appendix D, CAB 134/357.
153 'Action publicity' recommended by Ministerial Information Services Committee, IS(49)1, 25 March 1949, CAB 134/459.
154 Fraser, 'The Shaping of Film Proposals – Some Notes on Departmental Procedure', 25 September 1951, INF 12/542.
155 Niven McNicoll to Fraser, 11 October 1951, INF 12/542.
156 IH(O)(E)(49)18, Memorandum, Economic Publicity Policy, SC Leslie, 4 March 1949, CAB 134/369.
157 IH(O)(49)16, Memorandum, 2 March 1949, 'Newsreels and Official Publicity', CAB 134/358.
158 IH(O)(49)2nd, Minutes, 3 March 1949, CAB 134/358.
159 Meara to Stephenson, re Films Division, 12 August 1950, INF 12/355.
160 IS(50)7, Information Services Committee, Home Distribution of Official Films, 9 October 1950 – Note by COI, CAB 124/85.
161 Home Film Programme Committee (HFPC), 'Distribution of Official Films', extract from IH(O)(51) 2nd, Minute 9 (note 3 May 1951), MH 79/607.
162 Robert Fraser, 'The Film Programme', op. cit., 17 May 1949, INF 12/130.

4 'Information Management' Becomes a New Tool of Governance

1 Harold Macmillan (Conservative), Information Services Supply Debate, Parliamentary Debates, 13 May 1948, Vol. 450, Col. 2295–6.
2 'The Battle for Output', February 1947, CAB 124/909.
3 John Boyd Carpenter (Conservative), op. cit., Col. 2319–2320.
4 Macmillan, op. cit., Col. 2300.
5 SN Evans (Labour), op. cit., Col. 2351.
6 Kenneth Lindsay (Independent), op. cit., Col. 2388.
7 Gurney Braithwaite (Conservative), op. cit., Col. 2353.
8 See Patrick Gordon Walker, 19 March 1948, Parliamentary Debates, Vol. 448 Col. 2541.
9 Kenneth Pickthorn (Conservative), Vol. 450, Col. 2375.
10 Lindsay, Parliamentary Debates, 13 May 1948, Vol. 450, Col. 2388–2389.
11 Frederic Harris (Conservative), op. cit., Col. 2347.
12 Correspondence with Robert Fraser, from 25 February 1948, CAB 124/1029.

13 IS(48)6, Memorandum, Cost of Government Information Services, 12 April 1948, CAB 124/1029. Attlee to Commons 17 December 1945 and 7 March 1946. This did not even include Food and National Savings publicity which was substantial.

14 IS(48)6, op. cit.

15 Cabinet Conclusions, CM(48)66, 25 October 1948, CAB 128/13.

16 Morrison letter on 'Cost of Information Services', 15 December 1948, T245/6.

17 Fraser to Morrison, 23 May 1949, CAB 124/995.

18 Report of the Committee on the Cost of Home Information Services, Cmd. 7836, 1949.

19 This report was not published but was issued as an appendix to a Treasury instruction (Establishments circular 5/45 of August 20, 1949) – Whitley bulletin, October 1949, pp. 176–82.

20 Patrick Gordon Walker, *Restatement of Liberty*, (1951), p. 369.

21 Ibid. pp. 368–9

22 Ibid. p. 371

23 J.A.R. Pimlott, *Public Relations and American Democracy* (1951), p. 71.

24 Ibid., p. 80.

25 S.C. Leslie speech to Institute of Public Administration, 'The Work of the Economic Information Unit', 1949.

26 IH(O)(E)(48), Memorandum, 'Surveys of Public Opinion, Preliminary results of survey on opinions for May 1948', 5 July 1948, CAB 134/366.

27 Findings of the Survey on Colonial Affairs conducted for the Colonial Office, NS116, CO 875/72/2.

28 Mark Abrams to Robert Fraser, re interviews with readers of the *Daily Mail* and the *Daily Mirror*, 27 October 1947, RG 40/25. 'The figures are so startling that even if they were confirmed by a larger sample it would still be extremely unwise for them to be shown to anyone in the newspaper or advertising business'.

29 IH(O)(E)(48)11th, Minutes, 18 June 1948, CAB 134/364.

30 In an electoral experiment 'voting increased by 50 per cent with emotional propaganda, 35 per cent with rational, and 24 per cent in the control group which received neither', GK Evans to Fraser and Leslie, 'Some Comments Regarding Recent Publicity Surveys', 23 February 1949, CAB 124/81.

31 Ibid.

32 Morrison, Memorandum to Information Services Committee, 16 November 1950, CAB 124/81.

33 IH(O)(49) 2nd, Minutes, 3 March 1949, CAB 134/358.

34 'Note for French Committee – 'Free' Publicity for Home/Economic Production Themes', HI Kitchin, 11 January 1949, T245/6.

35 IH(O)(E)(49) 3rd, Meeting Minutes, 28 January 1949, T245/3.

36 See draft memorandum from Leslie to PMs office, 28 December 1950, CAB 124/79.

37 Ibid.

38 Max Nicholson was particularly anxious about the government, 'I suspect you are right in thinking that there is a good deal more to be done in educating the Government than is apparent', January 1951, CAB 124/79.

39 Hand written note from Morrison to Nicholson, 15 January 1951, 'PM agreed last night to my unofficial consultations on publicity line – home affairs in relation to rearmament, etc.' CAB 124/80.

40   Informal meeting of Chief Information Officers, minutes, 17 January 1951, CAB 124/80.
41   Ibid. Presumably the voluntary organisations they had dealt with in the past.
42   Ibid.
43   Leslie, sent by E.E. Bridges to Jordan, Armstrong, Henley, RB Marshall, Nicholson, Bligh, 23 January 1951, CAB 124/79.
44   Note from Leslie to Nicholson, 25 January 1951, CAB 124/80.
45   Ibid.
46   See John Dwight Jenks, 'Hot News/Cold War', op. cit., p. 135.
47   Gladwyn Jebb, 19 December 1949, CAB 130/37, cited in Dwight Jenks, op. cit., p. 134.
48   Lord President's Meeting, 8 February 1951, CAB 124/79.
49   Murray to D Le B Jones, Lord President's office, 15 January 1951, CAB 124/80.
50   AC(M)51, Morrison to Cabinet Ministerial Committee on Communism, 2 February 1951, CAB 124/80.
51   Ibid.
52   Gordon Walker memorandum, April 1948, send by Nicholson to Morrison, 7 February 1951, CAB 124/80.
53   Ibid.
54   COI, Regional Unit: Subversive Activities Policy (March-December 1951), INF 12/781.
55   Conference of Lecturers on National Defence, 30 March 1951, INF 12/781.
56   Note regarding 'Points at Issue', an IRD document containing facts and figures about what the Soviets had done, INF 12/781.
57   Philip Jordan to PM, 27 April 1951, FO 1110/422.
58   Defence Digest, September 1951, in Jacket 68/104, FO 1110/43.
59   Patrick Gordon Walker, Cabinet Paper, 5 June 1951, INF 12/577.
60   *Sunday Express*, 11 June 1950. A copy of which is also contained within the Colonial Office files, CO 875/72/2.
61   The budget for the Social Survey division for 1951–52 was £133,600. From Louis Moss, *Government Social Survey* (1991), p. 24.
62   Crookshank, 'Future of Ministry of Information and Government Publicity, MG(44)13, 6 June 1944, CAB 87/74. GPU – 'Glavnoje Politicheskoe Upravlenije', Soviet Political Police, precursor to NKVD and KGB.
63   Louis Moss, *Government Social Survey*, p. 24 (staff figures), and p. 265 (table 34), 'Survey Vote, Actual and Deflated'.

5   Neither Free nor Fair? Government Opinion of the Press

1   By 1950, 343,882 television licences had been sold. Perilli, in Curran & Porter, *British Cinema History* (1983).
2   Wilson Harris, *The Daily Press* (1943), p. 1.
3   Circulations for four weeks up to 29 June 1947 (Cmd. 7700, p. 12): 15,567,883 for national dailies, 12,982,099 for provincial dailies. 2004 figures from the Audit Bureau of Circulation.
4   *Hulton Readership Survey*, Hobson, Henry, and Abrams (1947).

5   Includes all 'general interest' daily newspapers in 1948, (Cmd. 7700, p. 7).
6   Circulations for four weeks up to 29 June 1947 (Cmd. 7700, p. 12).
7   At the prompting of Laurence Scott, the grandson of CP Scott. See David Ayerst, *Guardian, Biography of a Newspaper* (1971), p. 596.
8   Cmd. 7700, p. 14, paragraph 47, and *World's Press News*, 11 September 1947, circulation for first 6 months of 1947.
9   *New Statesman and Nation*, Editorial, 5 April 1947.
10 Herbert Morrison, Parliamentary Debates, Press (Ownership and Control), Vol. 428, Col. 556, 29 October 1946.
11 Figures taken from an analysis done by the *World's Press News* in June 1947 (5 June 47). Based on one week's coverage.
12 Minutes of Evidence, Royal Commission on the Press (ME-RCP), *News of the World*, Day 22 (19 February 48) q. 7411 & q. 7425, Cmd. 7398.
13 Andrew Thorpe, *The British General Election of 1931* (1991), Table 9.3, p. 193.
14 Ibid. p. 204.
15 Quoted in Huw Richards, *The Bloody Circus* (1997), p. 12.
16 'A Private Enquiry into the British Press', in *The Public's Progress*, Contact Publications, June 1947, contained in Morrison Papers, Part 1, Section 1–3, BLPES.
17 Duff Hart-Davis, *The House the Berry Built – Inside the Telegraph 1928–86* (1990). He was still throwing these parties for the Conservatives into the 1970s.
18 Ibid. 'Camrose later confided to one of the FT's managers that this was the greatest mistake he ever made', p. 120.
19 The *Daily Sketch* was an amalgamation of the *Daily Graphic* and *Daily Sketch* and changed its name from the *Sketch* to the *Graphic* and back again.
20 From Charles Wintour, *The Rise and Fall of Fleet Street* (1989), p. 41.
21 Reference to S.J. Taylor's biography, *The Reluctant Press Lord – Esmund Rothermere and the Daily Mail* (1998).
22 Under Associated Newspapers, of which the new Lord Rothermere became chairman in 1937 (Lord Camrose, *British Newspapers and their Controllers*, 1947, p. 54).
23 Stephen Koss, *Political Press Vol. II.* (1984), p. 621.
24 Hulton readership survey (1947).
25 The *Daily Mirror* was part of Daily Mirror Newspapers Ltd. With approximately 10,000 shareholders. *The Observer* was held by the Astor family but ownership was transferred to a trust by David Astor at this time. The *Manchester Guardian* was run by a trust.
26 Curran and Seaton, *Power without Responsibility* (5th Edition 1997), p. 44.
27 *The Economist*, 'The Government and the Press', 11 September 1943.
28 Wilson Harris, *The Daily Press* (1943), p. 16.
29 The report was edited by Max Nicholson. SC Leslie was also one of the members of the PEP Press group (Pinder, *50 Years of PEP*, p. 26).
30 Wickham Steed, *The Press* (1938), Norman Angell, *The Press and the Organisation of Society* (1933), Lord Camrose, *British Newspapers and their Controllers* (1947), Ivor Thomas, *The Newspaper*, Oxford Pamphlets on Home Affairs No. H2 (1943).
31 PEP, *Report on the British Press* (1938).

32 ME-RCP, Lord Layton and F.P. Bishop, Newsprint Supply Company, Day 24 (4 March 1948), Cmd. 7409.

33 PEP, *Report on the British Press* (1938), p. 132.

34 Net advertising revenue as a percentage of total net revenue, calculated by *The Economist*, 28 February 1948, 'Newspaper Revenues and Earnings', pp. 350–351.

35 From Tom Hopkinson's autobiography, *Of This Our Time – A Journalist's Story 1905–50* (1982), p. 243.

36 'Amid this chaos the transient nature of existing Parties and alignments becomes obvious, while the permanence of principles is plainer and more precious than ever. *The Observer* should not be a Party paper. It must be tied to no group, no sect, no interest. It should belong to no combine of journals. Its independence must be absolute' Ivor Brown, *The Observer*, 1942, quoted Koss (1984), pp. 621–22. Arthur Mann, the *Observer*, 'The primary purpose [of the Trust] is to secure independence from Government or Party control, and from being brought into a combine" ME-RCP, Day 9, (26 November 47), q. 2756, Cmd. 7339.

37 ME-RCP, interview with E.J. Robertson, General Manager of Express News, Day 16 (8 January 48), q. 4834 & q. 5062, Cmd. 7364.

38 Stephen Koss, *Political Press Vol. II* (1984), p. 616.

39 ME-RCP, Institute of Journalists, Day 6 (30 October 1947), q. 1663, Cmd. 7328.

40 McCallum and Readman, in their 1947 study of the 1945 election, first took issue with the idea that the newspapers were highly skewed to the right in *The British General Election of 1945* (1947). Since then, Koss and others have further questioned the partisan political consistency (*Rise and Fall of Political Press Vol. II*). Roy Greenslade has recently called McCallum and Readman's analysis 'badly flawed', underestimating the level of Tory support (*Press Gang*, 2003, p. 34).

41 Quoted in Derek Hudson, *British Journalists and Newspapers* (1945), p. 7.

42 Annual Address of William Redfern to the Institute of Journalists, 'Unfettered Press is Vital for World Peace', printed in *The Journal*, November 1944 (monthly publication).

43 '1944 Calls Journalists to Great Tasks', *The Journal*, January 1944.

44 *The Journal*, December 1944.

45 See, for example, the articles by 'Falcon', May–August 1944, in *The Journalist*.

46 *Sunday Express*, 29 July 1945, opinion column, 'Our hopes', p. 4.

47 *World's Press News*, 2 August 1945, p. 1 & p. 19.

48 *The Journalist*, Ernest Jay, September 1945, p. 1.

49 From 'Cost of Government Information Services', 12 April 1948, IS(48)6, Home Information Services: number of staff 1944/5 – 3,999, CAB 124/1029.

50 Donoughue and Jones, *Morrison*, p. 335.

51 Interviews with Ernest Jay, James Griffiths and Kingsley Martin. Ernest Jay said 'Herbert was very close to Percy Cudlipp, always playing around him'. Morrison Biographical Papers (Jones/Donoughue), BLPES.

52 *The Journalist*, 1 September 1945. 'Union has 20 MPs. NUJ Form 3rd Largest Group in New House'. 19 of the 20 were Labour (the twentieth, Vernon Bartlett, was an independent). The total of 40 journalists was calculated by Eric Harrison, a Parliamentary reporter for *The Times*, cited in Koss, p. 636.

53 Though all the newspapers reported Williams' salary as £2,000 a year, the original offer from Attlee was for £1,700 (Francis Williams Private Papers, letter from Attlee 27 September 1945). It is not clear whether this was increased after negotiations.

54 Francis Williams, *Press, Parliament and People* (1946), p. 85.

55 Ibid. p. 116.

56 Ibid. p. 129.

57 Review of *Press, Parliament and People*, *New Statesman and Nation*, 2 February 1946.

58 Review of *Press, Parliament and People*, *The Spectator*, 1 February 1946.

59 Jeremy Tunstall, *The Westminster Lobby Correspondents* (1970), p. 94, 'Regular daily briefings [from No. 10] ... only began in 1945'.

60 *World's Press News*, credited Williams with slimming down the number of departmental PROs but increasing their professionalism, 8 November 1945, p. 14.

61 Ibid.

62 Cabinet Paper, CP(46)360, 27 September 1946, CAB 129/13.

63 A newspaper conference on 'The Press and the Future' in November 1945 explicitly blamed the lack of Parliamentary news on the lack of newsprint. See 'Press and the Future', *World's Press News*, 29 November 1945.

64 Taken from range of newspapers, week beginning 11 March 1946.

65 Sessional Returns, House of Commons Public Bill Office, courtesy of House of Lords Library, September 2005.

66 The *Daily Telegraph*, Opinion, 1 February 1946.

67 James Margach, *The Abuse of Power* (1978), p. 8.

68 ME-RCP, Colonel J.J. Astor, Day 15, (7 January 48), q. 4681, Cmd. 7357.

69 *Sunday Times*, Opinion, 4 November 1945, p. 4.

70 *The Daily Sketch*, Candidus, 2 January 1946, p. 2.

71 *Daily Express*, 'The 1946 Campaign – This is the Policy and Purpose of the *Daily Express*', 1 January 1946, p. 2.

72 *Tribune*, 1 February 1946, 15 February 1946 and 8 March 1946.

73 *Tribune*, 1 March 1946, 15 February 1946 and 24 March 1946 respectively.

74 *World's Press News* noted in November 1945 that 'It seems about time that Whitehall dropped its wartime habit of "embargoing" every silly little hand-out their P.R.O.s issue', 22 November 1945, p. 10.

75 For example, before he left for Washington in January he said, "During 1946 I shall continue to do my utmost to provide more variety in our diet. We can look forward to some improvements, at any rate", quoted in *The Times*, 15 February 1946, p. 4.

76 The *Daily Mail*, Opinion, 1 February 1946.

77 *World's Press News*, 'Ministers Don't Use the Press Properly', 28 February 1946, p. 10.

78 Cabinet Conclusions, CM(46)10, 31 January 1946, CAB 128/5.

79 According to memorandum WFS(46)1, 2 February 1946, PREM 8/200.

80 WFS(46)6, Memorandum, Morrison, discussed at Food Supply Meeting, WFS(46)1, 4 February 1946, CAB 134/730 & 729.

81 'Yesterday was a black day for the people of Britain', *Daily Mail*, 6 February 1946. 'The Government has apparently never had a food policy worth the name', *Daily Sketch*, 7 February 1946. 'Why nation is resentful – not treated with frankness', 9 February 1946, *Daily Telegraph*.

82 WFS(46)17, Memorandum, Morrison, 11 February 1946, discussed on 12 February 1946, CAB 134/730 & 729.

83 'Statistics and documents relating to world grain position', February 1946, Cmd. 6737. This paper was only 10 pages long, provided very few statistics and none related to grain stocks held within Britain.

84 Anthony Eden; 'It does not seem to us that the Government took the proper steps to inform and warn the House and the country of what was impending', and Mr. Eccles; 'This food debate, and the crisis behind it, is one more proof that what the people really wanted from their Government were first-aid repairs in a state of emergency, and not a revolutionary upheaval in their economic system'. 14 February 1946, Vol. 419, Cols. 547–548 and 582.

85 *Daily Telegraph*, Editorial, 14 February 1946, p. 4.

86 WFS(46)17, Memorandum, Morrison, 11 February 1946. See, for example, 'Our Bread', in *Daily Express*, 12 February 1946, p. 2.

87 WFS(46)5th, Minutes, 5 March 1946, CAB 134/729.

88 WFS(46)53, Memorandum, Morrison, 'UK propaganda campaign', 4 March 1946, CAB 134/730.

89 See *Daily Express*, 19 March 1946, p. 2.

90 Ads taken from *Daily Express* and *Daily Mail* for February–May 1946. Issue of precedence highlighted by Sir Ben Smith to R.C. Griffiths, 10 March 1946, T223/249.

91 Shelton Smith to Edith Walker, Food Advice Division, 'Bread Economy Schemes', 8 March 1946, MAF 84/199.

92 WFS(46)57, Memorandum, Morrison, 8 March 1946, CAB 134/730.

93 *Daily Mail*, Opinion column – 'Food Facts Wanted', 11 March 1946.

94 *Daily Mail*, Front Page, 23 March 1946. It turned out that Shelton Smith had not been wrong and fats were indeed reduced subsequently.

95 Debate on World Food Shortage, 4 April 1946, Vol. 421. White Paper, 'The World Food Shortage', April 1946, Cmd. 6785.

96 Mr. Hudson, 'They [Labour Ministers] knew exactly the same thing as long ago as 4 September', Hansard, 4 April 1946, Col. 1417, Vol. 421.

97 Interview with Christopher Mayhew, 3 July 1968, Morrison Biographical Papers, Section 6–3, Donoughue and Jones, BLPES.

98 *Daily Express*, front page headline, 18 May 1946.

99 *Daily Mail*, opinion column, 'The "sheer gamble"', 20 May 1946.

100 *Daily Mail*, 'Morrison was Wrong – Say U.S.' 25 May 1946. Winston Churchill referred back to this snub when opening the food debate of 31 May 1946; "There is, I am sure, irony of fate in the right hon. Gentleman being ill-used by a public relations officer. It is rather like the case of the engineer being hoist with his own petard', Hansard, Col. 1490, Vol. 423.

101 Sir Ben Smith, Hansard, 22 May 1946, Oral Answers, Vol. 423, Col. 330.

102 'It can scarcely be denied that the long foreseen bread crisis is now upon us', copy of cable from British Food Mission in Washington dated 7 April 1946 to the Ministry of Food, AMAZE 7020, MAF 128/436.

103 The Cabinet approved, on 10 April 1946, 'the despatch of a telegram to Washington, which was prepared during the meeting, instructing the United Kingdom representative to state, at the meeting of the Combined Food Board, that Her Majesty's Government would be prepared to introduce bread rationing in the U.K., if it were also introduced in the U.S.', CM(46)32, CAB 128/5. Press Notice, 10 April 1946, in MAF 128/436.

104 Tom Williams to Attlee, 9 March 46, 'Any further sacrifice by us can have but a trivial practical effect on world food supplies. The importance of such a sacrifice would be in the main psychological and political', MAF 84/77.

105 Lord Halifax to F.O., 13 April 1946, MAF 128/436.

106 Note from Clinton Anderson written up in AMAZE 7091 from British Mission in Washington, 19 April 1946, MAF 128/436.

107 Ina Zweiniger-Bargielowska has also argued that the Labour government introduced bread rationing for political and psychological rather than practical reasons, in 'Bread rationing in Britain, July 1946–July 1948', *Twentieth Century British History*, Vol. 4, No. 1, 1993, pp. 57–85.

108 Attlee opening address to Imperial Press Conference, 3 June 1946, reported in *The Times*, 4 June 1946, p. 4.

109 Francis Williams, speech to Imperial Press Conference, 7 June 1946, reported in *The Times*, 10 June 1946, p. 6.

110 *Daily Herald*, Opinion – 'Food and Faction', 18 June 1946, p. 2.

111 *Daily Mail*, Opinion column, 26 June 1946, p. 2.

112 "Herbert could not take criticism. He was over sensitive to the press and very much annoyed at the way he was reported. He often complained of distortion. He had an insatiable urge for publicity which presented him in a good light" Interview with Ernest Jay, Morrison biographical papers, Section 6–2, Donoughue and Jones, BLPES.

113 *Sunday Times*, 'The People v. Socialism', 9 December 1945, p. 4.

114 *Truth*, 'Mr. Morrison's Triumph', 24 May 1946. See also references in *Daily Mail* and *Daily Express*.

115 Interview with Christopher Mayhew, op. cit., BLPES.

116 'This sensitivity [to Press criticism] was certainly one motive behind his support for setting up a Royal Commission to inquire into the press in October 1946. Over the next two and a half years while the Commission sat he carefully built up files of clippings illustrating press misrepresentations and personally submitted some of the items as evidence, Donoughue & Jones, *Morrison*, p. 359.

117 Herbert Morrison letter to *Daily Herald*, 12 June 1946, p. 2, 'Government of the Left – To The Editor'; regarding headline on 10 June 1946, p. 3.

118 The staff of the Herald were so appalled by his actions that they passed a resolution, placing on record their 'disapproval of the letter... It resents his [Morrison's] gratuitous advice on newspaper production', resolution from the *Daily Herald* Chapel, WAE Jones (Clerk, NUJ) to Morgan Phillips, 14 July 1946, CAB 124/1070.

6 Can Newspapers Be Made 'More Responsible'?

1 Orchestrated by Christiansen not Beaverbrook (see Francis Wheen, *The Soul of Indiscretion* (2001)), pp. 194–5.

2 In his evidence to the Royal Commission Maurice Webb of the NUJ, claimed that "The real genesis [of the idea for an independent investigation]... was when, towards the end of 1943, we sat down as a Union to consider our post war problems..." ME-RCP, Day 2 (16 July 47), q. 311, Cmd. 7317.

3 Driberg specifically referred to the preservation of the freedom of the press in his question, suggesting it be set up 'with a view to establishing

freedom of the press in Britain", Parliamentary Debates, 30 April 1946, Vol. 422, Cols. 28–29.

4   Clement Attlee, Parliamentary Debates, 30 April 1946, Vol. 422, Cols. 28–29.

5   From Morrison note to Prime Minister, 4 July 1946. 'The views of the Annual Delegate Meeting of the union were, of course, the subject of the question by Driberg on 30th April to which, on my advice, you gave a negative answer', CAB 124/1070.

6   Clement Bundock to Morrison, 2 July 1946, CAB 124/1070.

7   John Pimlott note to Morrison, 2 July 1946, CAB 124/1070.

8   Morrison to Attlee, 4 July 1946, CAB 124/1070.

9   As reported in *World's Press News*, 11 July 1946, p. 4.

10   Note from CM (assumed to be Christopher Mayhew given the context) to Morrison, 12 July 1946. The note also mentioned 'that it [the Royal Commission] should be timed to report before the next General Election', CAB 124/1070.

11   Cabinet Conclusions, CM(46)68, 15 July 1946. CAB 128/6.

12   Parliamentary Debates, Broadcasting, 16 July 1946, Vol. 425, Col. 1084.

13   Morrison memorandum regarding a Royal Commission, CP(46)298, 23 July 1946, CAB 129/11.

14   On 26 July Pimlott asked Morrison if he would like a question put forward about the Commission in the Commons so that he could make an announcement. However, on the 28th Clement Attlee sent the Lord President a personal minute (M251/46) telling him action should be postponed till after August, CAB 124/1070.

15   Cabinet Conclusions, CM(46)75, 30 July 1946, Morrison to Cripps, CAB 128/6.

16   Cabinet Conclusions, CM(46)84, 3 October 1946, 'in discussion doubts were expressed about the wisdom of initiating such an inquiry', CAB 128/6.

17   Ibid.

18   Ibid.

19   Hartley Shawcross, speaking in East Ealing, 30 July 1946, reported in *The Times*, 31 July 1946, p. 3. He had also, more famously, spoken in Battersea on the 19th, when he referred to the 'gutter press' and was forced, later, to apologise to Lord Kemsley (letter printed in *Sunday Times*, 11 August 1946).

20   Although with some notable absences from the Labour benches. Douglas Jay, for example, spoke against the motion, believing that the situation was a lot better than it had been, that the inquiry might be misunderstood by the public and abroad, and that it would not produce any results (Parliamentary Debates, Vol. 428, Col. 529).

21   Michael Foot, Parliamentary Debates, Press (Control and Ownership), 29 October 1946, Vol. 428, Cols. 469–470.

22   Derek Walker Smith, Ibid., Col. 544.

23   Major Sir David Maxwell Fyfe, Ibid., Col. 480.

24   Beverley Baxter, Ibid., Col. 488.

25   *World's Press News*, Editorial, 7 November 1946.

26   Particularly since this was the intention of some within government: Gordon Walker to Morrison, 8 October 1946, 'We want a Royal Commission to serve as a Grand jury or Grand Inquest', CAB 124/1070.

27 *World's Press News*, Editorial, 5 December 1946.
28 *The Economist*, 'Mr. Micawber's Crisis', 15 February 1947.
29 *World's Press News*, editorial, 13 March 1947.
30 Ibid.
31 'After February 15 there will be a suspension of publication of "at least" two consecutive issues of all periodicals irrespective of whether they are printed or published inside or outside the restricted area or from what source they draw their paper supplies', *Newspaper World and Advertising Review*, 15 February 1947, p. 193.
32 The instructions were 'voluntary' but carried out by almost periodicals. Only two defied the ban that there should be no duplicated substitutes, according to *Newspaper World and Advertising Review*, the *British Medical Journal* and *Liberal News* (8 March 1947, p. 227).
33 *The Economist*, 8 March 1947. *The Economist* was particularly cross at the government's illegal instruction – 'their "instruction",' it said 'for all its peremptory language, was without legal force', p. 313.
34 Reported in the *Sunday Express*, 'Threats to Freedom', 6 April 1947, p. 4.
35 *Daily Mirror*, 11 March 1947, p. 1. *World's Press News*, 20 March 1947, p. 24.
36 *World's Press News*, 3 April 1947, p. 3.
37 *The Economist*, 15 February 1947, op. cit., p. 267.
38 The first issue of the monthly periodical 'Coal' came out 1 May 1947. Its target circulation was 75,000 rising to 150,000. The fortnightly journal ROF News was being planned at the same time (*Newspaper World and Advertising Review*, 5 April 1947, p. 6, and 10 May 47, p. 150).
39 *The Times*, 5 March 1947.
40 *Picture Post*, 'Special Issue on the Crisis. Where Stands Britain?', 19 April 1947.
41 Minutes of Evidence, Royal Commission on the Press (ME-RCP), Lord Layton, Day 24 (4 March 48), q. 8116, Cmd. 7409.
42 As a result of the government's commitment to the US to return sterling to convertibility on 15 July 1947. For a dramatic account of the parlous state of the economy in the summer of 1947 see Hennessy, *Never Again*, pp. 299–305.
43 Cabinet Conclusions, CM(47)52, 5 June 1947, Chancellor, CAB 128/10. They returned to paper very briefly in the Cabinet discussion of 24 June 1947, only to say 'It was urged by Ministers that, while some cuts, e.g. those in paper, tobacco, and films, could be made without serious disadvantage, there was a danger that others, and particularly the proposed cut in food imports, would have an adverse effect on morale, and so on production' CM(47)56, CAB 128/10.
44 Hugh Dalton, Parliamentary Debates, 30 June 1947, Vol. 439, Col. 961.
45 The Chancellor met with the Newsprint Supply Company on the 7 July and said the cut would last six months. It ended up lasting much longer.
46 *The Economist*, 'What's Wrong with the Press', 26 1947.
47 *World's Press News*, Editorial, 4 September 1947, p. 8.
48 Until Harold Wilson, newly installed at the Board of Trade, told newspapers in May 1948 that they could expect to receive more paper, not less, in 1949.
49 Clement Davies sought to insert an additional sentence to the Bill reading; "Provided that nothing in this Act shall be held to authorise the suppression

or suspension of any newspaper, periodical, book, or other publication". Parliamentary Debates, Supplies and Services (Transitional Powers) Bill, 11 August 1947, Vol. 441, Col. 2093.

50 'Report to the Nation Campaign Begins Sunday', *World's Press News*, 9 October 1947, p. 30.

51 'Government's Eleven-Inch Doubles: Press Co-operates', *World's Press News*, 16 October 1947, p. 22.

52 Hugh Dalton, Budget Proposals, Parliamentary Debates, 12 November 1947, Vol. 444, Col. 401. Stafford Cripps, who took over as Chancellor after Dalton's resignation, postponed the new policy after lobbying by advertising firms. A special committee appointed to examine the tax eventually proposed a voluntary scheme rather than a compulsory P&L tax.

53 'Newsprint Cut Menace to Free Press', *World's Press News*, 2 October 1947, p. 4.

54 'The Stafford Fiasco', *World's Press News*, 23 October 1947, p. 4.

55 'Bevan Attacks Press: Morrison Wants Bigger Papers', *World's Press News*, 27 November 1947, p. 4.

56 Editorial, *World's Press News*, 11 December 1947, p. 8.

57 'Privileges Report – Committee says 'No Evidence to Justify Allighan Charges'', *World's Press News*, 31 July 1947, p. 3.

58 Herbert Morrison, Parliamentary Debates, 'Confidential Information (Disclosure)', 30 October 1947, Vol. 443, Col. 1228.

59 See Jeremy Tunstall, *The Westminster Lobby Correspondents* (1970), p. 48.

60 From memorandum by Stafford Cripps, on the paper of the British Union of Fascists, CP(47)54, 7 February 1947, CAB 129/17.

61 Cabinet Conclusions, CM(47)21, Paper for Fascist Periodical, 13 February 1947, CAB 128/9.

62 Cabinet Papers, CP(47)135, 'Supply of Paper for *Action*, Chuter Ede, 22 April 1947, CAB 129/18.

63 Cabinet Conclusions, CM(47)47, Paper for Fascist Periodical, 15 May 1947, CAB 128/9.

64 Cabinet Conclusions, CM(47)64, Paper for Fascist Periodical, 24 July 1947, CAB 128/10.

65 Stafford Cripps, Parliamentary Debates, 17 July 1947, Vol. 440, Col. 690.

66 Cabinet Conclusions, CM(48)24, Paper for Fascist Periodical, 22 March 1948, CAB 128/12.

67 Gordon Walker, Parliamentary Debates, Press (Ownership and Control), 29 October 1946, Vol. 428, Col. 484.

68 Herbert Morrison, Parliamentary Debates, Press, 29 October 1946, Vol. 428, Col. 558.

69 First in CP(46)298 in July 1946, CAB 129/11. Then in CP(46)360 in October, and finally in CP(46)379, again in October, CAB 129/13.

70 Gordon Walker note to Morrison, 8 October 1946, CAB 124/1070.

71 Morrison to Cabinet on 30 July 1946, CAB 128/6, and in CP(46)298, CAB 129/11. He referred back to the PEP report, saying it had given 'a fair idea of the ground to be covered' but was now not an adequate tool for action.

72 CP(46)360, 'Inquiry into the Press', Morrison, 27 September 1946, CAB 129/13. Discussed in Cabinet on 3 October 1946 (CM(46)84, CAB 128/6).

73 Gordon Walker to Morrison, 8 October 1946, the Royal Commission 'should not be obliged to make recommendations', CAB 124/1070.

74 Each of these proposals was either raised by contemporaries and considered by the Commission and/or included in the questionnaire they sent out to all the news groups. See Questionnaire NC1.

75 *The Guardian* 18 February 1969, reprinted in, *Kingsley Martin – Portrait and Self-portrait*, ed. Mervyn Jones (1969).

76 Kingsley Martin, *The Press the Public Wants* (1947), 'Truth and the Public', Conway Memorial Lecture, Conway Hall, 17 June 1945 (printed 1945).

77 Kingsley Martin, 'Truth and the Public', op. cit.

78 Kingsley Martin, *The Press the Public Wants*, p. 122.

79 Ibid. p. 107.

80 Memoranda of Evidence Submitted to the Royal Commission (RCP Memoranda), Replies to Questionnaire NC1, Daily Mirror Newspapers & Sunday Pictorial Newspapers, (20), response to q. 32(9).

81 Television Bill, No. 76, Parliamentary Papers 1953–54, Volume III, p. 463, 4 March 1954, Clause 3 (1)c, d, & h.

82 RCP Memoranda, Replies to NC1, Daily Mirror Newspapers and Sunday Pictorial Newspapers (1920) Ltd. (20), q. 32(6).

83 RCP Memoranda, Replies to NC1, Kemsley Newspapers (44).

84 RCP Memoranda, Replies to NC1, *Manchester Guardian* and *Evening News*. (54).

85 Broadcasting Bill, 5 February 1980, Bill 139, Parliamentary Papers 1979–80, Vol. 4, Part II, Clause 3(1)c.

86 Ibid. Clause 4(1)d.

87 RCP Memoranda, Replies to NC1, Berrow's Newspapers (3).

88 RCP Memoranda, Replies to NC1, *Manchester Guardian* and *Evening News* (54).

89 Morrison used the word 'socialisation' rather than nationalisation since he thought that the latter wA3 politically loaded and many of his concepts of government intervention involved public but not government control.

90 Described in detail in *The Economist*, lead article, 'State and Public', 18 September 1948.

91 Report of the Royal Commission on the Press, Cmd. 7700, p. 154 (paragraph 572).

92 Cmd. 7700, p. 131 (para. 483).

93 Cmd. 7700, p. 109 (para. 394).

7 'Press Freedom' Triumphs; Government Turns to Spin

1 Cmd. 7700, p. 155–156 (para. 578).

2 Cmd. 7700, p. 160 (para. 597).

3 Cmd. 7700, p. 165 (para. 617).

4 Lord Layton told the Commission that 'The British public is definitely becoming an *ill-informed* public' as a consequence of paper rationing. ME-RCP, memorandum by Newsprint Supply Company, Day 24 (4 March 48), Cmd. 7409 [*his italics*].

5 Preparation for memorandum CP(46)379, Morrison, 9 October 1946, CAB 124/1070.

6 A judge was first suggested by Morrison in CP(46)360, 27 September 1946, CAB 129/13.

7 'In view of objections to inviting a judge to preside over the enquiry, we thought it would be wise to abandon the idea of a having a judge for this purpose' CP(46)379, 'Inquiry into the Press', Morrison, 14 October 1946, CAB 129/13.

8 Thomas Johnston, Sir Hector Hetherington and Sir Philip Morris all rejected invitations from Morrison. Johnston to Morrison, 9 November 1946; Hetherington to Morrison 8 December 1946, CAB 124/1071. Morris to Morrison, 11 January 1946, CAB 124/1072.

9 Calculated by adding up all the suggested names from the files of the Lord President and the Prime Minister (CAB 124/1070–1071, PREM 5/249).

10 Williams to Attlee, 16 October 1946, PREM 5/249.

11 Williams to Attlee, 17 February 1947, PREM 5/249. Williams wrote that he spoke to the Lord President who recognised that there were weaknesses of the current list and was willing to agree changes.

12 Reported in *The Times*, 27 March 1947.

13 The Royal Commission first sent out a questionnaire with 32 questions directed to the editors of all the newspaper and periodical publishers in Britain (NC1). They sent slightly different questionnaires to proprietors, advertisers (B1) and advertising agents (B2).

14 The questionnaire was so disordered that Odhams Press (owner of *Daily Herald, News Review, Illustrated, The People,* and *John Bull*) re-ordered them under its own headings (RCP Memoranda, No. 63).

15 Clement Bundock in *The Journalist*, January 1945.

16 Gordon Walker note to Morrison, 14 November 1946, CAB 124/1071.

17 *Evening Standard*, 'The Londoner's Diary', 13 December 1946, p. 4.

18 Evidence of the NUJ submitted to the Royal Commission by J.E. Jay (President) and Clement Bundock (General Secretary), 3 June 1947.

19 Cmd. 7700, p. 61 (para. 217). Lord Rothermere sold off his controlling interest in the *Daily Mirror* and *Sunday Pictorial* in 1931. Lords Kemsley, Camrose and Illife divided their news empire in 1937.

20 RCP Memoranda, Replies to NC1, Berrow's Newspapers (3).

21 Curran and Seaton, *Power without Responsibility* (1997), p. 45.

22 ME-RCP, memorandum submitted by Viscount Kemsley, Day 36 (27 May 48), p. 3, Cmd. 7503. This is despite Kemsley once boasting to Canadian journalists that 'I dictate all the leading articles printed in my papers', quoted in Stephen Koss, *Political Press Vol. II.* (1984), p. 1010.

23 ME-RCP, Lord Kemsley, Day 36 (27 May 48), q. 12,009, Cmd. 7503.

24 Cmd. 7700, p. 118 (para. 432). Quote applied specifically to by-election but consistent with report's comments on other cases.

25 Cmd. 7700, p. 88 (para. 312).

26 Cmd. 7700, p. 143 (para. 528).

27 RCP Memoranda, Replies to Questionnaire B2 (Advertising Agents), London Press Exchange.

28 ME-RCP, NUJ, J.E. Jay, Day 1 (16 July 47), q. 129, Cmd. 7317.

29 RCP Memoranda, written evidence of Advertising Association.

30 On 18 July 1947 Morrison met with the advertising managers of the daily and Sunday newspapers at 11 Downing Street and appealed to them to maintain the amount of space they gave to the government advertisements, in proportion to the newspaper page reduction, INF 12/13.

31 The Commission told the government that 'twenty-seven organisations have referred in their written evidence either to PROs or in general terms to the Government information services'. Attachment to letter from J.J. Nunn to D.J. Wardley at the Treasury, requesting representatives for interview, 16 March 1948, CAB 124/1073.

32 ME-RCP, Guild of Newspaper Editors, Day 4 (16 October 1947), q. 1061, Cmd. 7322.

33 Ibid. q. 1007.

34 ME-RCP, Guild of Newspaper Editors, Day 4 (16 October 1947), q. 997, Cmd. 7322. Based on results of a questionnaire survey the Guild sent out to all local newspapers and journals.

35 Ibid.

36 ME-RCP, Daily News, Robin Cruikshank, Day 24 (4 March 1948), q. 8218, Cmd. 7409.

37 ME-RCP, Institute of Journalists, quoted from submitted evidence, A.T. Penman, Day 6 (30 October 1947) q. 1725, Cmd. 7328.

38 ME-RCP, Sir Stephen Tallents, Day 25 (17 March 1948), q. 8341, Cmd. 7415.

39 ME-RCP, A.L. Cranfield, Daily News Ltd., Day 24 (4 March 1948), q. 8218, Cmd. 7409.

40 RCP Memoranda, Replies to NC1, *The Economist*, Geoffrey Crowther (27).

41 RCP Memoranda, Replies to NC1, *Tribune* Publications (83). *Gleischaltung* was specifically related to the Nazification process of alignment or coordination within Germany in the 1930s.

42 ME-RCP, Northcliffe Newspapers Group, Day 17 (21 January 1948), q. 5442, Cmd. 7373.

43 NUJ to J.J. Nunn (Royal Commission), 11 July 1947, HO 251/154.

44 Examples cited in letter from Sir Thomas Balogh to Sir David Ross, 3 December 1947, HO 251/155.

45 RCP Memoranda, submitted by the Institute of Journalists.

46 Sir Geoffrey Vickers, memorandum on interim report to Sir David Ross, 8 December 1947, HO 251/216.

47 R.C.K. Ensor, memorandum (Paper 89), 5 January 1948, HO 251/216.

48 G.M. Young, memorandum (Paper 115), 14 February 1948, HO 251/216.

49 Ibid.

50 G.M. Young, memorandum to the Policy Committee of the Royal Commission, December 1947, HO 251/213.

51 G.M. Young, memorandum (Paper 115), 14 February 1948, HO 251/216.

52 There are 'two main schools of thought among members' Sir David Ross wrote to Commission members, 12 March 1948, HO 251/216.

53 Ibid.

54 J.J. Nunn to Wardley (Treasury), 16 March 1948, CAB 124/1073.

55 James Crombie (Treasury) to Robert Fraser (COI), 23 February 1948, CAB 124/1073.

56 Note from Fraser to David Stephens (LP's Office), 31 March 1948, CAB 124/1073.

57 Note from Stephens to Morrison about Home Information Services Meeting, 2 April 1948: 'At this morning's meeting there was strong support for the view that the first and most essential task was not so much the selection and briefing of suitable witnesses as the preparation of a government

statement which would describe the work of the Departmental information services in their relations with the press and would also constitute the brief to which the selected witnesses would speak', CAB 124/1073.

58 The IH(O) committee initially discussed the request of the Royal Commission and the response on 2 April 1948. The Ministerial committee discussed the request and a draft response (attached to Lord President's memorandum) on 14 April. Note from David Stephens to Morrison, 20 April 1948, says that 'Mr. Jordan is getting the PM's approval concurrently', CAB 124/1073.

59 Point raised at IS(48)4 when they discussed Jordan's memo, 14 April 48, CAB 124/1073.

60 Gordon Walker to Morrison, 22 April 1948, CAB 124/1073.

61 J.I.C. Crombie wrote to J.J. Nunn, LO.215/06, 23 April 1948, telling her that the Commission would receive the government response 'in the next day or so', CAB 124/1073.

62 The official information services committee, IH(O)(48)5th, 30 April 1948, talked about what they thought the Commission might ask (for example, about scoops and about attribution of sources). The Ministerial committee then discussed the issues further at its next meeting; IS(48)3rd, 11 May 1948, CAB 124/1073.

63 ME-RCP, Government, Day 35 (26 May 48), questions 11,700 to 11,830, Cmd. 7500. Interview with Viscount Kemsley and Lionel Berry Day 36 (27 May 48), questions 11,831 to 12,429, Cmd. 7503.

64 Ibid., q. 11,744, Cmd. 7500.

65 Ibid. "There has been a very great development of that over the last twenty years; there was a very rapid development between the years 1939 and 1944; the year 1944–45 represented the peak year", JIC Crombie, q. 11,818, Cmd. 7500.

66 Ibid. q. 11,806.

67 Ibid. q. 11,799.

68 Ibid. q. 11,820.

69 The Commission did ask if there was a 'more definite code' being drawn up for PROs. Jordan bristled and replied that the 'rules that govern the conduct of civil servants apply to CIOs just as much'. This was not entirely true since most PROs were not yet civil servants. The Commission continued briefly with this line of inquiry then dropped it. Ibid. q. 11,757, Cmd. 7500.

70 Outside the Soviet Union this included Hungary, Rumania, Bulgaria, France, Chile, Argentina, Guatemala, China and India. According to *The Times*, January–March 1948.

71 'Press Threat in Hungary', *The Observer*, 29 June 1947, p. 1.

72 Reported in *The Times*, 30 January 1948, p. 3.

73 G.M. Young Memorandum (Paper 115), 14 February 1948, 'On the Possibility of an Interim Report and Discussion of Progress', HO 251/216.

74 *The Times*, 25 February 1948, p. 5.

75 *The Sunday Times*, Editorial Comment, 29 February 1948.

76 *The Observer*, Editorial, 7 March 1948.

77 Statement printed in *The Times*, 3 March 1948, p. 4.

78 *The Observer*, Editorial, 7 March 1948.
79 *Newspaper World and Advertising Review*, 'Czech Crisis – Editors Deprived of Livelihood and Newspapers Suspended', 6 March 1948, p. 240.
80 '"Freedom of Press Not Assured" says Sir George Waters', *World's Press News*, 17 June 1948, p. 3.
81 Ensor writing as 'Scrutator' in the *The Sunday Times*, 29 February 1948 and 7 March 1948.
82 Reported in the *The Times*, 31 March 1948, p. 4.
83 Hector McNeil, speaking on 29 March, reported in *The Times*, 30 March 1948.
84 *World's Press News*, 'Templar', 8 April 1948.
85 This offer emerged from material published in the US, not in Britain and was raised in the short debate on the loan in the House of Commons on the evening of Monday, 3 May 1948. This was reported in *The Times* the following day.
86 *The Times*, 6 May 1948.
87 *World's Press News*, Editorial, 27 May 1948.
88 *The Observer*, 9 May 1948, p. 5.
89 Herbert Morrison, speech to the Labour Conference, Monday afternoon session, 17 May 1948, from the Report of the Conference (Transport House, London, 1948).
90 'Soskice on Press Role Under Nationalisation', *World's Press News*, 6 May 1948, p. 3.
91 'Morgan Phillips Says – Labour Does Not Want State Press Control', *World's Press News*, 3 June 1948, p. 18.
92 Chuter Ede, Parliamentary Debates, 29 July 1948, Vol. 454, Col. 884.
93 *The Economist*, 'Shorter Notes', 31 July 1948, p. 179.
94 Herbert Morrison, speech at Fife, reported in *World's Press News*, 25 November 1948, p. 9.
95 *Manchester Guardian*, 'Friend and Protector of the Press', 17 November 1948, p. 6.
96 Hartley Shawcross, speaking in Oklahoma, 28 June 1949, reported in the *Spectator*, 1 July 1949, p. 4, 'Verdict on the Press'. Sir Stafford Cripps, speaking to East Bristol constituents, reported in *Manchester Guardian*, 21 November 1949, p. 5, 'Chancellor denounces Tory "Gloom-Makers" – Hopeful Signs in Economic Crisis – Press Accused of Setting Out to Mislead People'.
97 *Manchester Guardian*, 'Press Freedom – "Fight by No Means Over"', 22 October 1949, p. 3.
98 *Daily Express*, 30 June 1949, front page.
99 Report of the Royal Commission on the Press, Cmd. 7700, p. 151 (para. 559).
100 Cmd. 7700, p. 147.
101 *World's Press News*, 8 July 1948, p. 18.
102 This seriously backfired. All Gordon's sub-editors resigned en masse and Gordon had to apologise for his criticisms before they would return to work (*World's Press News*, 22 January 1948).
103 ME-RCP, Government, Day 35 (26 May 48), q. 11,727, Cmd. 7500.

8 A Model Communicator? The BBC Objects to Being a Mouthpiece of the State

1 Board of Governors (BoG) Papers 1948. Comparison of numbers of pre-war and present staff, Note by director of administration G69/48–1939: 4,300 (total) 1948: 11,349, R1/84/3, BBC Written Archives Centre (BBC-WAC).
2 Lochhead to Crossley, in response to question in the House of Commons, 6 February 1946, CAB 124/401.
3 Herbert Butcher, Parliamentary Debates, Broadcasting, 16 July 1946, Vol. 425, Col. 1168.
4 William Haley broadcast, 'The Place of Broadcasting' (Third Programme), November 1947 (25th Anniversary), HALY 16–52, Churchill Archives Centre (CAC).
5 Peter Hennessy, *Never Again* (1993), p. 327.
6 RCP Minutes, Kingsley Martin, Day 10 (27 November 47), q. 3222, Cmd. 7369.
7 Haley diaries, 22 July 1947, HALY 13–34, CAC.
8 Miss Benzie to Vincent Alford, 25 October 43, Talks: Reconstruction (The World We Want), R51/448/2, BBC Written Archives Centre (BBC-WAC).
9 *The Listener*, Editorial 'New Programmes', 26 July 1945, p. 92.
10 William Haley, 'Cultural Forces in British Life Today', British Institute of Adult Education, 20/21 September 1946 HALY 16/52, CAC.
11 BBC Memorandum, 'General Survey of the Broadcasting Service', Cmd. 8117, 1951, p. 5, para. 12. Cited in Asa Briggs, *Volume IV – Sound and Vision* (1995), p. 562.
12 Haley diaries (reference to speech), 16 March 1947, HALY 13–34, CAC.
13 Mrs. Goldie to Miss Quigley, 'Suggestions for Autumn Programmes: "Facts First"', 1 August 1945, R51/158 BBC-WAC.
14 Vincent Alford (Acting Asst Director of Talks) to David Bryson, 4 January 1946, 'Facts First', R51/158, BBC-WAC.
15 See BBC files on 'Political Broadcasting, Lists of Broadcasts by MPs', File 1 1943–46, File 2a 1947–48, File 2b 1949–50 etc. R51/414. Also in Ministerial Broadcasts. BBC-WAC.
16 Herbert Morrison, Parliamentary Debates, Broadcasting, Vol. 425, Col. 1089, 16 July 1946.
17 Morrison to Gordon Walker, 25 June 1946, CAB 124/411.
18 Herbert Morrison, Parliamentary Debates, Broadcasting, Vol. 425, Col. 1078, 16 July 1946. Morrison had even modelled his London Passenger Transport Board on the BBC when he served as Minister of Transport in 1931.
19 Haley broadcast, 'The Place of Broadcasting' op. cit., HALY 16–52, CAC.
20 Ibid.
21 The Crawford Committee in 1925 (Cmd. 2599) and the Ullswater committee in 1936 (Cmd. 5091).
22 Broadcasting Policy meetings, GEN 81, 29 August 45, 12 September 45, 10 October 45, CAB 78/37.
23 Coalition Committee on Broadcasting; detailed in note from Martin Flett to Morrison 26 June 1946, CAB 124/25.
24 Flett to Morrison, Memorandum, 27 August 1945, CAB 124/399.

25 Ibid. And, Broadcasting Committee Meeting minutes, GEN 81/1, 29 August 1945, 'The opinion of the meeting was that there was no need for a public enquiry on the present occasion', CAB 78/37.

26 Cabinet Minutes, CM(45)63, 17 December 1945, CAB 128/2.

27 Call noted in Haley's diaries, 23 December 1945: 'I asked him [Bamford] if there was to be a Charter inquiry. He said not but the Govt. would probably issue their findings as a White Paper', HALY 13–35, CAC.

28 Maurice Gorham, *Sound and Fury, 21 Years at the BBC* (1948), p. 189.

29 And even then only for domestic services. BBC Overseas Services were to continue to be funded by a grant-in-aid. Haley note to Board of Governors (BoG), 31 December 1947, Ga2/48, BoG Papers, R1/84/6, BBC-WAC.

30 William Haley, *The Public Influence of Broadcasting and the Press*, Clayton Memorial Lectures, XCV (1953–54), No. 2, p. 3, HALY 16/52, BBC-WAC.

31 Haley speech at Columbia University; 'Broadcasting, Government & Freedom of the Press', 1971, HALY 16–54, CAC.

32 The Postmaster General, acting under the authority of clause 4(iii) of the 1927 Licence (which stated the Postmaster General may from time to time... require the Corp to refrain from sending out broadcasts) 'informed the BBC on 11 January 1927 that he required the BBC to refrain from broadcasting the following matter:- "(a) statements expressing the opinion of the Corporation on matters of public policy; and (b) speeches or lectures containing statements on topics of political, religious or industrial controversy."', MOI memorandum, 27 August 1945, CAB 124/408.

33 'In January 1928 the BBC made a formal application to the Postmaster General for a relaxation in these restrictions. The Corporation [said that]... the power, if granted, would not be misused. No partisanship would be shown and any new controversial matter would be introduced gradually and experimentally. There would be no expression of views contrary to the interests of the State'. The rules were relaxed shortly after, MOI Memorandum, IH(46)8, 25 June 1946, CAB 124/408.

34 'The history of political broadcasting before the war was decidedly chequered', Herbert Morrison, (IH(46), 22 June 1946), CAB 124/408. See also 14 page MOI memorandum on the history of political broadcasting 27 August 1945 (CAB 124/408) and 'Reith and the Denial of Politics', in Curran and Seaton, *Power without Responsibility* (1997).

35 Haley diaries, 10 November 1945, HALY 13–35, CAC.

36 Cabinet Conclusions, CM(45)64, 20 December 1945, CAB 128/2.

37 Meeting recorded in BoG minutes, 24 January 1946, Min.19, R1/14/1, BBC-WAC, and in Haley diaries, 3 February 1946. Haley commented that 'this is delightful from a Labour government', HALY 13–35.

38 Haley diaries, 30 September 1945, HALY 13–35, and in separate diary entry 30 September 1945, HALY 13–5, and reference in BoG Minutes, 4 October 1945, R1/13/1, BBC-WAC.

39 Haley diaries, 15 October 1945, HALY 13–35.

40 BoG Minutes, Minute 229, 18 October 1945, R/1/13/1, BBC-WAC.

41 Asa Briggs, *Volume IV* (1995), p. 564.

42 Haley diaries, 30 September 1945, 'The revelation one gets of being enmeshed in government is to see how many things that ought to be done remain undone simply for lack of decisions', HALY 13–5, CAC.

43 According to Lord Listowel, House of Lords Debates, 26 June 1946 (reported in *The Times*, 27 June 1946, p. 8). The number of households paying a BBC Radio Licence Fee passed 10 million in January 1946. See BBC Programme Policy Meeting minutes, 29 January 1946, R34/615/4, and *Radio Times* 24 February 1946.

44 'List B', 'Public Service broadcasts for Home listeners' November 1945. Research provided to Martin Flett by the BBC for the July debate, 8 July 1946, CAB 124/25.

45 Correspondence between BBC and MOI, June to December 1945. The MOI was not happy to give up the slots as seen from MOI telephone call to Tony Rendall, 18 December 1945, R28/84/3, BBC-WAC.

46 E Bamford to Haley, 18 August 1945, R34/534/5, BBC-WAC. Procedure outlined in Cabinet Papers, CP(45)100, 8 August 1945, CAB 66/67. CP(46)199 laid out that Ministers inform the PMG of subject, length and date. The PMG then contacted the PM for sign-off.

47 Margin, Flett to Morrison, 'Ministerial Control of Broadcasting', 26 September 1945, CAB 124/400.

48 Flett to J.A.R. Pimlott, 1 October 1945, CAB 124/400.

49 Between 1939 and 1948 the number of live hours broadcast by the BBC overseas services each week rose from 99 to 481. Over the same period the number of staff rose from 323 to 4,161, G69/48, R1/84/3, BBC-WAC.

50 See Asa Briggs, *Volume IV* (1995), 'Overseas Broadcasting', pp. 125–147.

51 Sian Nicholas, regarding 'Kitchen Front' 1942, *Echo of War*, p. 79.

52 AP Ryan, obituary, *The Times*, 3 July 1972.

53 E.J. Williams told Parliament the Licence Fee would double on 22 January 1946 (Vol. 418, *Col. 34*). Attlee told Janner there would be no inquiry into the BBC on 19 February 1946 (Vol. 419, Col. 952–3).

54 Flett and Bamford visited Haley on 14 February 1946 about working more collaboratively and worked with the Corporation from then until the broadcasting debate in July. See Flett to Morrison, 20 February 1946, and subsequent memoranda in CAB 124/402.

55 Haley diaries, 25 June 1946, HALY 13–35, CAC.

56 Policy, Coordinating Committee Meeting Minutes, 8 August 1945, Minute 136, 'Broadcasts by MPs', R34/320/1, BBC-WAC. The second comment is scribbled by Haley beside the first (his underlining).

57 'Liaison with Government Departments' (unsigned), 1946, R51/205/4, BBC-WAC.

58 Record of Telephone Conversation, 3/4 July 1946, R.A. Rendall (Controller, Talks) with Sir Drummond Shiels re Strachey desire to broadcast on bread rationing on Sunday 21 July, R34/534/5, BBC-WAC.

59 'What Listeners think of the BBC', *News Chronicle* poll, 25 June 1946, p. 2.

60 'Ministerial Broadcasts', R34/553/2, BBC-WAC.

61 Haley diaries (his underlining), 10 November 1945, HALY 13–35 CAC.

62 Home Service, 11 November 1945, 9.15 pm, printed in *The Listener*, 15 November 1945, p. 549.

63 Strachey, Home Service, 16 June 1946, 9.15 pm, printed in *The Listener*, 20 June 1946, p. 801.

64 Assistant Controller (Talks), GR Barnes, to C(T), re: Suggested Broadcast by the Lord President of the Council, 16 March 1946, R34–534, BBC-WAC.
65 Boon to Morrison, re production broadcast, 19 March 1946, CAB 124/904, PRO.
66 Haley diaries, 9 February 1946, HALY 13–35, CAC.
67 Pethick-Lawrence on 1 January, Ben Smith on 5 February and Shinwell on 9 February itself, R34/553/2, BBC-WAC.
68 'Extract from Minutes of Programme Policy meeting', 21 May 1946, R51/205/4, BBC-WAC. Haley proposed that he go and speak to the Post Office 'as [a] first step towards [a] proper working arrangement'.
69 Full list of Ministerial broadcasts for 1945–46 in R34/553/2, BBC-WAC.
70 Note by DG, 6 May 1948 to BoG, G41/48, 'Broadcast on Matters before Parliament', BoG Papers, R1/84/2, BBC-WAC.
71 This became formalised in Clause 6(iv) of the Aide Memoire on political broadcasting in 1947 and, in 1948, was expanded to explain that this meant the BBC could not have discussions on any issues for a period of a fortnight before they are debated in either House, nor could MPs be involved in discussions on subjects regarding ongoing legislation. See Briggs, *Volume IV*, pp. 582–3.
72 From analysis of the *Radio Times* 1945–46 and *The Listener* 1945–46.
73 Ben Smith (5 February 1946 on world food shortage), Tom Williams (22 February 1946 food production), Edith Summerskill (10 March 1946 on food shortages), Tom Williams (27 March 1946 – Battle for Food – Women's Land Army), Tom Williams (30 May 1946, wheat off farms quick), John Strachey (16 June 1946 review of food), from R34/553/2, BBC-WAC.
74 Arthur Salter, 'The Shadow of World Famine', Home Service, printed in *The Listener* 11 April 1946 (p. 453), Maurice Webb also wrote an article for The Listener on 'Hunger in Europe', 30 May 1946 (not clear if broadcast first, p. 709), DG Bridson, 'UNRRA – The battle against starvation and want in Europe', Home Service, 30 June 1946, 9.30 pm, *Radio Times* 30 June–6 July.
75 Recorded in Haley's diaries, 4 July 1946, HALY 13–35, CAC.
76 'Britain Gets Going Again', Morrison, Home Service, 9.15 pm, 30 June 1946. Transcript in *The Listener*, 4 July 1946.
77 Ibid.
78 Cabinet Paper, CP(46)255, 2 July 1946, Morrison believed the broadcast 'could hardly have been less controversial in either matter or manner' CAB 129/11.
79 Churchill had already started informal discussions about political broadcasting (e.g. meeting of 18 March 1946 in LP's office) – but the Morrison broadcast forced the issue, CAB 124/408.
80 Barnett Janner, Parliamentary Debates, 13 December 1945, Vol. 417, Col. 606–7.
81 *Daily Mirror*, 'The BBC's Quid Pro Quo', Editorial, 24 January 1946.
82 Barnett Janner, Parliamentary Debates, 29 January 1946, Vol. 418, Col. 693–4. And, 19 February 1946, Vol. 419, Col. 952–3.
83 *The Times*, leader article, 'BBC Prospects', 8 April 1946, p. 5. 'BBC News Policy', letter from Arthur Mann, also p. 5.

84 James Stuart to leader of the Opposition, 5 June 1946, in Churchill 2/5, Correspondence A-C, Churchill Papers, CAC.

85 Parliamentary Debates, House of Lords, 26 June 1946, Vol. 141, Col. 1173–1218.

86 *The Spectator*, 'Scrutiny of the BBC', 28 June 1946, p. 650.

87 *The Times*, leader article, 'A BBC Inquiry', 27 June 1946, p. 5c.

88 Arthur Mann argued that news and Parliamentary affairs were not receiving enough airtime. He had a history of taking principled stances when editor of the *Yorkshire Post* in the 1930s and later over Suez. See heated correspondence in BoG papers 1946, between G2/46 and G33/46, R1/82/1, BBC-WAC

89 BoG Papers 1948. Comparison of numbers of pre-war and present staff, Note by director of administration G69/48–1939: 4,300 (total) 1948: 11,349, R1/84/3, BBC-WAC.

90 Ogilvie had been effectively dismissed as DG of the BBC in January 1942 because the Governors did not think him capable enough. This was kept secret at the time and subsequently. Haley told Morrison prior to the Broadcasting debate after Ogilvie began writing to *The Times*. See Flett to Morrison, 'Sir Frederick Ogilvie', 13 July 1946, re Haley note. CAB 124/25.

91 *Time and Tide*, 'No BBC Commission – Why?', 6 July 1946, p. 627.

92 *The Times*, 'BBC Select Committee', 22 June 1946.

93 Haley diaries, 25 June 1946, HALY 13–35, CAC.

94 Parliamentary Papers, Broadcasting Policy White Paper, Cmd. 6852, Vol. XX., 2 July 1946.

95 *The Spectator*, 'Bad News About Broadcasting', 5 July 1946, p. 2.

96 *Time and Tide*, 'No BBC Commission – Why?', 6 July 1946, p. 627.

97 Ian Orr–Ewing, Parliamentary Debates, Broadcasting Debate, 16 July 1946, Vol. 425, Col. 1086. P.P. Eckersley, ex-chief engineer of the BBC, also asserted that there was not a limit on wavelengths, as the government suggested: 'there are no real technical limitations whatsoever barring the expansion of broadcasting'. Eckersley letter to *The Times*, 16 July 1946.

98 *Time and Tide*, op. cit., p. 627.

99 Based on note from Flett to Morrison, 21 June 1946, CAB 124/25.

100 Flett to Morrison, 24 June 1946. From appointment to White paper – fourteen months. The committee itself took eight and a half months, CAB 124/25.

101 Haley diaries, 25 June 1946, HALY 13–35, CAC.

102 See above, memorandum from Flett to Morrison, 27 August 1945, CAB 124/399.

103 Morrison made the contrast between broadcasting and the press explicit during the Broadcasting debate when he called for an inquiry into the latter, Parliamentary Debates, 16 July 1946, Vol. 425, Col. 1084.

104 Note from CPM (privy council office) to Morrison re speech to PLP, 12 July 1946, CAB 124/25.

105 During the Commons debate Henderson Stewart, Brendan Bracken, Lady Megan Lloyd George, WJ Brown, KWM Pickthorn and Herbert Butcher all questioned the nature of the relationship between the BBC and the government. Parliamentary Debates, 16 July 1946, Vol. 425, Col. 1118.

106 Lord Brabazon, 'Is this the way the mines are going to be run – in a spirit of perpetual self-satisfaction?'... Do they really want these organisations kept up to date by inquiry and improvement...?' Parliamentary Debates, House of Lords, 26 June 1946, Vol. 141, Col. 1182.

9 'Necessity' Justifies New Techniques of Manipulation

1 BBC Licence, Cmd. 6975, 29 November 1946, Clause 4(3).
2 Ibid. BBC Licence, Clause 4(2).
3 Ibid. BBC Licence, Clause 4(4).
4 Ibid. BBC Licence, Clause 5, 'The Corporation shall observe and perform such stipulations conditions and restrictions and do such acts and things in relation to the Television Broadcasting Stations or the Television Service as from time to time may be prescribed by the Postmaster General in writing'.
5 *Time and Tide*, 'The BBC Charter', 14 December 1946, p. 1212.
6 Ibid., p. 1212.
7 *The Spectator*, 'The Government and Broadcasting', 19 July 1946, p. 53. Though written before the ratification of the Licence, this article is referring specifically to the proposal that the BBC be compelled to broadcast "any pronouncement or other matter which a Department of his Majesty's Government may require".
8 Haley told the Board of Governors that he had only a few days in which to suggest amendments to the Charter and Licence, BoG Minutes, 27 November 1946, R1/14/1, BBC-WAC.
9 'Postmaster-General's Right of Veto', G15/47. Note by DG to Governors, 26 February 1947, BoG Papers, R1/83/1, BBC-WAC.
10 Cyril Radcliffe to BBC, quoted in G15/47 PMG's right of veto. Note by DG 26 February 1947, R1/83/1, BBC-WAC.
11 Herbert Morrison, Parliamentary Debates, Broadcasting, 16 July 1946, Vol. 425, Col. 1079.
12 Morrison, Parliamentary Debates, Broadcasting, 16 July 1946, Vol. 425, Col. 1080.
13 The list included George Orwell, Note to EE Bridges, 7 March 1946. Herbert Morrison sent his five recommendations to the PM on 12 March 1946, and forwarded it to the Post Master General, CAB 124/413.
14 Lord Listowel to Morrison, 14 March 1946, CAB 124/413.
15 Morrison to Attlee, 14 October 1946, CAB 124/413. Morrison thought this might be slightly balanced by a vice-Chairman who was 'moderately to the Right or non-political'.
16 'E' (presumably Ellen Wilkinson), Ministry of Education, re Lord Inman to Morrison, 24 October 1946, CAB 124/413.
17 Haley diaries, 25 May 1947, HALY 13–34, CAC.
18 Haley diaries, 13 May 1947, HALY 13–34, CAC.
19 Haley diaries, 13 May 1947, '[Ernest Simon] told me he had been talking to Morrison about his possible investigations into how public corporations should be organised as between Board and Executive. Morrison had said that the DG of the BBC was too powerful' HALY 13–34, CAC.

20 As well as recommending greater power for the Governors ('the Governors of the future should have as much authority as possible' Cmd. 8116, p. 177, paragraph 591), the report suggested the Governors take a bigger role in programme policy making – for example by attending Board of Management meetings (paragraphs 581–2).

21 Ministerial Broadcasts, R34/553/2, BBC-WAC.

22 Letter from Lord Woolton to James Stuart, copied to Winston Churchill, 12 November 1946, Churchill Correspondence 2/38 (Public and Political: General 1946–51) Political Broadcasting, CAC.

23 Copy of Conservative Central Office Statement; Politics and the BBC. An Analysis of Broadcast Talks, Ga1/47, 25 January 1947, R1/83/4, BBC-WAC.

24 The BBC claimed that the Conservative figures only related to the Home Service broadcast from London and excluded the appearance of Conservatives on programmes which were less explicitly political (like 'Brains Trust'). BBC statement in *The Times*, 30 January 1947.

25 Haley to Pimlott, 19 November 1946, regarding alleged verbal directive, CAB 124/33.

26 Pimlott to Morrison, regarding the number of Ministerial broadcasts and the procedure surrounding them, 19 December 1946, CAB 124/33.

27 Morrison to Attlee, 24 December 1946, regarding the number of Ministerial broadcasts and recommending the use of alternative means of publicity, CAB 124/33.

28 Ibid.

29 This sentence was specifically added to Rowan's draft of CP(47)7, 3 January 47, by Morrison's office, see JAR Pimlott to Morrison, 30 December 1946 and Pimlott to Rowan, 1 January 1947, CAB 124/33.

30 Cabinet Paper, CP(47)7, 3 January 1947, 'Ministerial Broadcasting', CAB 129/16.

31 IH(47)1ˢᵗ, Minutes, Morrison, 31 July 1947, CAB 134/354.

32 Morrison to Attlee, regarding conversation of the 16ᵗʰ about possible Cripps' broadcasts, 17 November 1947, CAB 124/33.

33 Morrison to Attlee, 25 November 1947, CAB 124/33.

34 Haley to Board of Governors, BoG Papers, G13/48, 29 January 1948, R1/84/1, BBC-WAC.

35 Ibid.

36 Ibid. Cripps eventually had to cancel this broadcast, planned for 22 January.

37 Minutes of meeting between government and BBC, 17 February 1948, CAB 124/410.

38 Ibid.

39 Note by Editor (News) to Board of Governors, 5 May 1947, G36A/47, R1/83/1, BBC-WAC.

40 Isaacs to DG (BBC), contained within papers to Board of Governors, G43/47, 21 May 1947, R1/83/2, BBC-WAC.

41 Philip Noel-Baker to PM, 28 January 1949, CAB 124/33. Approved by Attlee the next day although subsequently cancelled for other reasons, then rearranged for later that year (Noel–Baker to Attlee, 5 May 1949, CRA reply 5 May 1949).

42 There were 31 Labour ministerial broadcasts in 1948 compared with 26 in 1949 and 18 in 1950 (not including Party Political Broadcasts), R51/414/1 to R51/414/4.

43 Ibid.

44 A.P. Ryan letter to DG (BBC) re Production drive, 18 March 1947, R34/701, BBC-WAC.

45 Prosperity Campaign Meeting, Minutes, 20 March 1947, CAB 124/909.

46 R.A. Rendall letter to Professor Robert Rae, MAF, 16 April 1947, R51/205/5, BBC-WAC.

47 Ibid.

48 PC(O)C(47) 17th, Minutes, 8 May 1947, CAB 124/910.

49 *The Listener*, Editorial, 'Britain's Crisis', 8 May 1947, p. 702.

50 'Broadcasts on the Crisis', September 1947, R51/55, BBC-WAC.

51 Haley Diaries, 18 September 1947, referring to Governors' Board Meeting, HALY 13–34, CAC.

52 BoG Minutes, Minute 224, 'BBC and the National Crisis', 18 September 1947, R1/15/1, BBC-WAC.

53 Haley Diaries, 15 September 1947, referring to special meeting of Board of Governor's on 18 September, HALY 13–34, CAC.

54 'The BBC and the Crisis', note by the DG, 30 September 1947, R34/339, BBC-WAC.

55 Extract, Programme Policy Meeting Minutes, Minute 199, 'Economic Bulletin', 2 December 1947, R51/205/5, BBC-WAC.

56 IH(47)2nd, Minutes, 'Terms and Timing of Government Announcements', 12 November 1947, CAB 124/404.

57 Programme Policy Meeting Minutes, min. 192, 'Wording of News', 18 November 1947, R34/615/6, BBC-WAC.

58 Minutes to meetings in CAB 124/408.

59 'The Chairman and Director-General reported that at the meeting on 5 November they had been faced with complete unanimity of view between the two parties', BoG Minutes, 18 November 1946, R1/14/1, BBC-WAC.

60 Haley diaries, 5 November 1946, HALY 13–34. This was despite Churchill's comment in 1938 that "the idea that no public man not nominated by Party Whips should be allowed to speak on the radio is not defensible in public policy". Cited by Haley in BoG Papers, G61/46 Political Broadcasting, R1/82/2, BBC-WAC.

61 As Morrison pointed out in a note to Attlee, 16 January 1947, CAB 124/409.

62 Haley diaries, 5 November 1946, HALY 13–34, CAC.

63 Haley diaries, 13 August 1947, HALY 13–34, CAC.

64 Haley diaries, 10 November 1945, HALY 13–35, CAC.

65 A summary of their attempts can be found in a Foreign Office memorandum, 'Memorandum on Radio Luxembourg', 6 January 1947, CAB 124/407.

66 Flett to Pimlott, 19 February 1946: 'The BBC themselves have taken steps to counteract this [the popularity of Radio Luxembourg] and in fact one of the main purposes of the new Light Programme is to kill any demand for the sort of thing which used to be put out by Radio Luxembourg', CAB 124/407.

67 Flett to W.E. Phillips (Treasury), 7 June 1946, CAB 124/407.

68 Board of Trade letter to Flett, telling him that they are going to be unable to block the export of records to Radio Luxembourg, 11 July 1946, CAB 124/407.

69 Preparatory notes for response of Morrison to Parliamentary question from Wilson Harris. Unsigned and undated. June 1946, CAB 124/411. See also Harris to Morrison, Parliamentary Debates, 10 July 1946, Vol. 425, Col. 385.

70 P.H. Boon to Morrison, 13 February 1946, CAB 124/407.

71 P.H. Boon to Morrison, 22 May 1946, CAB 124/407

72 Morrison to Flett, 12 June 1946, 'I trust the Treasury can find a suitable amdmt to the DR's. It is important. If not try a new clause in the Finance Bill. It is an important evasion and shd not be tolerated' written on bottom of note from Flett to Christie (Treasury), 7 June 1946, CAB 124/407.

73 Haley to Flett, 12 June 1946 and 20 June 46, informing him that companies were not buying space on Radio Luxembourg because they knew the government was trying to shut it down. Stephens letter of 11 November 1947 shows that Morrison's office were still actively pursuing this course a year after the station re-opened, CAB 124/407.

74 Quoted above. Morrison to Gordon Walker, 25 June 1946, CAB 124/411.

75 Churchill to Morrison, 17 February 1948, Churchill correspondence, Churchill 2/38, Political Broadcasting, CAC.

76 Political Broadcasting meeting, 25 February 1948, CAB 124/31.

77 Research submitted by Woolton to BBC, re excessive broadcasts and publicity for communists, in R34/313/2, BBC-WAC.

78 Norman Brook to David Stephens, 22 March 1948, CAB 124/31.

79 Ibid. 'This, for obvious reasons, was not recorded in the Cabinet minute; but the LP undertook to look into the point', CAB 124/31.

80 Haley diaries, 10 April 1948, HALY 13–34, CAC.

81 Stephens to Morrison, 30 March 1948, Stephens description of his conversation with Haley, CAB 134/31. Reiterated by Haley in a letter to Churchill, 5 May 1950; 'No entrant to the BBC for the past 12 years therefore, has come into the Corporation without check', R34/313/3, BBC-WAC.

82 Haley diaries, 10 April 1948, HALY 13–34, CAC.

83 The BBC did just that, and the references can be found in the file 'Parliament, Communists in News Output, Returns 1948–1954', R31/28, BBC-WAC.

84 BoG Minutes 1948, R1/16/1, BBC-WAC.

85 BoG Minutes, 1 April 1948, Minute 87, R1/16/1, BBC-WAC.

86 Haley diaries, 12 April 1948, HALY 13–34, CAC.

87 Haley refers briefly in his diaries to the candidate, called 'Mr. Gater'. Gater does not appear in other files relating to this episode. Haley diaries, 14 April 1948, HALY 13–34, CAC.

88 Ibid.

89 'Mr. Morrison continues his antics. He is now demanding a report of the Governors attendances. I hope they will refuse them. The are independent and he is not their schoolmaster', Haley diaries, 17 July 1948, HALY 13–34, CAC.

90 'He [Simon] who should be in a position to be 100 per cent independent is appallingly susceptible', Haley diaries, 14 April 1948, HALY 13–34, CAC.

91 On 4 April 1950 the government and Opposition raised the issue of communism again after receiving a letter from the Listeners' Association, CAB 124/31.

92 See BBC file on, 'Policy, Communism, File 3: 1950–51', R34/313/3, BBC-WAC. During the preliminary stages of the rearmament re-education campaign in early 1951 Clem Leslie and others were keen to enrol the BBC in promoting anti-communism. See Leslie to Nicholson 25 January 1951, CAB 124/80.

93 *The Spectator*, 'BBC For Ever', 19 January 1951, p. 67. *New Statesman and Nation*, 'No Revolution at the BBC', 20 January 1951, pp. 54–55.
94 Report of the Broadcasting Committee 1951, Cmd. 8116, para. 205.
95 Ibid. para. 167.
96 Ibid. 'We believe therefore that the Government should retain powers of direction in relation to television greater than those possessed by it in the older field of sound broadcasting', para. 342.
97 Ibid. p. 8, para. 29.
98 Ibid. p. 166, para. 553.
99 Ibid. Para. 171.
100 Ibid. Para 591 and para. 554. and title to page 166.
101 Ibid. Para. 552.
102 Parliamentary Debates, House of Lords, 25 July 1951, Vol. 172, Col. 1260.
103 Asa Briggs, *Volume IV* (1995), p. 364.
104 Cmd. 8550, 15 May 1952, quoted in Asa Briggs, *Volume IV* (1995), p. 391.
105 Haley diaries, 29 July 1945, HALY 13–35, CAC.
106 Haley diaries, 19 May 1947, HALY 13–34, CAC.
107 Selwyn Lloyd Minority Report, Report of the Broadcasting Committee 1951, Cmd. 8116, p. 202.
108 D.R. Thorpe, *Selwyn Lloyd* (1989), p. 142.
109 Minority Report, Cmd. 8116, p. 202.

Conclusion: Communication Moves Centre Stage

1 S.C. Leslie to Morrison, 30 June 1947, T 245/2.
2 IS(48)1, Memorandum, Morrison, 21 January 1948, CAB 134/354.
3 A.P. Ryan letter to DG (BBC) re Production drive, 18 March 1947, R34/701, BBC-WAC.
4 'I am advised that the Department find it useful and in fact essential to have machinery available to maintain sample investigations under the three heads which I have specifically mentioned and, in particular, that the Survey of Sickness is producing information which will be of great value in connection with the NHS. The investigations to check the results of the Department's educational campaigns are a useful test of efficiency and help secure improvement in presentation and selection of media', Bevan to Morrison, 6 May 1946, CAB 124/637.
5 GK Evans to Fraser and Leslie, 'Some Comments Regarding Recent Publicity Surveys', 23 February 1949, CAB 124/81.
6 Dorothy Johnstone (Treasury Chambers) to Sir Robert Fraser, 17 December 1951, INF 12/691.
7 Note by Treasury, 'Government Information Services: the Central Agency', 12 January 1952, INF 12/691.
8 From 1,413 (1 October 1951) to 974 (1 April 1952), Written Answers, Parliamentary Papers, Vol. 499, Col. 103–4, 1951–2.
9 David Gammans (MP) letter to Viscount Swinton, 27 May 1952, quoting from Newspaper Association, FICA 2/2/1 Fife Clark papers, CAC.
10 Drogheda Report, Cmd. 9138, Parliamentary Papers, Vol. XXXI, 1953–54, p. 7.

11 Gross Totals (estimates), 1954–55: £1,289,400, 1959–60: £2,691,550, Select Committee on Estimates, Sub Committee F, Estimates, COI 1959–60, Parliamentary Papers, Number 259, Vol. 5. Figures also taken from Sir Fife Clark, *Central Office of Information* (1970), p. 172, Appendix VI, although these figures do not exactly match thoQe of the Select Committee.
12 Lord Hill, *Both Sides of the Hill* (1964), p. 208.
13 Butler and Sloman, *British Political Facts 1900–1979*, Fifth Edition (1980), p. 462.
14 Lord Hill, op. cit. (1964), p. 207.
15 Patrick Gordon Walker, *Restatement of Liberty* (1951), p. 369.

Bibliography

Primary Sources

Unpublished

Official Documents, Public Record Office, Kew

CAB 21 Cabinet Office and Predecessors: Registered Files (1916–1965)

CAB 78 War Cabinet and Cabinet: Miscellaneous Committees, Minutes & Papers

CAB 87 War Cabinet and Cabinet: Committees on Reconstruction, Supply and other matters: Minutes and Papers

CAB 124 Lord President's Office, including:

396–405: Broadcasting, Future Policy

408–410: Discussion between Government, members of Opposition and the BBC on political broadcasting

904–910: Prosperity Campaign Committee

985–996: Post War Organisation of Government Publicity

1025–1028: Central Office of Information and Documentary Films Problem

1029–1030: Proposals for Economies in Expenditure on Government Information Services

1070–1074: Appointment of Royal Commission to inquire into the control, management and ownership of the Press

CAB 128 Cabinet Conclusions

CAB 129 Cabinet Memoranda

CAB 134 Cabinet: Miscellaneous Committees, Minutes and Papers, including:

354, 458–460: Ministerial Information Services Committee, Minutes and Memoranda

355–360: Home Information Services (Official) Committee, Minutes and Memoranda

361–373: Economic Information Committee, Minutes and Memoranda

FO 1110 Foreign Office, Information Research Department: General Correspondence

HO 251 Royal Commission on the Press (1947–1949): Evidence and Papers

INF 1 Ministry of Information: Files of Correspondence

INF 5 Central Office of Information: Crown Film Unit Files

INF 6 Central Office of Information and Predecessors: Film Production Documents

INF 8 Central Office of Information: Monthly Division Reports 1946–1963

INF 12 Central Office of Information: Registered Files 1943–1994

INF 21 MOI and COI: Personal Files 1940–1967

MAF 84 Ministry of Food: Supply Department: Cereals Group

MAF 99 Ministry of Food: Services Department: Distribution Group

MAF 128 Ministry of Food: Senior Officers' Papers

MH 79 Ministry of Health: Information Services, including:

577–609: Home Information Services (Official) Committee and Subcommittees – Minutes and Memoranda

PREM 8 Prime Minister's Office: Correspondence and Papers
RG 23 Government Social Survey Department: Social Survey
RG 40 Central Office of Information, Social Survey Division: Social Survey
T 222 Treasury: Organisation and Methods Division
T 245 Treasury: Economic Information Unit
T 273 Treasury: Papers of Lord Bridges

Archives

British Broadcasting Corporation, Written Archives Centre, Caversham
  R1 Board of Governors, Minutes and Papers
  R9 Audience Research
  R28 News
  R34 Programme Policy
  R51 Talks
British Film Institute
Newsreel Association, Meeting Minutes 1937–1952
Conservative Party Archives, Bodleian Library, Oxford University
Imperial War Museum, Film Archive
Labour Party Archives, Manchester
National Union of Journalists, 308 Gray's Inn Road
The Times Archive, News International Archive and Record Office, London
Tom Harrisson Mass–Observation Archive, University of Sussex

Private Papers & Correspondence

Clement Attlee; correspondence and papers, Oxford University: Bodleian Library
Lord Beaverbrook; correspondence, House of Lords Record Office
Winston Churchill; correspondence and papers, Cambridge University, Churchill Archives Centre
Sir Thomas Fife Clark; correspondence and papers, Cambridge University, Churchill Archives Centre
Patrick Gordon Walker; diaries, correspondence and papers. Cambridge University, Churchill Archives Centre and correspondence and papers. PRO, CAB 127/296–325
Sir William Haley; diaries, correspondence and papers 1929–1970. Cambridge University, Churchill Archives Centre
Selwyn Lloyd; correspondence and papers 1929–1970. Cambridge University, Churchill Archives Centre
Herbert Morrison; Biographical Papers (Jones/Donoughue), London University, BLPES
Francis Williams; correspondence and papers 1929–1970. Cambridge University, Churchill Archives Centre

Published

Official Publications

Parliamentary Debates, House of Commons, Hansard, Fifth Series
Parliamentary Debates, House of Lords, Hansard, Fifth Series

Cmd 2756: BBC Charter & Licence 1926
Cmd 5329: BBC Charter & Licence 1936
Cmd 5091: Ullswater Committee Report 1935–6
Cmd 6852: White Paper on Broadcasting, July 1946
Cmd 6974: BBC Charter 1946
Cmd 6975: BBC Licence 1946
Cmd 7046: Economic Survey for 1947
Cmd 7700: The Royal Commission on the Press 1947–49
Cmd 7836: Report of the Committee on the Cost of Home Information Services
Cmd 8116: Report of the Broadcasting Committee 1949 (Beveridge)
Cmd 8117: Appendix H. Memoranda submitted to the Broadcasting Committee

Unofficial Contemporary Publications

Arts Enquiry, The Factual Film, A Survey sponsored by the Dartington Hall
    Trustees (Oxford University Press, 1947)
BBC Quarterly
Hulton Readership Survey
Political and Economic Planning, Broadsheets
P.E.P., Report on the Press (1938)
*A Free and Responsible Press – A General Report on Mass Communication: Newspapers,
    Radio, Motion Pictures, Magazines and Books*, The Commission on the Freedom
    of the Press (US), (University of Chicago Press, Chicago, 1947)

Speech Collections

Forward from Victory – Labour's Plan (London, Victor Gollancz, 1946)
Can Planning be Democratic? (London, Routledge, 1944)
The Peaceful Revolution (London, Allen & Unwin, 1949)

Newspapers

Daily Express
Daily Herald
Daily Mail
Daily Mirror
Daily Sketch/Graphic
Daily Telegraph
Evening Standard
Manchester Guardian
News Chronicle
The Observer
Sunday Express
Sunday Times
The Times

Journals, Trade Press and Magazines

Documentary Film Letter
Documentary Film News
The Economist

The Listener
Newspaper World and Advertising Review
New Statesman and Nation
Picture Post
Sight and Sound
The Spectator
Time and Tide
Truth
World's Press News & Advertiser's Review

Films

The Balance (Films of Fact for COI, 1947). BFI
Berlin Airlift (British Movietone for Air Ministry, 1949). Film Images
Britain Can Make It Nos 5, 6, 11, 12 (Films of Fact for COI). IWM & BFI
The Centre (For the Foreign Office, 1947). Film Images
Charley's New Town (Halas & Batchelor for Ministry of Town and Country Planning, 1948). Film Images
Cumberland Story (CFU for COI/Ministry of Fuel and Power, 1947). BFI
Designing Women (Merlin Films for Council of Industrial Design, 1947). Film Images
Dim Little Island (For the COI, 1948). Film Images
Getting On With It (Merlin and Films of Fact for COI, 1946). BFI
From the Ground Up (CFU for COI/EIU, 1950). BFI
Life in Her Hands (CFU for COI/Ministry of Labour, 1951). BFI
Pop Goes the Weasel (CFU for EIU, 1947). Film Images
Report on Coal (CFU for EIC 1947). BFI
Robinson Charley (Halas & Batchelor for Board of Trade, 1948). BFI
This Modern Age, No. 16, 'The British Are They Artistic?' (1947). BFI
Turn it Out (Greenpark for Prime Minister's Office, 1946). BFI
Waverley Steps (Greenpark Films for the Scottish Office, 1948). Film Images
What a Life (Public Relationship Films, COI, 1949). BFI
The Wonder Jet (CFU for COI/EIU). BFI
Wonders of the Deep (CFU for COI/EIU, 1949). IWM
A Yank Comes Back (CFU for COI, 1948). IWM.
Your Very Good Health (Halas & Batchelor for Ministry of Health, 1948). Film Images

Newsreels

British Pathé, ITN Archive, www.itnarchive.com
British Movietone News, BFI
British News, BFI

Sound Archives

BBC Radio recordings, British Library (Ministerial broadcasts)

Memoirs and Diaries

Christiansen, Arthur, *Headlines All My Life* (London, Heinemann, 1961)

Clark, William, *From Three Worlds: Memoirs* (London, Sidgwick and Jackson, 1986)

Cockett, Richard (ed.), *My Dear Max: The Letters of Brendan Bracken to Lord Beaverbrook, 1925–58* (London, The Historian's Press, 1990)

Dalton, Hugh, *High Tide and After: Memoirs 1945–60* (London, Muller, 1962)

Gorham, Maurice, *Sound and Fury, 21 Years at the BBC* (London, Percival Marshall, 1948)

Grisewood, Harman, *One Thing at a Time* (London, Hutchinson, 1968)

Hamilton, Denis, *Editor-in-Chief, Fleet Street Memoirs* (London, Hamish Hamilton, 1989)

Hopkinson, Tom, *Of This Our Time – A Journalist's Story 1905–50* (London, Hutchinson, 1982)

Jay, Douglas, *Change and Fortune: A Political Record* (London, Hutchinson, 1980)

Mayhew, Christopher, *Time to explain* (London, Hutchinson, 1987)

Morrison, Herbert, *An Autobiography* (London, Odhams Press, 1960)

Pimlott, Ben (ed.), *The Political Diary of Hugh Dalton 1945–60* (London, Jonathan Cape, 1986)

Shawcross, Hartley, *Life Sentence: The Memoirs of Hartley Shawcross* (London, Constable, 1995)

Shinwell, E., *Conflict without Malice* (London, Odhams Press, 1955)

Stuart, Charles (ed.) *The Reith Diaries* (London, Collins, 1975)

Turner, John, *Filming History – the Memoirs of John Turner, Newsreel Cameraman* (London, BUFVC, 2001)

Walker, Patrick Gordon, *Political Diaries, 1932–71* (London, Historian's Press, 1991)

Williams, Francis, *Nothing so Strange* (London, Cassell, 1970)

Williams, Philip M. (ed.), *The Diary of Hugh Gaitskell 1945–56* (London, Cape, 1983)

Contemporary Works

Angell, Norman, *The Press and the Organisation of Society* (Cambridge, Minority Press, 1933)

Butler, David, *The British Election of 1951* (London, Macmillan, 1952)

Camrose, Lord, *British Newspapers and their Controllers* (London, Cassell and Company, 1947)

Contact Book, *The Changing Nation*, (London, Contact Publications, 1947)

Coase, RH, *British Broadcasting – A Study in Monopoly* (Longmans, London, 1950)

Cummings, A.J., *The Press and a Changing Civilisation* (London, The Bodley Head, 1936)

Gallup, George, *Public Opinion in a Democracy* (Princeton, Princeton University, 1939)

Hardy, Forsyth (ed.), *Grierson on Documentary* (London, Collins, 1946)

Harris, Wilson, *The Daily Press* (Cambridge, Cambridge University Press, 1943)

Hudson, Derek, *British Journalists and Newspapers* (London, Collins, 1945)

Hayek, F.A., *The Road to Serfdom* (London, Routledge and Keegan Paul, 1944)

Layton, Sir Walter, *Newsprint – A Problem for Democracy* (London, The Hollen Street Press, 1946)

Lippman, Walter, *Public Opinion* (1922) (New York, Free Press Paperbacks, 1997)

McCallum, Ronald and Alison Readman, *The British Election of 1945* (Oxford, Oxford University Press, 1947)

Martin, Kingsley, *The Press the Public Wants* (London, Hogarth's Press, 1947)

Mass–Observation, *The Press and its Readers* (London, Art and Technics, 1949)

Morrison, Herbert, *Socialisation and Transport* (London, Constable, 1933)

Nicholas, Herbert George, *The British Election of 1950* (London, Macmillan, 1951)

Noble, Peter (ed.), *British Film Yearbook, 1949–50* (London, Skelton Robinson, 1949/50)

Pimlott, J.A.R., *Public Relations and American Democracy* (Princeton, Princeton University Press, 1951)

Rotha, Paul, *Rotha on the Film – A Selection of Writings about the Cinema* (London, Faber & Faber, 1958)

Simon, Lord, *The BBC from Within* (London, Victor Gollancz, 1953)

Sinclair, Robert, *The British Press – The Journalist and his Conscience* (London, Home and Van Thal, 1949)

Steed, Henry Wickham, *The Press* (London, Penguin, 1938)

Thomas, Ivor, 'The Newspaper', Oxford Pamphlets on Home Affairs, No. H2 (London, OUP, 1943)

Vallance, Aylmer, 'Control of the Press', *Current Affairs*, No. 12, September 1946

Walker, Patrick Gordon, *Restatement of Liberty* (London, Hutchinson, 1951)

Williams, Francis, *Press, Parliament and People* (London, Macmillan, 1946)

Williams, Francis, *The Triple Challenge* (London, Heinemann, 1948)

Williams–Thompson, Richard, *Was I Really Necessary? Chief Information Officer, Ministry of Supply, 1946–49* (London, World's Press News Publishing, 1951)

Williams-Thompson, Mike [sic], *'Tell the People!'* (London, World's Press News Publishing, 1955)

Weidenfeld, A.G. (ed.), *The Public's Progress* (London, Contact Books, 1947)

Secondary Sources

Published

Reference

Alford, B.W.E., Rodney Lowe and Neil Rollings, *Economic Planning 1943–51 – A Guide to Documents in the Public Record Office* (London, HMSO, 1992)

The British Imperial Calendar and Civil Service List (London, HMSO, Annual)

Butler, D.E., and Jennie Freeman, *British Political Facts 1900–1968* (London, Macmillan, 1969)

Cook, Chris, Jane Leonard and Peter Leese, *The Longman Guide to Sources in Contemporary History Vol. 2: Individuals* (London, Longman, 1994)

Illingworth, Frank (ed.), *British Political Yearbook 1947* (Kingston–Upon–Thames, Knapp, Drewett & Sons, (1947)

Biography

Boyle, Andrew, *Poor, Dear Brendan: The Quest for Brendan Bracken* (London, Hutchinson, 1974)

Bryant, Chris, *Stafford Cripps: The First Modern Chancellor* (London, Hodder and Stoughton, 1997)

Bullock, Alan, *The Life and Times of Ernest Bevin, Vol II* (London, Heinemann, 1983)

Campbell, John, *Nye Bevan and the Mirage of British Socialism* (London, Weidenfeld and Nicholson, 1987)

Chisholm, Anne & Michael Davie, *Beaverbrook: A Life* (London, Hutchinson, 1992)

Clarke, Peter, *The Cripps Version, The Life of Sir Stafford Cripps 1889–1952* (London, Penguin, 2002)

Ellis, Jack, *John Grierson: Life, Contributions, Influence* (Carbondale, Southern Illinois University Press, 2000)

Foot, Michael, *Aneurin Bevan: A Biography Vol. 2, 1945–60* (London, Davis-Poynter, 1973)

Hardy, Forsyth, *John Grierson: A Documentary Biography* (1979)

Harris, Kenneth, *Attlee* (London, Weidenfeld and Nicholson, 1982)

Jones, G.W. and Bernard Donoughue, *Herbert Morrison: Portrait of a Politician* (London, Weidenfeld and Nicolson, 1973, 2001 edition)

Pearce, Robert, *Attlee* (London, Longman, 1997)

Pimlott, Ben, *Hugh Dalton* (London, HarperCollins, 1985/1995 edition)

Thorpe, D.R., *Selwyn Lloyd* (London, Cape, 1989)

Wheen, Francis, *The Soul of Indiscretion, Tom Driberg* (London, Fourth Estate, 2001)

Williams, Francis, *A Prime Minister Remembers: the war and post war memoirs of the Rt. Hon. Earl Attlee... based on his private papers and on a series of recorded conversations* (London, Heinemann, 1961)

Williams, Francis, *Ernest Bevin, Portrait of a Great Englishman* (London, Hutchinson, 1952)

Other Studies

Addison, Paul, *The Road to 1945: British Politics and the Second World War* (London, Cape, 1975)

Addison, Paul, *Now the War is Over: A Social History of Britain 1945–51* (London, BBC, 1985)

Aitken, Ian, *Film & Reform: John Grierson & the Documentary Film Movement* (London, Routledge, 1990)

Ayerst, David, *Guardian, Biography of a Newspaper* (Glasgow, William Collins Sons & Co., 1971)

Balfour, Michael, *Propaganda in War 1940–45: Organizations, Policies and Publics in Britain and Germany* (London, Routledge and Kegan Paul, 1979)

Ballantyne, James (ed.), *Researcher's Guide to British Newsreels, Vol. I* (London, BUFVC, 1983)

Black, John, *Organising the Propaganda Instrument: The British Experience* (The Hague, Martinus Nijhoff, 1975)

Boyce, George, James Curran and Pauline Wingate, *Newspaper History from the Seventeenth Century to the Present Day* (London, Constable, 1978)

Briggs, Asa, *The History of Broadcasting in the United Kingdom, Volume 4, Sound and Vision* (Oxford, Oxford University Press, 1979)

Briggs, Asa, *The BBC: The First Fifty Years* (Oxford, Oxford University Press, 1985)

Brivati, Brian, and Harriett Jones (ed.), *What Difference did the War Make?* (New York, St. Martin's Press, 1993)

Bulmer, Martin (ed.), *Essays on the History of British Sociological Research* (Cambridge, Cambridge University Press, 1985)

Calder, Angus, *The People's War: Britain 1939–45* (London, Jonathan Cape, 1969)

Calder, Angus, and Dorothy Sheridan (eds) *Speak for Yourself: a Mass–Observation Anthology 1937–49* (London, Cape, 1984)

Chapman, James, *The British at War: Cinema, State and Propaganda 1939–45* (London, IB Taurus, 1995)

Cockett, Richard, *Thinking the Unthinkable: Think–Tanks and the Economic Counter–Revolution 1931–1983* (London, Harper Collins, 1994)

Cockett, Richard, *Twilight of Truth: Chamberlain, Appeasement and the Manipulation of the Press* (London, Weidenfeld and Nicholson, 1989)

Cockerell, Michael, Peter Hennessy and David Walker, *Sources Close to the Prime Minister – Inside the Hidden World of the News Manipulators* (London, Macmillan, 1984)

Crofts, William, *Coercion or Persuasion? Propaganda in Britain after 1945* (London, Routledge, 1989)

Cruikshank, Charles, *The Fourth Arm: Psychological Warfare 1938–45* (Oxford, Oxford University Press, 1981)

Cudlipp, Hugh, *Publish and be Damned: The Astonishing Story of the Daily Mirror* (London, Dakers, 1953)

Curran, James and Vincent Porter (eds), *British Cinema History* (London, Weidenfeld and Nicolson, 1983)

Curran, James and Jean Seaton, *Power without Responsibility – The Press and Broadcasting in Britain* (London, Routledge, 1997, Fifth Edition)

Dickinson, Margaret, and Sarah Street, *Cinema and the State: The Film Industry and the Government 1927–84* (London, BFI, 1985)

Eatwell, Roger, *The 1945–1951 Labour Governments* (London, Batsford, 1979)

Edelman, Maurice, *The Mirror: A Political History* (London, Hamish Hamilton, 1966)

Engel, Matthew, *Tickle the Public: 100 Years of the Popular Press* (London, Victor Gollancz, 1996)

Fielding, Steven, Peter Thompson and Nick Tiratsoo, *"England Arise!" The Labour Party and Popular Politics in 1940s Britain* (Manchester, Manchester University Press, 1995)

Fife Clark, Sir Thomas, *The Central Office of Information* (London, Allen and Unwin, 1970)

Franklin, Bob, *Packaging Politics – Political Communications in Britain's Media Democracy* (London, Edward Arnold, 1994)

Goldie, Grace Wyndham, *Facing the Nation. Television and Politics, 1936–1976* (London, Bodley Head, 1977)

Grant, Mariel, *Propaganda and the Role of the State in Inter–War Britain* (Oxford, Oxford University Press, 1994)

Greenslade, Roy, *Press Gang: How Newspapers Make Profits from Propaganda* (London, MacMillan, 2003)

Hart-Davis, Duff, *The House the Berrys Built: Inside the Telegraph 1928–1986* (London, Hodder and Stoughton, 1990)

Hennessy, Peter and A. Arends, *Mr. Attlee's Engine Room: Cabinet Committee Structure and the Labour Government 1945–51* (Glasgow, Strathclyde University, 1983)

Hennessy, Peter, *Never Again: Britain 1945–51* (London, Cape, 1992)

Ingham, Bernard, *The Wages of Spin* (London, John Murray, 2003)

Jefferys, Kevin, *The Attlee Governments* (London, Longman, 1992)

Jefferys, Kevin, *The Labour Party since 1945* (Basingstoke, Macmillan, 1993)

Jones, Harriet and Michael Kandiah (eds) *The Myth of Consensus: New Views on British History 1945–64* (Basingstoke, Macmillan, 1996)

Koss, Stephen, *The Rise and Fall of the Political Press in Britain, Vol. 2: The Twentieth Century* (London, Hamish Hamilton, 1984)

Lashmar, Paul and James Oliver, *Britain's Secret Propaganda War* (Stroud, Sutton Publishing, 1998)

Mackenzie, John M., *Propaganda and Empire: The Manipulation of British Public Opinion 1880–1960* (Manchester, Manchester University Press, 1984)

McKernan, Luke (ed.), *Yesterday's News: the British Cinema Newsreel Reader* (London, BUFVC, 2002)

McLachlan, Donald, *In the Chair, Barrington–Ward of the Times, 1927–48* (London, Weidenfeld, 1971)

McDonald, Iverach, *The History of the Times, Vol. V, Struggles in War and Peace 1939–1966* (London, Times Books, 1984)

McLaine, Ian, *Ministry of Morale: Home Front Morale and the Ministry of Information in World War II* (London, Allen and Unwin, 1979)

McNair, Brian, *Journalism and Democracy: An Evaluation of the Political Public Sphere* (London, Routledge, 2000)

Margach, James, *The Abuse of Power: the war between Downing Street and the Media from Lloyd George to Callaghan* (London, WH Allen, 1978)

Marr, Andrew, *My Trade: A Short History of British Journalism* (Basingstoke, Macmillan, 2004)

Mayer, Frank, *The Opposition Years: Winston S. Churchill and the Conservative Party 1945–51* (New York, P Lang, 1992)

Middlemas, Keith, *Politics in Industrial Society: the Experience of the British System since 1911* (London, Deutsch, 1979)

Mitchell, Austin, *Election '45: Reflections on the Revolution in* Britain (London, Bellew, 1995)

Morgan, Kenneth O., *Labour in Power, 1945–1951* (Oxford, Clarendon, 1984)

Morgan, Kenneth O., *Labour People: Leaders and Lieutenants, Hardie to Kinnock* (Oxford, OUP, 1987)

Morgan, Kenneth O., *Britain Since 1945 – The People's Peace* (Oxford, OUP, 2001, Third Edition)

Moss, Louis, *The Government Social Survey – A History* (London, HMSO, 1991)

Negrine, Ralph, *Politics and the Mass Media in Britain* (London, Routledge, 1994, Second Edition)

Nicholas, Sian, *The Echo of War: Home Front Propaganda and the Wartime BBC 1939–45* (Manchester, Manchester University Press, 1996)

Norris, Pippa, et al., *On Message: Communicating the Campaign* (London, SAGE, 1999)

Ogilvy–Webb, M., *The Government Explains: A Study of the Information Services* (Royal Institute of Public Administration, HMSO, 1965)

Orwell, George, *Orwell and Politics* (London, Penguin, 2001)

Pegg, Mark, *Broadcasting and Society 1918–1939* (London, Croom Helm, 1983)

Pelling, Henry, *The Labour Governments, 1945–51* (London, Macmillan, 1984)

Pinder, John (ed.), *Fifty Years of Political and Economic Planning: Looking Forward 1931–81* (London, Heinemann, 1981)

Pronay, Nicholas, and Spring, D.W. (eds), *Propaganda, Politics and Film, 1918–1945* (London, Macmillan, 1982)

Ramsden, John, *An Appetite for Power: A History of the Conservative Party Since 1830* (London, HarperCollins, 1999)

Ramsden, John, *The Making of Conservative Party Policy: The Conservative Research Department since 1929* (London, Longman, 1980)

Rawnsley, Gary (ed.), *The Sword and the Pen: Propaganda and the Cold War in the 1950s* (Macmillan, 1999)

Reeves, Nicholas, *Official British Film Propaganda during the First World War* (London, Croon Helm, 1986)

Rose, Jonathan, *The Intellectual Life of the British Working Classes* (New Haven, Yale University Press, 2002)

Scammell, Margaret, *Designer Politics: How Elections are Won* (Basingstoke, Macmillan, 1995)

Seaton, Jean (ed.), *Politics and the Media – Harlots and Prerogatives at the Turn of the Millennium* (Oxford, Blackwell, 1998)

Seymour–Ure, Colin, *The British Press and Broadcasting since 1945* (Oxford, Blackwell, 1991)

Seymour–Ure, Colin, *The Press, Politics and the Public* (London, Methuen and Co., 1968)

Seymour–Ure, Colin, *Prime Ministers and the Media: Issues of Power and Control* (London, Blackwell, 2003)

Shaw, Tony, Eden, *Suez and the Mass Media: Propaganda and Persuasion during the Suez Crisis* (London, IB Taurus, 1996)

Silvey, Roger, *Who's Listening? The Story of BBC Audience Research* (London, Allen & Unwin, 1974)

Sissons, Michael and Philip French (eds), *Age of Austerity* (London, Hodder and Stoughton, 1963)

Sked, Alan and Chris Cook, *Post War Britain: A Political History* (Harmondsworth, Penguin, 1990)

Swann, Paul, *The British Documentary Film Movement, 1926–46* (Cambridge, Cambridge University Press, 1989)

Taylor, Philip M., *British Propaganda in the Twentieth Century: Selling Democracy* (Edinburgh, Edinburgh University Press, 1999)

Taylor, Philip M., *Munitions of the Mind: A History of Propaganda from the Ancient World to the Present Era* (Manchester, Manchester University Press, 1995)

Taylor, Philip M., *The Projection of Britain: British Overseas Publicity and Propaganda 1919–1939* (Cambridge, 1981)

Tiratsoo, Nick (ed.), *The Attlee Years* (London, Pinter Publishers, 1991)

Tunstall, Jeremy, *The Westminster Lobby Correspondents – A Sociological Study of National Political Journalism* (London, Routledge and Kegan Paul, 1970)

Weiler, Peter, *British Labour and the Cold War* (Stanford, Stanford University Press, 1988)

Williams, Francis, *Dangerous Estate – The Anatomy of Newspapers* (London, Longmans, Green and Co., 1957)

Zweiniger–Bargielowska, Ina, *Austerity in Britain: rationing, controls, and consumption, 1939–1955* (Oxford, OUP, 2000)

Articles

Adamthwaite, Anthony, '"Nation shall speak unto nation": the BBC's Response to Peace and Defence Issues, 1945–58' in *Contemporary Record*, Vol. 7, (1993), pp. 557–77

Adamthwaite, Anthony, 'The British Government and the Media, 1937–38', in *Journal of Contemporary History*, Vol. 18:2, (1983), pp. 281–98

Anstey, Caroline, 'The Projection of British Socialism: Foreign Office Publicity and American Opinion 1945–50' in *Journal of Contemporary History*, Vol. 19:3, (1984), pp. 417–51

Crofts, S.W., 'The Attlee Governments' Economic Information Propaganda' in *Journal of Contemporary History*, Vol. 21:3 (1986) pp. 453–71

Fielding, Steven, 'What did "The People" Want? The Meaning of the 1945 General Election' in *Historical Journal*, Vol. 35:3, (1992), pp. 623–39

Fielding, Steven, 'Labourism in the 1940s' in *Twentieth Century British History*, Vol. 3:2, (1992), pp. 138–53

Goldman, Aaron L., 'Press Freedom in Britain during World War II' in *Journalism History*, Vol. 22:4, (1997), pp. 146–55

Gorman, J., 'The Labour Party's Election Posters in 1945' in *Labour History Review*, Vol. 61:3 Winter, (1996), pp. 299–08

Grant, Mariel, 'Towards a Central Office of Information: Continuity and Change in British Government Information Policy 1939–51' in *Journal of Contemporary History*, Vol. 34:1 (1999), pp. 49–67

Gunn, JAW, 'Public Opinion', in Terence Ball, James Farr, Russell Hanson (eds), *Political Innovation and Conceptual Change*, (Cambridge, Cambridge University Press, 1989)

Hennessy, Peter, 'Major Attlee and his Party' in *Modern History Review*, Vol. 1:3, (1990), pp. 9–12

Hennessy, Peter, The Quality of Political Journalism', in *The Royal Society of the Arts*, November, 1987, pp. 926–34

Hollins, T.J., 'The Conservative Party and Film Propaganda between the Wars', in *English Historical Review*, 96:379, 1981, pp. 359–69

Kandiah, Michael, 'Television Enters British Politics: The Conservative Party's Central Office and Political Broadcasting, 1945–55', in *Historical Journal of Film, Radio and Television*, 15:2, 1995, pp. 265–84

Lucas, W.S. and C.J. Morris, 'A Very British Crusade: the IRD and the Beginning of the Cold War' in *British Intelligence, Strategy and the Cold War*, Richard Aldrich (ed.) (London, Routledge, 1992)

O'Malley, Tom, 'Labour and the 1947–49 Royal Commission on the Press', in Michael Bromley and Tom O'Malley (ed.), *A Journalism Reader* (Routledge, London, 1997)

Pronay, Nicholas, 'British Newsreels in the 1930s: 1 – Audience and Producers', in *History*, 56, October 1971, pp. 411–18

Pronay, Nicholas, 'British Newsreels in the 1930s: 2 – Their Policies and Impact', in *History*, Vol. 56, February 1972, pp. 63–72

Robins, Kevin, Frank Webster and Michael Pickering, 'Propaganda, Information and Social Control', in *Propaganda, Persuasion and Polemic*, Jeremy Hawthorn (ed.), (Edward Arnold, London, 1987), pp. 1–18

Shaw, Tony, 'The British Popular Press and the Early Cold War' in *History*, Vol. 83, (1998), pp. 66–85

Shaw, Tony, 'Government Manipulation of the Press during the 1956 Suez Crisis', in *Contemporary Record*, Vol. 8, (1994), pp. 274–88

Smith, Lyn, 'Covert British Propaganda: IRD 1947–77', in *Millennium*, Vol. 9:1, (1980), pp. 67–83

Summerfield, P., 'Mass Observation: Social Research or Social Movement? in *Journal of Contemporary History*, 20 (1985) pp. 439–52

Taylor, Philip M. '"If War should Come": preparing the Fifth Arm for Total War, 1935–39', in *Journal of Contemporary History*, 16:1 (1981), pp. 27–52

Tiratsoo, Nick, 'The Attlee Years Revisited' in *Modern History Review*, Vol. 5:3, (1994) pp. 31–3

Weiler, Peter, 'British Labour and the Cold War: the Foreign Policy of the Labour Governments 1945–1951', in *Journal of British Studies*, Vol. 26:1, (1987), pp. 54–82

Weiler, Peter, 'Britain and the First Cold War: Revisionist Beginnings', in *Twentieth Century British History*, Vol. 9:1, (1998), pp. 127–38

Wildy, Tom, 'The Social and Economic Publicity of Labour Governments of 1945–51' in *Contemporary Record*, Vol. 6, (1992), pp. 45–71

Wildy, Tom, 'British Television and Official Film 1946–51' in *Historical Journal of Film, Radio and Television*, Vol. 8, (1988), pp. 195–202

Wildy, Tom, 'From the MOI to the COI – Publicity and Propaganda in Britain 1945–51: the National Health and Insurance Campaigns of 1948' in *Historical Journal of Film, Radio and Television*, Vol. 6, (1986) pp. 2–17

Wilford, Hugh, 'The IRD: Britain's Secret Cold War Weapon Revealed' in *Review of International Studies*, Vol. 24:3, (1998), pp. 353–69

Willcox, Temple, 'Projection or publicity? Rival concepts in the pre–war planning of the British Ministry of Information', in *Journal of Contemporary History*, 18:1 (1983), pp. 97–116

Willcox, Temple, 'Towards a Ministry of Information', in *History*, 69 (1984), pp. 398–414

Wring, Dominic, 'Political Marketing and Party Development: a "Secret" History' in *European Journal of Marketing*, Vol. 30, (1996), pp. 100–11

Wring, Dominic, 'Machievellian Communication – the role of spin doctors and image makers in early and late twentieth century British politics' in Phil Harris, Andrew Lock and Patricia Rees (eds), *Machiavelli, Marketing and Management*, (London, Routledge, 2000)

Wring, Dominic, 'Power as well as Persuasion: Political Communication and Party Development' in John Bartle and Dylan Griffiths (eds), *Political Communications Transformed – From Morrison to Mandelson*, (Basingstoke, Palgrave, 2001)

Wring, Dominic, 'Media Messiahs' in *Tribune* (5 April, 1996)

Young, Michael and Peter Hennessy, 'The 1945 General Election and Post War Period Remembered' in *Contemporary Record*, Vol. 9:1, (1995), pp. 80–98

Zweiniger-Bargielowska, Ina, 'Bread rationing in Britain, July 1946–July 1948', in *Twentieth Century British History*, Vol. 4, 1993, pp. 57–85

Unpublished

Theses and Dissertations

Anstey, Caroline, Foreign Office Efforts to Influence American Opinion 1945–49, Ph.D. Thesis, LSE, 1984

Crofts, S.W., 'Techniques of Information and Persuasion Employed by Her Majesty's Government 1945–51', Ph.D. Thesis, Open University, 1983

Enticknap, LDG, 'The Non-Fiction Film in Britain, 1945–51', Ph.D. Thesis, Exeter University, 1999

Hogenkamp, Albert, 'The British Documentary Movement and the 1945–51 Labour Governments' Ph.D. Thesis, Westminster College, 1991

Hollins, Timothy, The Presentation of Politics: the Place of Party Publicity, Broadcasting and Film in British Politics, 1918–39, Ph.D. Thesis, Leeds, 1981

Jenks, John Dwight, Hot News/Cold War: The British State, Propaganda and the News Media 1948–53, Ph.D. Thesis, University of California, Berkeley, 2000

Laurence, Alistair, 'Propaganda, Planning and the Economy: A Study in Government Public Relations 1945–49', M.Phil. University of Leeds, 1982

Smith, David, 'Politics through the microphone: BBC Radio and the 'New Jerusalem', Ph.D. Thesis, London, Queen Mary and Westfield College, 2000

Thorpe, Keir, "The Missing Pillar": Economic Planning and the Machinery of Government during the Labour Administrations of 1945–51, Ph.D. Thesis, London, Queen Mary and Westfield College, 1999

Wildy, Thomas, 'Propaganda and Social Policy in Britain 1945–1951: Publicity for the Social Legislation of the Labour Government', Ph.D. Thesis, Leeds, 1985

Index